Reforming the Kirk:
The Future of the Church of Scotland

Reforming the Kirk:

The Future of the Church of Scotland

An expanded version of the Chalmers Lectures 2017

Doug Gay

SAINT ANDREW PRESS

First published in 2017 by
SAINT ANDREW PRESS
121 George Street
Edinburgh EH2 4YN

British Library Cataloguing in Publication Data
A catalogue record for this book is available from the British Library.

978-0-86153-901-7

Typeset by Manila Typesetting Company
Printed and bound in the United Kingdom by
CPI Group (UK) Ltd

For the Kirk, with love,
and for these congregations
to which, in various ways I have belonged
and in which I have worked and
ministered:

St Andrew's and St Ringan's, Castle Douglas
Martyrs Church, St Andrews
Ruchazie Parish Church
St George's and St Peter's, Easterhouse
Lansdowne Church
Wellington Church
Borgue Parish Church
Ruchill Parish Church
Kelvinside Hillhead Parish Church

Contents

Introduction:
Decline and Fail?
On Being Consumed . . .

Times are hard and spirits are low. Tell someone you are writing a book on the future of the Kirk and their instant response is likely to be some version of the quip 'So it has one?' Take it from me.[1]

Since my return to Scotland in 2002, after my second (happy) exile in east London, I have been troubled and fascinated by the state of the Kirk. Educated and licensed for ministry by the Church of Scotland, I was ordained into the United Reformed Church (URC) in Hackney in 1995 and spent the next decade first working as a local minister and undertaking a PhD in Scotland funded by the URC.[2] I moved back from the URC to the Church of Scotland in 2005 and have spent the past decade working for the church in various guises as a Sunday school teacher (unpaid), supply preacher (paid), locum minister (paid), associate minister (unpaid) and as Principal of Trinity College, Glasgow (unpaid) while also working as a lecturer at the University of Glasgow since the end of 2005 (paid). In 2013 I took up a part-time appointment as a locum minister, which after a year became a non-stipendiary associate role, working in a congregation in the west end of Glasgow which has been without a permanent minister since 2008.

Although not a cradle presbyterian (I came to the Church of Scotland age 16) I have now become something of an insider. For myself and many of those who will read this book, reflecting from inside the Kirk lends a particular existential urgency to the

---

1 Others include: 'Short book then?'
2 In case I seem ungrateful, they declined my offer to serve them in an academic position at the end of my studies. I remain very grateful to them for the Millennium Scholarship!

questions at stake. What has happened to the church we have loved, served and belonged to for so many years? What will happen to it in future? These are not just questions for insiders. The state and fate of the Kirk is a topic which should be of wider interest within Scottish society and beyond. The Church of Scotland, in its Reformed guise, has had a profound social and cultural influence on Scottish life for some 450 years. The steady decline of that influence and the rapid institutional decline of the Kirk are therefore key historical and sociological questions for all those interested in how Scotland has changed and is changing.[3]

The impetus to write this book came in large part from frustration at the lack (with some honourable exceptions) of enough serious intellectual and theological work on possibilities for reform. This is of course a painful irony in a tradition often badged with the motto *semper reformanda* – 'always to be reformed'. Within the church I had been aware of huge amounts of complaint, a fair amount of bitterness, a good deal of mutual recrimination, a lot of sarcasm, a pile of unfunny jokes and a deep and wide sense of foreboding about the future. What I was not coming across was enough serious intellectual and theological engagement with some of the key questions facing the church. Many intelligent and otherwise thoughtful ministers and elders I met seemed to be treating their presbyterian identity and its institutional expression as a running joke; apparently content to ironise it endlessly, without putting serious effort into devising constructive options for reform. My growing suspicion has been that this reaction reflected a sense of disempowerment and distress. People were laughing instead of crying because they did not know what else to do. It was also, of course, because many people were so busy.

A number of things have driven this project. First, I was interested in why the conversation about reform was in such a poor state. Were people already so deeply discouraged, so institutionally depressed that they had lost hope of anything changing? Were a generation of clergy and elders (most of whom had never known

---

3 In a February 2014 seminar on culture and the independence debate at Glasgow School of Art, commentator Alex Massie referred to 'the death of the Church of Scotland' as a key factor in the changing nature of Scottish identity and culture.

a growing church) resigned to a future in which the bush was burning out and the Kirk[4] was finally being consumed?

Second, I was interested to know what people would say in response to such questions if they were asked. Having not been the most empirical of practical theologians up to this point, it seemed as if this might be a good time to do some field work and interview some key actors.

I approached the Church of Scotland and asked for official co-operation in writing the book, which I received. On my own initiative I made certain commitments: there would be no *ad hominem* attacks, there would be no 'off the record' interviews or briefings. Someone else may write a more provocative, whistle-blowing or 'racy' book which does include such things; I wanted to see what could be done in an open, transparent and irenic way.

The coming decade, from 2020 to 2030, will be a decisive one for the Church of Scotland in terms of its historic status and character as a national church. Continuous and rapid decline since 1958 is already bringing it close to a tipping point, when it will simply no longer be possible for the Kirk to carry on as it has done until now. In recent years there have been challenges linked to schism and division, with some congregations and ministers leaving over disputed points of doctrine and ethics. However, up to this point, these have been relatively minor factors compared to the broad overall challenge posed by an ageing and declining membership. The most acute symptom of this in the past decade, has been the dwindling supply of new ministers. When this is combined with projections for retirement of the existing population of ministers (the so-called ministerial 'cliff') a continuation of existing trends will create a very significant shortfall of ministers by the early 2020s. The supply of full-time stipendiary ministers is set to decline at an even faster rate than the number of members, the number of congregations or the amount of money available to pay for them.

---

4 The Kirk's motto *nec tamen consumebatur* (which means 'yet it was not consumed') is a quote from the Latin translation of Exodus 3.2, referring to Moses' encounter with the bush 'which burned yet was not consumed'.

A significant shortfall of ministers poses a major challenge to the dominant paradigm of ministry as it has existed within the church for the past two centuries and as it was aspired to in the two and half centuries before that. The aspiration within the medieval parish system, to a priest in every parish, was taken over by the sixteenth-century reformers in Scotland. While it seems that the Kirk has often felt itself short of ministers, it has for the past two centuries mostly been able to maintain what we could call the basic social-ecclesial imaginary[5] of a minister in every parish, in a Scotland covered by parishes of a manageable size, in which every parishioner was within reach of a local church with their own local minister. That way of imagining Scotland is fading before our eyes and seems likely to become increasingly foreign to rising generations.

To make that basic and uncontentious observation about the Church of Scotland is also to assert that the concerns of this book affect a broader public than the Kirk itself. The system of presbyterian parish churches is also a very basic element of how much of Scottish society has imagined itself since the Reformation. The fact of its being attacked, lampooned, critiqued, satirised in poetry and prose (both novels and commentary), drama, film and television, is a witness to the power of this social imaginary in Scotland's past. To that extent, understanding why it is now changing so rapidly within contemporary society also raises important questions for social historians, sociologists of religion and critical/cultural theorists. The concerns of this book are inevitably framed by how we understand a broader debate about the secularisation of Scottish society.

Some commentators will rejoice that Presbyterian Scotland is melting before them like 'sna aff a dyke', as the warmer temperatures of a secular spring arrive and allow new life and growth to flourish, free from the deadening influence of the 'frozen chosen'. For others, even some who are agnostic or sceptical about religion, the decline of a major institution of Scottish life might be seen as part of a worrying trend in which a range of key institutions has

---

5 For the concept of a social imaginary, see Taylor, 2004; also James K. A. Smith's use of the concept in Smith, 2009.

been in steep decline: not just churches but trade unions, political parties[6] and a range of voluntary societies has been dissolving before our eyes. Their more cautious judgement might be that the acids of global capitalism and consumerism are dissolving key institutions which have been vital for our ethical capacity and our social well-being. For all the baleful persistence of social evils and economic injustice within our societies, without these institutions and the ways in which they shaped law, politics, the operations of the market and the formation of families, things might have been a whole lot worse in the past and might yet become significantly worse in the future.[7]

While a radical secular vision for Scotland might applaud the Kirk's decline with a cry of 'Good riddance' and a critical appraisal by theological conservatives might name it as judgement for various kinds of apostasy,[8] this book and the lectures on which it is based have taken a different approach. As someone working in practical theology, I understand what I do as the Christian theological practice of reflecting from within the church, on practice in the world (including the church's practice) for the sake of practice in church and world, in its relation to the mission of God.

While the broad orientation of reflection is retrospective,[9] there is also a prospective dimension to practical theology which is concerned, in Elaine Graham's words, with 'transforming practice'.[10] The South African missiologist David Bosch spoke in Barthian tones of the decisive task of theology as being 'to critically accompany the church in its mission to the world'.[11] Such critical accompaniment will always involve review, but sometimes it will also

---

6 The jury is still out on interpreting the trend-bucking dramatic rise in membership of the SNP post the 2014 indyref and the rise in membership of Labour associated with the Corybn debates.

7 An unexpectedly insightful and nuanced reflection on this, related primarily to the Church of England, was printed in the *Guardian* on 27 May 2016: www .theguardian.com/commentisfree/2016/may/27/the-guardian-view-on-disappearing -christianity-suppose-its-gone-for-ever.

8 Various Free Church of Scotland commentators could be cited here, some of whom I will not dignify with a citation.

9 In the methodology of Liberation Theology, theological reflection is a 'second step' which follows practice.

10 Graham, 1996.

11 Bosch, 1982, p. 27.

involve preview. Historians can always say the future is not their period, but theologians cannot.

In Galatians 6.11, Paul famously quips, 'see what large letters I am making when writing to you in my own hand'.[12] This book is in part some kind of ethnography, written in large letters, since it is eschewing the usual close-up focus of congregational studies and entering the wider angle and less common format of 'denominational studies'. It offers reflection informed by listening to and interviewing a variety of stakeholders within and beyond the contemporary Church of Scotland. It also reflects its origins in my appointment to the Chalmers Lectureship, offering a certain kind of unapologetic church theology, which is part diagnosis, part thought experiment about reform, and part advocacy for some courses of action.[13]

I am grateful to the General Assembly for appointing me as Chalmers Lecturer and to the Principal Clerk and the trustees of the Lectureship for their patience in awaiting the belated production of the lectures, which finally took place in February 2017 over three weeks in St Giles' Cathedral, Edinburgh, from where they were also live streamed and archived on YouTube.[14] Thanks are also due to Rev. Calum MacLeod, minister of St Giles and to the Kirk Session there for their gracious hospitality. As part of the work of preparing both lectures and book, I wrote a series of six articles for the Church of Scotland's monthly magazine, *Life and Work*, which appeared between October 2014 and March 2015. I am grateful to its editor Lynne McNeill for this opportunity to engage directly with a wider church public. Thanks are also due to both the University of Glasgow and Trinity College for part-funding a study trip to the USA which included time at the Presbyterian Church (USA) – PCUSA – offices in Louisville, KY, in the summer of 2014. I am indebted to Michael Jinkins, Amy Pauw, Cliff Kirkpatrick and Lisa Lee Williams of Louisville Seminary, as

12 The implication is that he has previously been dictating through an amanuensis who has had smaller, neater handwriting.

13 The Chalmers Lectures, offering an abridged version of the arguments presented here, were delivered over three nights in St Giles' Cathedral, Edinburgh, during February 2017.

14 Lectures can be viewed at www.youtube.com/watch?v=u5_mLIvvzRU.

well as Gradye Parsons, Stated Clerk of the PCUSA, for hospitality and time discussing the life and work of their church. A further trip to the USA in November 2015 gave me opportunities to meet with staff at Princeton and Columbia Seminaries of the PCUSA, and again I am grateful to the University and Trinity College for financial support, as well as to James Kay, Kait Dugan, Anna and David Carter Florence, and Leanne Van Dyk for hospitality and insight. Steve Salyers (aka GA Junkie on Twitter) gave invaluable advice on aspects of the governance and structure of the PCUSA.

I owe a particular debt of gratitude to Fiona Tweedie, Peter McEnhill, Neil Glover and Allan Vint for advice on various aspects of this project.

As a practical theologian, I try to write for the sweet spot which spans church and academy, aware I am running the risk of pleasing neither. The discussion in this book will move between the languages of theology and of religious studies, but I have also made the decision to give the lectures and write the book in the first person. The days are gone when most academics aspired to the narrative voice of the disembodied universal and today more of us aspire to an honest and reflexive standpoint epistemology. This means recognising that 'where we sit affects what we see'. I have written this book as someone who is part of the problem and wants to be part of the solution. I remain inspired by the task Fearghas MacFhionnlaigh names in his wonderful poem 'The Midge': 'I am only a cell in Scotland's body, struggling to be a brain cell'.[15] As with *Honey from the Lion*[16] in which I reflected on the state of the nation, so in this book it is with just as much trepidation and awareness of my own limitations that I offer these reflections on the state of the Kirk.

Stated simply, my thesis is that the systems architecture of the Kirk needs a (partial) redesign. This will not be a silver bullet, only God holds those, but I think it could make a positive contribution to the wise stewardship of our institutions which is a crucial part of discipleship in the world and in the churches.

---

15 Published in *Cencrastus*, 1982.
16 Gay, 2014.

To invoke the idea of wisdom is to draw on a theological tradition which draws together experience and reason, which is open
to borrowing from any area of human life and work, recognising
that 'all truth is God's truth'.[17] Organisational psychology, management theory and political science may offer rich sources of
insight to add to divinity's traditional mix of disciplines. There is
an appropriate theology of institutional reform which goes along
with this, neither harbouring 'pelagian' ambitions for the church,
nor engaging in 'docetic' fantasies about it. Humble, imaginative,
wise reform, according to holy scripture, interpreted under the
guidance of the only-wise Holy Spirit – that is what the Church of
Jesus Christ aspires to. To work hard at improving how an institution operates, at reforming its processes, structures and policies,
need not be seeking to do things 'in our own strength'; it can, in
its own way, also be divine service.

The redesign is possible, because there are no definitive blue-
prints in the New Testament for how the church should be organised. Church polity is underdetermined by the biblical witness and
I will argue (ecumenically) that we should embrace that as a gift of
providence. Sam Wells says that reading Stanley Hauerwas helped
him to understand that 'God intended the church'.[18] To that I
would add the claim that God also intended that members of the
church would be involved in shaping, negotiating and continually reforming its polity. This task belongs to Christian freedom,
albeit that freedom is not unconstrained. The call to exercise that
freedom comes to the church within the *missio Dei* and is itself
a response to the *missio Dei*; it belongs to the evangelisation of
human life, the redemption of human culture.

In the case of the Kirk, the redesign is necessary because past
decisions about structure and governance, which belonged to the
contextual discipleship of previous generations, are no longer the
best options for addressing the contextual, missional challenges
facing the Church of Scotland today. In particular, I will argue
here that:

---

17 Holmes, 1977; Amy Plantinga Pauw of Louisville Seminary opened up these
themes from her current work on wisdom ecclesiology in the Kerr Lectures, delivered in Glasgow in 2015.

18 Wells, 1998, p. xvii.

- the creation of the eldership and of Kirk Sessions reflected a contextual response to ecclesial and societal challenges in the sixteenth century, which needs to be rethought and reworked today;
- the designation of ministers of word and sacrament reflects a series of contextual understandings from the sixteenth century onwards and needs to be reviewed and reworked for the twenty-first century;
- the current degree of centralisation, bureaucratic and economic, reflects the legacy of a nineteenth-century contextual response, the Disruption project of creating a new, national denomination (the Free Church) from scratch and is not best suited to tackling issues of pervasive national decline;
- the number of presbyteries is the legacy of a series of contextual reforms linked to the size of the national church, the degree of centralisation and the civic administrative divisions decided upon by the UK/Scottish state. It no longer works or makes sense and is hindering the church's witness.

I am aware that this may seem like an ambitious or even overambitious thing to attempt, but I want to argue that there is no hubris involved here. I set out in Chapter 5, the reasons why I think the reform agenda has to be approached in a systemic and holistic way. An individual academic has the freedom to do this, to say and think things which might not survive the rigours of a council or committee's drafting processes. The hope is that what this lacks in accountability and authorisation, it may make up for in creativity. Although many of my theological leanings will be obvious, the book is not written to score theological points. I believe that what I argue for here is a habitable vision of the Kirk's future, which could continue to accommodate the needs of a broad and diverse church, including those to the left and right of myself theologically.

The book is offered to the Kirk as a thought experiment in the face of complex and demanding challenges. If this book has some gifts to offer to the church, I am sure among them will be the gift of being wrong. There is no shame in that. There are no definitively right answers available when it comes to institutional reform; only choices which can be made with as much wisdom and grace as we can receive from the hand of God. I want to play a part in developing and deepening a conversation that needs many voices to take it forward; voices institutional, academic, artistic and civic. What follows is not a programme I expect to be implemented or a blueprint I expect to be followed. We do, I believe, urgently need such a programme and such a blueprint, but this is only one draft, one sketch of what it might look like. The work of reform belongs to the whole church. As a theologian commissioned in the service of the church, I hope this book can serve that work. My hopes for this were raised by the remarkable response to the lectures and the many messages I received after they were delivered. The response was by no means uncritical, nor did I expect or want it to be, but it was overwhelmingly positive and constructive. What was clear was the shared sense of urgency about the issues covered in the lectures. These issues are explored in more depth and detail in the following chapters.

I

What Just Happened?

The story of how we got here is inextricably bound up with our account of where we are...

Charles Taylor[1]

One of the strong arguments in favour of the kind of educated ministry the Church of Scotland has long been committed to, is the importance of historical perspective for those who are leaders and teachers within the church. There is a pithy observation attributed to church historian Henry Sefton, that 'the Seceding Churches planted strategically, while the Free Church planted competitively'. This explains a lot about the state in which the Church in Scotland entered the twentieth century and about the streetscape of many of Scotland's cities and towns.[2] Move forward two generations from the 1840s, through the post-Disruption explosion of church building, to the Church of Scotland in the 1920s, and you will encounter the unflattering portrait of these years, assembled above all by Stewart J. Brown, depicting the Kirk's past complicity in anti-Irish prejudice and sectarian propaganda.[3] My own doctoral thesis noted the change in tone between the 1920s and the 1930s, when the wiser leadership and analysis of figures such as John Baillie began to prevail over the toxic tendencies of John White. After the shameful episodes of the 1920s, the witness of the Church of Scotland was clearer and stronger during the Second World War, with the Baillie Commission offering visionary leadership which contributed to post-war initiatives on the

---

1 Taylor, 2007 p. 772.

2 I have been unable to find a citation for this.

3 Brown, J. S., 1990; see also on this Bruce, 2014, especially Chapters 3–5 where he offers some correctives and supplements to Brown's account of the 1920s and 1930s. Brown's story is undoubtedly the truth, though not the whole truth, about the Kirk in this period.

reconstruction of the economy and the creation of the welfare state.[4]

The period immediately after the Second World War was one of immense energy and activity, in which a youthful Iona Community was growing alongside the ambitious missional activities of 'Tell Scotland'.[5] The pioneering Scottish sociologist of religion, John Highet, documented this activity in his 1960 study *The Scottish Churches: A Review of Their State 400 Years After the Reformation*.[6] He could not have known (although arguably he intuited) that he was writing at the hinge point, when the Church of Scotland had already reached its all-time membership high and was beginning its relentless decline from the early 1960s. Table 1 sets out the turning point and the onset of decline in membership from this mid-century peak.

Table 1. Church of Scotland membership 1950–2015.

Year	Membership
1950	1,271,247
1956	***1,319,574***
1960	1,301,280
1970	1,154,211
1980	953,933
1990	786,787
2000	607,712
2010	445,646
2011	432,343
2012	413,488
2013	398,389
2014	380,163
2015	363,597

* AU-time peak membership

---

4 See Gay, 2006; see also Newlands and Baillie, 2002.

5 For information on 'Tell Scotland' see Sandy Forsyth's 2017 doctoral thesis.

6 Highet, 1960; for brief information on Highet's career, see www.brin.ac.uk /commentary/drs/appendix8/; this period is also discussed briefly in Burleigh, 1983, p. 413: his analysis, written in 1960, claims that 'Never in its history has there been more of the missionary spirit in the Church expressing itself in active churchly evangelism.'

Tracing the pattern of decline which set in from the early 1960s is not just a statistical and a sociological task, it is also a spiritual challenge for the Kirk. Forty years ago the downward trend was well established, but there were still just over a million members of the Church of Scotland worshipping in some 2,000 congregations and served by over 1,600 ministers of word and sacrament. Today, in 2017, we have around 350,000 members in 1,331 congregations, served by some 800 ministers. Not everywhere, but in most congregations, it has been a story of relentless decline. The Church of Scotland has lost the equivalent of an average-sized congregation each week for the past ten years.[7] It is psychologically significant that most people in the Kirk, along with most ministers, are now unlikely to have ever had the experience of being part of a growing congregation.

A tale of two censuses

Questions on religion were only finally included in the UK Census in 2001. The Church of Scotland was already braced for results which would highlight its decline, but the numbers in 2001 were not nearly as bad as some had feared. More than two million Scots identified their religion as 'Church of Scotland' in the Census returns, representing 42 per cent of the population, while just 27.5 per cent or 1.4 million said they had 'no religion'. While this undoubtedly represented a substantial decline on what the levels of identification would have been in 1971 or 1981, it still bore witness to a prior Scotland, which had understood and felt itself to be culturally presbyterian. However, when the results of the 2011 Census came out, with the church again braced for bad news as its own numbers continued to plummet, there was little comfort to be found. The number of those identifying as 'Church of Scotland' had fallen by 20 per cent to just over 1.7 million, while the number of those identifying as having 'no religion' had risen by 38 per cent to 1.94 million. Presbyterian Scotland was

---

7 The comparison was made to me by Rev. Dr Fiona Tweedie, Statistics for Mission adviser to the Church of Scotland.

not yet entirely gone, but it was fading fast. The Census, which perhaps functions best as a measure of a residual, cultural religiosity, was charting a rapid process of secularisation across Scotland, and the Kirk was topping the charts for religious decline.

What just happened?

The question, 'What just happened?' is a question which I think many people in Church of Scotland congregations are asking. Men and women who are 60 years old this year, who were born in 1957, were baptised into a church which had just reached its peak membership and which was still a formative and pervasive force within Scottish society. The churches they knew as children and which their parents and grandparents knew, were still very well stocked with children and young people. Sunday schools with numbers in the hundreds were not uncommon. Stories from the 1950s speak of fleets of buses taking youngsters on Sunday school trips, of queues outside evening services held by popular preachers, of hundreds of people attending evangelism schools linked to 'Tell Scotland' and of large gatherings attending meetings to hear about what had gone on at 'World Council of Churches' assemblies!

Social historian Callum Brown places the hinge between growth and decline at the beginning of the 1960s and argues that more and more people (particularly the women who had been staunchly holding things together, despite their exclusion at this stage from ordination to ministry and eldership) found that the message of the Kirk was not one that resonated with their lives and identities in a changing Scotland and a changing world.[8] Scotland's *makar*[9] between 2011 and 2016, Liz Lochhead (b.1947), is an example of Callum Brown's generation of women who came of age in the 1960s. She left a Church of Scotland (where her father had been Elder and Session Clerk) which in too many ways did not seem to rhyme or resonate with her understanding of being a woman in

---

8 See Brown, 1997.
9 The Scots word used for Scotland's Poet Laureate.

a changing Scotland.[10] 'Her poem 'The Offering' begins: 'Never in a month of them would you go back./Sunday, the late smell of bacon/then the hard small feeling of the offering in the mitten.' The language is striking: the insistence on never going back, the crystallising of what church gave into the language of 'the hard, small feeling'.[11] It is one of a few post-1960 literary texts which are essential resources for understanding the decline of the Kirk in terms of what happened inside people's psyches, their hearts and minds. If you came of age in the 1960s and you wanted to live a life which was open, creative and expansive, this did not seem to be a space in which women could flourish.

From the 1960s, membership began to decline, numbers of church weddings declined, numbers of infant baptisms declined and attendances at worship declined. That such decline has been a painful and dispiriting experience for hundreds of thousands of Scots is beyond question. Some of the ministers retiring now or who retired in the past decade, especially those who were ordained in the 1970s, have spent their whole ministries with declining congregations. For them and for many older folk in the Kirk, there is a certain sense of disbelief, mingled with a deep sense of grief at the scale of the losses within congregations they have known and loved and served. As the decline progressed, in a country over-churched in building terms as a result of the Disruption, there has been an ongoing programme of 'unions and readjustments', in which much-loved church buildings have been closed and sold on for other uses or for demolition. In many cases, the palpable attachment of local people to 'their kirk' has been a source of great pain. Not uncommonly, its demise has led to bitterness. Along with the sociology and the statistics have come the spiritual and theological questions for church members. What just happened? Why has this happened? Where is God in this? What is God saying to us through this?

---

10 In conversation with her at Solas Festival in 2015, she told me her father had been Session Clerk.

11 Lochhead, 2011. For a brief critical commentary on 'The Offering', see Crawford and Varty, 1993, pp. 71-2.

There has been no shortage of people over the years ready to offer competing and conflicting diagnoses of the causes of decline. Some of the most common ones from across the spectrum include:[12]

It's divine judgement on an unfaithful church which has neglected God's Word and failed to preach the gospel . . . It's a healthy human response to an institution which dragged its feet over issues of justice and equality . . . It's a sad but predictable cultural response from young people to an institution which feels boring and irrelevant . . . It's a creative spiritual move beyond the life-denying, philistine shapes of reformed worship and piety. . .

The blunt and outspoken US theologian Stanley Hauerwas once said, 'God is killing Protestantism and perhaps Christianity in America and we deserve it.'[13] While that may resonate with some, others may feel more like joining the lament of the worshippers in Psalm 44: 'All this has come upon us, yet we have not forgotten you, or been false to your covenant. Our heart has not turned back, nor have our steps departed from your way, yet you have broken us.' Through the past six decades of decline it would be hard to find a parish where in any given week there was not some story, and sometimes many stories of selfless and loving service, of enriching Christian community, of spiritual inspiration, of costly discipleship, of generous hospitality. Nor would it be hard to find examples of prophetic witness: sharing in the struggle against apartheid, campaigning against the spread of nuclear weapons, setting up some of the first stalls in Scotland to sell fairly traded goods, joining in the Millennium Jubilee 2000 campaign for the cancellation of third world debt, supporting women and men struggling with addiction, opening buildings and creating projects to welcome and support refugees and asylum seekers. The ministers of word and sacrament, whose identities and confidence have been much assailed in these years, have engaged in faithful visiting, carrying Communion to housebound folk, sitting with

---

12 Here I paraphrase.
13 Hauerwas, 1995, p. 39.

the dying and their families, conducting baptisms and weddings and funerals. In some, though not all places, there has been a rich weekly diet of faithful and creative worship, passionate preaching, thoughtful and beautiful liturgy, heartfelt prayer, empowering involvement of members in worship and uplifting music.

Given the many things in the life of the Kirk which deserve to be celebrated, honoured and given thanks for, the scale of decline may seem galling and might indeed provoke some worshippers to remonstrate with God. The Old Testament theologian Walter Brueggemann uses Psalm 44 as an example of the vigorous dialogue which takes place between YHWH and Israel across the texts of the Hebrew scriptures.[14] For Brueggemann, such a dialogue can be a sign of spiritual health. Across the canon of scripture, there are some texts which show arguing with God as a form of denial and self-deception, but others which celebrate it as a form of faithfulness, patience and hope. Ironically perhaps, for an institution which takes care of so many through death and dying, I am not sure that the Kirk has yet done its own grief work over the huge losses it has experienced. 'What just happened?' is a theological, a spiritual and a psychological question, but since the discussion in this book will move between the languages of theology and of religious studies, I also want to ask how the question 'What just happened?' can be answered from a religious studies/ sociological and philosophical perspective.

Secularisation and its discontents

Theories of secularisation have been evolving within Western culture since the intellectual challenges of the Enlightenment and the political challenges of the French Revolution made their presence felt. They took on a more systematic form in the latter half of the nineteenth century, as the theories of Karl Marx and Charles Darwin began to break open the self-understanding of Western Christendom. The classic forms of secularisation theory which were to become almost an article of faith for many within the

---

14 Brueggemann, 2005, p. 8.

developing social sciences, reflected strong modernist assumptions about the trajectory of historical development. Western European societies, seen by their nineteenth and early twentieth century intellectuals as the most advanced civilisations which had ever existed, were undergoing deep transformations: industrialisation, urbanisation, social differentiation, mass education. Under the tutelage of Enlightenment theories of progress and, not least, the influences of Marx and Marxism, a 'classic' theory of secularisation became dominant across the social sciences, according to which a decline in the social significance of religion was seen to be an inevitable concomitant to the rise of modernity. Western European societies, on this understanding, were simply going to grow out of religion. The predictions of most secularisation theorists until the 1990s were that institutional forms of Christianity, which had been powerful in Europe for 1,400 years, were now facing a relentless decline.

In contemporary Scotland, secularisation theory has been challenged and revised in significant ways by the work of the social historian Callum Brown, now a professor at the University of Glasgow.[15] Brown's work offered some important challenges to classic accounts of secularisation, from the perspective of postmodern understandings of historical and cultural change. He argued against a deterministic philosophy of history in which secularisation was inevitable, in favour of a more open and flexible account of 'religious change'. He argued against the idea of a continuous process of secularisation from the nineteenth century onwards, suggesting that this analysis was driven by the assumptions of secularisation theory, but did not fit the statistics. Brown's analysis of church membership and attendance redated secularisation in Scotland, arguing that it did not really begin in earnest until after the Second World War and even offering a single year, 1963, as the putative starting point. Along with his reconceptualising and redating came a new theory of causation in which gender played a decisive role. Brown argued that religious life in Scotland had been marked in the nineteenth century by a 'feminisation of piety'

---

15 See Brown, 1997; Brown, 2005; Brown, 2009.

and that secularisation in the twentieth century was triggered by a 'de-pietisation of femininity'.[16]

Brown's analysis has been critiqued and contested from various angles, with 'old-school' secularisation theorists resisting his redating and others resisting his rather singular focus on gender as the key explanatory factor. From the perspective of this book, it is interesting to note that while his rejection of the inevitability of secularisation might be welcomed by those of us within the churches, he does believe that secularisation is happening, that it has taken hold of Scotland and Britain with a vengeance since the 1960s and that it is to be very much welcomed. In the past decade, Brown's own stance seems to have hardened against religion and he increasingly sounds less like the academic fascinated by religion and more like a determined evangelist for atheism.[17]

There have been other challenges to secularisation theory which have also contested its ideology of historical inevitability. Peter Berger produced what the University of Aberdeen sociology professor Steve Bruce has called 'an unnecessary recantation', when he suggested that classic secularisation theory had become the province of European intellectuals.[18] What Berger was pointing to, alongside other analysts like José Casanova, was the persistence and emergence of various phenomena which challenged a 'one size fits all' secularisation theory. Christianity was still growing in global terms, particularly in the global south, across three continents: Latin America, Africa and Asia. Post-1989, with the collapse of Soviet communism, there was evidence of a 'desecularisation' of former communist countries and a resurgence of the religious allegiances and behaviours which communist regimes had tried to suppress. A further challenge could be found in the notable differential apparent between the USA and Europe. As an advanced industrial society which scored as highly on all of the indicators of modernity as any European country, surely levels of religiosity should be falling just as quickly in the USA as

16 To translate roughly: from the late nineteenth century, religion came to be seen increasingly as a women's thing – and then, from the 1960s, women increasingly came to see religion as not their thing.

17 See Brown, 2017.

18 Berger's essay appeared as Chapter 6 in Woodhead et al., 2001.

they were in Europe? The fact that they were not was a further challenge offered back to secularisation theory. These currents of debate which were swirling around in the 1990s and the first decade of this century, saw a massive intervention in 2007, with the publication of *A Secular Age* by the Canadian liberal Catholic philosopher Charles Taylor.[19] Taylor's magnum opus offered an extended reflection on the changing place of religious belief within the West over roughly five centuries between the early modern era and the present day. Taylor's hugely learned enquiry is sympathetic to faith without denying the enormity of the change which has taken place. He charts a broader range of losses which have come in the wake of a loss of faith in religious explanations and experiences of life, and he pauses to wonder if the experience of these other losses may yet cause new generations in search of an elusive 'fullness' to life, to turn back to religion.

Linda Woodhead and Paul Heelas's *The Spiritual Revolution*[20] tracked the religious behaviour and attitudes of the population of Kendal, a market town in the north of England. Guided by Charles Taylor's 'subjectification theory' they undertook research which confirmed their hypothesis that inherited, traditional 'life as' forms of organized religion were increasingly giving way to chosen forms of 'subjective life' religion. Alongside growth in the 'holistic milieu' which was particularly strong among women over 40, the forms of denominational Christianity which were doing best were those shaped by charismatic evangelicalism. Both these forms of religiosity shared a stress on experience, emotion and an affirmation of personal subjectivity: on people 'finding themselves' and experiencing themselves through religion. Their book has rightly been much discussed and admired. Its academic confirmation of increasing numbers saying 'I'm not religious, but I am a spiritual person' resonates as strongly in Scotland as in England or Wales. Where Scotland's experience diverges, is that the Kirk has been influenced less by successive waves of the charismatic renewal than the Church of England. Given Woodhead and Heelas's findings, this is potentially significant and likely to

---

19 Taylor, 2007.
20 Woodhead and Heelas, 2005.

reduce the appeal of the Kirk further, unless the Scottish population were shown to be less drawn to that form of subjective life spirituality for cultural reasons.[21]

What just happened . . .?

This has been very deliberately posed here as a question. My claim is that it is not one we will be easily done with, but one which demands serious engagement. Taking a cue from Walter Brueggemann, there is a place for 'lament', but we should understand that biblical traditions of lament consist in more than handwringing and nostalgia. They include serious and searching prophetic reflection on what has gone wrong (and right). I have been a strong supporter of the need for more empirical research into patterns of church attendance and participation in Scotland. A good deal of valuable work has been done, under the aegis of the Statistics for Mission Working Group and subsequently by Rev. Dr Fiona Tweedie, but there is more to be done. It can be easy to delude ourselves that things are better than they are (or sometimes worse) based on our own anecdotal awareness. Very often a bracing dose of statistics is essential if we are to gain a broader and fuller picture and set what we know in a national (and international) context. But the kind of reflection needed will also have to go beyond statistics, to ask about the social, cultural and spiritual meanings of the experiences which the numbers direct our attention to. To explore these, we need to draw on literary treatments from a Liz Lochhead or a James Robertson and we need to undertake broader initiatives in what academics call 'qualitative research', based on interviews with individuals and groups. We need to listen to the stories and the interpretations of decline which come to us from the mouths of members, elders and ministers, as well as from those indifferent or even hostile to

---

21 No one has attempted anything like the Kendal project in Scotland, so we have no secure research data on which to base conclusions. Steve Aisthorpe's research described in his 2016 book *The Invisible Church* offers some important insights, but was designed to address different questions.

the Church. We also need, in the best traditions of theological reflection (and preaching) and of the other humanities, to attempt our own interpretations as we seek to 'know the times' and to understand, as Marvin Gaye said, 'what's goin' on'.

What it means for Scotland

To date we have seen relatively little discussion among historians and sociologists about what the decline of the Kirk means for Scottish identity, culture and society. At a pre-Referendum event in Glasgow School of Art in 2014, journalist and commentator Alex Massie was an exception to this, connecting the decline of an older Unionist sensibility in Scotland to the decline of the Kirk.

There has been noisy commentary from the rival mini denominations of the Scottish Secular Society and the Edinburgh Secular Society, along with a more moderate tone from the somewhat larger Humanist Society of Scotland; but the activists behind these represent very small groups within contemporary Scotland. A more general attitude seems to be the feeling that this is a matter of private grief for the Kirk and its members, but something other people in Scotland view with benign indifference. Grace Davie, another leading voice in contemporary English, UK and European sociology of religion debates, has given support to theories of 'vicarious Christianity'.[22] This interesting and, to me, persuasive analysis registers the existence in post-Christendom Europe of significant (even if declining) numbers within the population who want the Church to exist, but do not themselves want or intend to play any active part in it, either through attendance, 'membership', or regular giving. In other European countries, these are the people who, when faced with the choice to pay or not to pay their 'church tax' will, more often than not, opt to pay it. For this section of the Scottish population, their feelings about the church go beyond indifference. They want the Church of Scotland to be there, will regret its passing and feel diminished by its absence, but are mostly not prepared to do anything much or indeed, anything

---

22 Davie, 2002, pp. 19–20.

at all to avert this. More conservative and evangelical commentators within the Kirk tend towards a strongly negative view of such people, arguing that membership statistics from the 1950s were inflated by what they dismiss as mere 'nominalism'. For them, the pruning of such people from the rolls of parish churches may be a helpful purification of the church.

A very different perspective has been espoused by Linda Woodhead, who argued in a series of articles in the *Church Times* during 2014–15, that the Church of England was too focused on congregational growth and needed to pay more attention to its rarely attending Anglican fringe; those who still felt some weak identification with and had some weak ties to the denomination.[23] In an article in *The Spectator* in the summer of 2015, Mark Greaves described the tensions between those who tend to Woodhead's position and those, backed by Justin Welby, who were hot for strategy and congregational growth.[24] The positions I will develop in this book reflect my belief that folk on both sides of this debate have a point and should not try to cancel one another out.

Linda Woodhead has developed her views in conversation with data from an extended series of YouGov polls exploring public attitudes towards Church,[25] belief and religious participation in England. While this method of sampling opinion has its limitations, it does offer useful snapshots and indications of how public attitudes are shifting and changing. There is no comparable data in Scotland at present. The nearest we have is the data from the Scottish Social Attitudes Survey, whose 2015 survey is fairly grim reading for the Kirk, reporting a decline in belonging and attendance which is affecting the Church of Scotland more acutely than other religious groups.[26]

---

23 See among others, www.churchtimes.co.uk/articles/2015/23-january/comment /opinion/the-challenges-that-the-new-c-of-e-reports-duck.

24 www.spectator.co.uk/features/9583672/gods-management-consultants -the-church-of-england-turns-to-bankers-for-salvation.

25 Mainly the Church of England.

26 www.ssa.natcen.ac.uk/media-centre/latest-press-releases/ssa-2015-two -thirds-of-religious-scots-don-t-attend-services.aspx.

This points to a wider set of questions as to 'What Just Happened?' in relation to Scottish society as a whole. The 2014 Referendum on independence for Scotland led to a remarkable mobilisation of political energies and revitalisation of political discourse, including a revival of public meetings (a good many of them held in churches or church halls) on a scale few had thought possible. The 55:45 result for No was a clear outcome, but within days it became obvious that it had not taken the momentum away from the Yes campaign which had risen from around 30 per cent to 45 per cent over the course of the campaign. The effects of this were seen in the remarkable rise in SNP membership post-Referendum and the extraordinary SNP landslide in the 2015 General Election. The scale of public movement towards the SNP and the popular enthusiasm for Nicola Sturgeon during the General Election campaign bore witness to a Scotland which in some respects was changing faster than pundits or pollsters could keep up with. While support for the SNP and Scottish Green Party had remained high, the 2016 Brexit Referendum was a profound shock to the political system, with the 62 per cent of the Scottish electorate voting Remain being overwhelmed by Leave voters in England and Wales. As a result, a second independence referendum is now being sought by some, although the 2017 General Election saw something of a backlash against this. With Brexit negotiations still to be worked out over 2018 and 2019, further political turbulence seems inevitable.

It is tempting to place within the same frame the Referendum on Same-sex marriage held in Ireland on 22 May 2015, which resulted in a decisive victory for those who supported change. In this case, arguably, the result was anticipated by those such as religious studies scholar Gladys Ganiel, who had already begun in 2014 to speak about a 'post-Catholic Ireland'.[27] Although the Referendum in Scotland was not one which involved voters in any kind of clash with a position taken by religious authorities, there may be a similar sense of 'generational shift' in both countries. What analysis there has been of the religious identities of those who voted in the indyref suggested that most Church of Scotland members voted No

---

27 Ganiel, 2016.

and most Roman Catholics voted Yes. Age is likely to have been a key factor in this, as support for Yes was lower among the older demographic, who make up the majority of Kirk members.[28]

The trope of invoking the ethos and values of 'presbyterian Scotland' was revived in print journalism after 1997, in response to the rise of Gordon Brown, to be first Chancellor, then between 2007 and 2010, Prime Minister of the United Kingdom. However, it was already by then barely understood by many of those who used it and after this last outing, it seems likely to have a diminishing effect.[29] Presbyterianism no longer casts the same shadows over the Scottish psyche as it once did. This is both because it no longer carries the same social power and visibility and because the twenty-first-century Church of Scotland and its members no longer carry or deserve the same reputation for dourness or severity. The Scotland of the 2014 Independence Referendum campaign and its aftermath, particularly the younger half of its population, is no longer the culturally presbyterian Scotland experienced and imagined by previous generations. This change is creating a new situation for the Kirk, which those of us within it are struggling to understand and respond to. On the one hand, the change comes with what are perceived as negative consequences: people no longer attending church, people unable to sing supposedly familiar hymns at funerals, widespread ignorance of Christian doctrine and increasing biblical illiteracy. On the other hand, the reduction in hostility to the Kirk and the rise of indifference may bring some new possibilities for the rediscovery of Christian faith and church practice by rising generations in a post-presbyterian Scotland.[30]

Commentators like the Aberdeen University sociologist Steve Bruce remain convinced that secularisation is a steady, cumulative and invincible process within Scotland as it is, broadly speaking,

---

28 www.brin.ac.uk/2014/scottish-independence-and-other-news/.

29 See my discussions of this in relation to Gordon Brown in Gay, 2007 and Gay, 2009.

30 Secularisation may take different forms in different countries, and this may be related to which religious traditions were dominant. I say 'may' because we don't understand this phenomenon well enough as yet, but a working hypothesis would be that historically Roman Catholic and historically Protestant populations may show distinctive patterns of secularisation. So Ganiel's title could be adapted to speak of a post-Protestant or post-presbyterian Scotland.

across the whole of western Europe.[31] Scotland, they say, is leaving the Kirk and never coming back. Charles Taylor offers a subtly different perspective. 'Our age', he claims, 'is very far from settling in to a comfortable unbelief.'[32] Taylor suggests that as secularisation advances within Western societies, we may reach a kind of fragile equilibrium, which is capable of tipping in different directions. In some societies, he believes there may still be further movement towards a more secular outlook, with increasing numbers of people identifying religion as a problem and gravitating towards a self-contained, 'immanentist' view of life.[33] However, Taylor also offers a distinctive reading of 'secularisation and its discontents',[34] suggesting that in the twenty-first century the most secular societies may find that 'many young people will begin again to explore beyond the boundaries' of a 'waste land' of immanence. In these societies, blaming a relatively weak religious domain for human ills will seem increasingly implausible and the record and capacities of a now dominant humanism and secularism for meeting human aspirations to 'fullness' of life will be increasingly questioned.[35] Those of us living in the most secularised societies in the world may find that beyond the post-Christendom period we are currently living through, we may be about to experience, even if this happens patchily across Europe, a post-secular and post-atheist phase in our culture.[36] This, we should note, would not be the same as a revival of religion, although it might create conditions favourable to that. In the first instance, it would represent a feeling, a *zeitgeist* or cultural mood, in which secularism and atheism no longer felt so much like progressive forces,

---

31 www.gold.ac.uk/faithsunit/reimaginingreligion/landmark-interviews /steve-bruce/.

32 Taylor, 2007, p. 727.

33 Taylor, 2007, p. 770.

34 The phrase, a punning paraphrase of Freud's 1929 book *Civilisation and its Discontents*, has been used by multiple authors, so no single attribution seems possible.

35 See Smith, 2014 for critical reflections on reading Charles Taylor.

36 The ideas explored here are on the borderlands between sociology of religion, prophetic spirituality, and missiology and need to be held within an overarching understanding of divine providence. There is no claim of inevitability and no claim that technique or strategy can secure outcomes.

which had the cultural winds in their sails, but were themselves the object of increasing critique, scepticism and disillusionment. A key challenge then, to which I will return in the final chapter, is understanding the forms which Christian witness and church practice should take, if they are to bear faithful witness to an eternally innovative God in what may turn out, paradoxically, to be both a post-Christendom and a post-secular Scotland.[37]

Conclusion

The first and hardest task for the Church of Scotland is to honestly face up to what just happened, to count the cost and to make a sober assessment of what has been lost and what is left. The Kirk is not yet done with that task, but even as work continues on it, we can look around at the changing equilibrium in Scotland. Writing in 2006, Callum Brown observed that:

> By the end of the twentieth century, Britain was one of the most secular places that the world had ever known . . . With Sweden and the Netherlands, Britain was sharing an approach to religion that had virtually removed the going to church, and the cultural accessibility of religious narratives, from the lives of most people and from the narrative of the nation.[38]

What this means is that, like most of their peers across Europe, the rising generation of young Scots is embarked on a massive social and psychological experiment, into how far it will be able to negotiate life – birth and death, suffering and celebration, beauty and cruelty, joy and despair – without the challenges and consolations of religion.[39] One of the most significant comparisons from the Census data, which only became possible from February 2014, compares identification with the Church of Scotland with age (Table 2).

---

37 See also the arguments of Dutch missiologist Stefan Paas, 2016.
38 Brown, 2006, pp. 317, 319.
39 Aisthorpe, 2016, is a thought-provoking resource here.

Table 2. *2011 Census: age versus religion.*

The results are no surprise to any informed observer, but none-theless the 'graphic' confirmation of expectations makes sobering viewing. The table offers a clear picture of a rapidly secularising Scotland and a steadily ageing and shrinking church.

How far will this rising generation be able to craft satisfying and meaningful new rituals and ceremonies to mark life transitions? What kind of story or stories will it tell itself about who it is and where it has come from and will these stories prove to be 'thick' enough to offer the depth of meaning and inspiration which the Christian story has over many centuries?[40] And, if a world without religion as a dominant force or a present reality proves to be just as violent, cruel, unjust and depressing as one in which religion was a powerful force, how will people respond? These are some of the questions Charles Taylor carefully and thoughtfully offers to us at the end of his panoramic survey of secularisation. In doing so, without ignoring the sins and follies of religion and without complacency, he quietly opens a door

---

40 I am influenced here by the ideas of the anthropologist Clifford Geertz on 'thick' description and his memorable comment that 'Culture is the ensemble of stories we tell ourselves about ourselves'. Geertz, 1975, p. 448.

of hope to the future, which might on other grounds look over-whelmingly bleak for the Christian churches in countries such as Scotland.

In a chapter which has focused on the decline and failure of the church, it is helpful to be aware of that opening, and I will return to it at the end of the book. Before then, however, I want to take time to explore how the Church of Scotland could and should respond to the situation it finds itself in. What just happened? And what next?

2

Being Presbyterian

The polity of presbyterianism – with its strong insistence on the rule of the majority and the rights of the minority – is indeed the way in which Presbyterians affirm their unity and their diversity. This polity not only organizes dissent and diversity, it is itself a product of dissent, diversity, compromise and the creative resolution of bitter conflict.[1]

It may be that Presbyterianism asked too much and gave too little . . .

G. D. Henderson[2]

What does it mean to be presbyterian? It seems important to tackle this question head on, because some of the proposals for reform of the Church of Scotland which have been canvassed in recent years and some which will be commended again in this book have been accused of leading the church away from its true *presbyterian* identity, towards one of two potential falls from presbyterian grace: either a *congregationalist* polity or an *episcopalian* one.

As important as that rather specialised, insider debate about systems of church polity, or even more important, are three other questions. What has presbyterianism come to mean in Scotland? What is presbyterianism for? and what future does presbyterianism have in Scotland?

---

1 Report of Special Committee on Historic Principles, Conscience and Church Government, to the 1983 General Assembly of the PCUSA, quoted in Chapman, 1999, p. 2.
2 Henderson, 1954, p. 154.

The roots of presbyterianism

Presbyterianism is a form of church government which evolved out of the sixteenth-century Protestant Reformation. A standard narrative might refer to the reorganisation of church structures developed by the Reformer Martin Bucer in Strasbourg in the 1530s, to their implementation and refinement by John Calvin in Geneva from 1541 onwards and to their translation to Scotland in the 1560s by John Knox and his colleagues. Within Scotland, the polity evolves through various phases from the *Scots Confession* and *First Book of Discipline* in 1560, through the *Second Book of Discipline* in 1578, the 'Golden Act' of 1592, and the document entitled *The Form of Presbyterial Church Government* agreed by the Westminster Assembly in 1645; all of these leading up to the definitive settlement of 1690 in which presbyterianism was finally secured in law and in fact as the polity of the Church of Scotland. Donald MacLeod, former Principal of the Free Church of Scotland College in Edinburgh, writes of the development of presbyterianism in Scotland:

> John Knox, of course, set up no presbyteries, and this can easily lead to the conclusion that he was no Presbyterian. But Presbyterianism is not government by Presbyteries, but government by *presbyters*, and the essential principles of such a polity were already set in place by Calvin in Geneva. Here already it was perceived that the words *presbyters* and *bishops* referred to one and the same office; and here, too, it was laid down that churches must be governed not by one individual, but by a plurality of such presbyter-bishops. There had to be a *presbyterion*: a college or council of presbyters, 'which was in the church what a council is in a city.' (Calvin, *Institutes*, IV.XI.6). Hence the Scottish presbytery, the Genevan consistory and the Dutch classis.[3]

---

3 Article on Donald MacLeod's website, published 6 April 2015: www.donald macleod.org/?p=483.

MacLeod identifies Alexander Henderson's *Notes on the Government and Order of the Church of Scotland*, published in 1641, as 'the best succinct exposition of Scottish Presbyterianism'. In particular, he is drawn to what he calls Henderson's brilliant summary of the genius of presbyterian polity; that it offers 'superiority without tyranny, parity without confusion, subjection without slavery'.[4]

As a product of the Reformation, the elements of what would become presbyterianism emerged in critical reaction to the hierarchical structures of the Roman Catholic Church and then in an ongoing critical differentiation from both the modified episcopalianism of the Church of England and the radical congregationalism of anabaptists and independents. The main intellectual work of devising and refining presbyterian polity was undertaken over the course of a century, between Bucer and Calvin's crucial early moves and the 'fixing' of the main features of Scottish/British presbyterianism in the 1640s. Its early theorists and champions were almost all careful about distancing themselves from radical and anti-monarchical political movements, as they fought to gain the support of civil powers for the establishment of reformed protestantism in various territories in Europe. Nevertheless, despite their wary insistence on distinguishing spiritual and civil spheres, the polity they proposed for governing the church stood as a radical alternative to most civil polities in early modern Europe.

Glasgow Professor Willy Maley, in a discussion of John Milton's critical view of presbyterianism, quotes historians Roger Mason and Brian Tierney:

> For Roger Mason . . . it is precisely the Scottish radical and republican roots of Presbyterianism as epitomised by Knox that is at issue, as it was for Charles I's father at the dangerous moment of Anglo-Scottish union: 'James . . . responded to the inherent anti-imperialism of Presbyterian thought by embracing whole-heartedly the imperial ideology developed in England

---

4 Quotation from Alexander Henderson's 1641 *Notes on the Government and Order of the Church of Scotland*, via www.freescotcoll.ac.uk/images/files/Classics /Hendersongovernmentandchurch order.pdf.

to underwrite the Tudor monarchy's assertions of supreme authority over both church and state' . . . As Brian Tierney notes, 'James I of England understood the matter well enough when he said, "a Scotch presbytery agree-eth as well with monarchy as God with the Devil".'[5]

Milton's distaste for presbyterianism reflected his disappointment at its failure to build upon the radical and regicidal roots he saw in the work of Knox and also what he saw as its own nascent tyrannical tendencies in co-opting the civil powers to enforce religious settlements in its favour. In this discussion, we see something of the ambivalence of sixteenth and seventeenth century Scottish presbyterianism as a political system. On the one hand it was subversive of personal hierarchies, on the other hand it was keen to maintain corporate discipline and national unity. To enable this, it restricted both the role and prerogatives of the whole congregation in relation to the eldership and the rights of individual congregations in relation to the presbytery. It prized its independence from the state, but expected the state to uphold a more or less monopolistic reformed settlement in religion. In these influential early designs of its polity, calibrated in relation to specific geographical and historical contexts, we can see the seeds of future discontent and weakness, some of which are surfacing today and need to be addressed.

Layers and levels of governance

Presbyterian governance is built around a tiered, hierarchical system of courts and councils, which is designed to offer 'superiority without tyranny'. In addressing this, it addresses a perennial political problem, which is not so different in form, whether it is within the church or within wider civil and political society: how to unite, represent and involve people in governance. Particularly within more recent Scottish historical and cultural commentary, there has been too little recognition of the importance of presbyterianism in shaping a broader political imagination, both

---

5 Maley and Swann, 2013, p. 142.

at home and wherever in the world presbyterian influence has been spread.[6] Versions of this political problem can be found in every translocal political system in history. The genealogy of presbyterianism looks back to the descriptions in the Old Testament of how the tribes of Israel were organised and on through the classical legal and political traditions of Greco–Roman culture, to the small-scale beginnings of a 'conciliar' tradition in the New Testament writings.[7] Of course, it has often imagined those traditions retrospectively in its own image, but it has drawn inspiration and sought validation from them at different times. Marianne Wolfe suggests that 'the foundation stone of Reformed polity is the conviction that the church is "the body of Christ" (1 Corinthians 12) and that all authority in the church belongs to Jesus Christ, head of the church'.[8] Since both those affirmations would be accepted by those who prefer other forms of church polity, the key question is *how* the church's identity as body and Christ's role as head are to be acknowledged in the design of a church polity. Presbyterians have tried to recognise the 'body', all of whose parts are important, by ensuring each local congregation was fairly and equally represented in the higher courts and by giving each member of a congregation a single, equally weighted vote in the processes of calling a new minister and the election of elders.[9] This represents the bottom up/whole body element of the polity. Presbyterianism has expressed the top down/sovereign headship of Christ over the whole church, through its hierarchy of courts. Marianne Wolfe puts it succinctly: 'Each governing body makes its decisions by majority vote, the representatives of the larger part of the church having the power of review over

---

6 Elwyn Smith writes that Genevan patterns of church order 'in more fully evolved forms, [were] powerfully influential in the formation of Western political and economic institutions'. McKim (ed.), 1992, p. 293.

7 The Jerusalem 'council', etc.

8 See her article on 'Polity', in McKim (ed.), 1992, p. 283.

9 Though it is important to note that initially only men were allowed to vote as heads of households, so as with any narrative of political democracy in the West, we need to remember with shame the exclusions which undermined theories of equality and liberty or doctrinal ideals of a spiritual body within which every member was valued.

governing bodies representing a smaller part of the church.'[10] The weighting and calibration of the system has changed in different places and at different times, but these family resemblances have persisted. The power of review, is the presbyterian form of *episkope* or oversight, which is exercised communally by the courts and their representatives, not in a personal form by a bishop.

Representative democracy and participatory democracy

Presbyterianism contains elements of both representative democracy and participatory democracy, but the representative element has always been stronger. In his 1954 book, *Presbyterianism*, the Scottish scholar G. D. Henderson notes that 'Calvin would have called his system aristocratic and representation does develop rather an aristocratic principle of government.'[11] This representational aspect of presbyterianism is what is most likely to be unpopular with congregationalists, as it qualifies and reduces the autonomy and involvement of the local congregation. From a PCUSA perspective William Chapman comments that 'It is axiomatic that to be Presbyterian is to be in a union of churches. This means that a particular Presbyterian church may not operate as an independent entity [at variance with the provisions of the *Book of Order*].'[12] It is, of course, possible for congregationalists to be part of a union,[13] but such a union will leave more power with congregations and will significantly restrict the *episkope* of higher courts. The differences between congregationalism and presbyterianism are significant and intriguing. Although they share much in common, particularly their rejection or limitation of forms of personal *episkope*, and their broadly democratic instincts, they each represent differently calibrated answers to the question of subsidiarity, that is, which powers belong at which level of a

---

10 In McKim (ed.), 1992, p. 283.
11 Henderson, 1954, p. 61.
12 Chapman, 1999, p. 23.
13 http://conglib.co.uk/collections/congregational-unionchurch-archives/.

political system. These different answers have implications for how their systems operate. A General Assembly which has significant power to bind presbyteries and local congregations/kirk sessions is likely to be given more significance and taken more seriously than an assembly which is more used to simply connecting, considering and commending.

Where power lies within a system is critically important and crucial to determining the questions of where money is raised and spent.[14] A system like that of the Church of Scotland, in which money is distributed according to a centrally determined formula, has a different power map from the system which prevails in the PCUSA, in which more money is raised and spent locally. David Foxgrover has suggested that a congregationalist 'concern about local autonomy is a characteristic of all American churches'.[15] Miroslav Volf, in *After Our Likeness*, spoke of a growing 'congregationalisation' of traditional Protestant and Catholic churches:[16]

> Today's global developments seem to imply that Protestant Christendom of the future will largely exhibit a Free Christian form . . . It seems clear to me that we are standing in the middle of a clear and irreversible 'process of congregationalization'.[17]

If Volf was right, and I think he was, denominations like the Church of Scotland need to find ways to adjust to this, accepting that these forms of polity are not fundamentally opposed but are more like points on a continuum of differently weighted *federal* systems. Viewed in that way, the emergence of or transition to a more congregationalist form of presbyterianism can be seen as a wise adjustment, not a betrayal of principle. I will return to this later in Chapter 5, when I offer detailed suggestions about reform of the church's structures.

---

14 This is considered in more detail in the next chapter.
15 McKim (ed.), 1992, p. 79; a similar point was made to me in conversation by Professor James Kay of Princeton Theological Seminary in November 2015.
16 Volf, 1998, p. 12.
17 Volf, 1998, p. 13.

Leaving

It is intentionally hard for individual congregations to secede from a presbyterian system. Even where there is local funding of ministry, the ownership of buildings may be vested in a regional or national trust, so that congregations who wish to leave find it very difficult to take their buildings with them. This vesting of ownership of property in presbyteries and/or the national church reflects the materialist dimension of presbyterian ecclesiology, rooted in Reformed instincts about people being sinful and schismatic. The blunt message is that individual congregations should count the cost before they leave their sisters and brothers and opt for independency, or pay the cost afterwards. The great historical demonstration of that is of course the Disruption of 1843, in which hundreds of thousands of Scots presbyterians made a costly and sacrificial exit from the Church of Scotland to form the Free Church, with many leaving their church buildings and manses behind. It is hard to say other than that this is an intentional form of constraint and coercion, designed to curb the schismatic instincts which Protestants are so prone to, by imposing a high cost on walking away from the denomination. Where there is a parish system, as in Scotland, it also works to safeguard a place for local people to meet within a congregation which is recognised and approved by the national denomination.[18] While this feature of the polity was not particularly visible in the period 1929 to 1999, it has been more visible in the twenty-first century in the face of some deep divisions over the church's position on human sexuality. The limited moves the Kirk has made to accept and accommodate ministers in same-sex relationships have led some congregations to leave the denomination, and in some well-publicised cases the congregations' wish to take 'their' building with them have been frustrated by the denomination

---

18 Another 'material' dimension is that it also keeps bequests and legacies within the denomination they were offered to.

asserting its title and desire to retain it for the mission of the Church of Scotland.[19]

Did I ask too much?[20]

G. D. Henderson's intriguing reflection (made in 1954) on the history of presbyterianism in the USA, placed at the head of this chapter, raises the question of the demands which any polity makes upon its members and ministers. He suggests that 'Presbyterianism asked too much and gave too little.' From the outset, the Scottish tradition of presbyterianism asked a lot of its members. In certain contexts, that has been one of its chief attractions and main strengths. Reformed Christians, developing their traditions in a newly formed print culture, were passionate about education and literacy, about giving whole populations the tools they needed to read scripture in the vulgar tongue. Just as Aristotle believed that the optimum operation of the *polis* required effective formation of citizens who were able to participate fully in political life, so the Calvinist Reformed tradition has from the beginning been deeply exercised over forming laypeople who were able to play their full part as presbyters. This formation was educational as well as spiritual, political as well as ecclesial. It required citizen presbyters who were able to take part in the deliberations of consistories and Kirk Sessions and to cast their votes in a way which was informed by their reading of scripture and their understanding of doctrine. The wider political influence of presbyterianism, which I have already referred to, resulted from men and women who had been inducted into organised forums of deliberation and decision-making within the local and regional church, taking those skills and understandings out of the church

---

19 The case of St George's Tron in central Glasgow was widely reported in the media. Most of the congregation and the former parish minister left the Church of Scotland to form an independent congregation, but the building has been retained as a parish church with a new and creative evangelical ministry in place and a growing congregation.

20 '. . . more than a lot', from the song 'One' by U2.

and into the secular political arena, where they were used both to design new constitutional and political arrangements and to participate in them. In Scotland, between the sixteenth and nineteenth centuries, a significantly broader social range of men were able to speak and vote in session and congregational meetings than were able to vote in local government and national parliamentary elections.

There are multiple overlapping stories to be told about the role of presbyterianism in Scottish culture, but here I want to consider two broad types. One is a story of an *empowering* presbyterianism. In this (which is certainly too little told in modern Scotland) we encounter a presbyterianism which, because it asks a lot of those who are enlisted to run the system, also directly and indirectly empowers and equips them with skills which are transferable into other social and political contexts. Presbyterians in this story become accustomed to having a voice and a vote, to being at least selectively involved in decision-making, to being culturally enfranchised.[21]

The other story is of an *exhausting* and perhaps exhausted presbyterianism. In this, characterised by what Henderson described as 'asking too much', we find the demands of administering presbyterian polity become a cultural liability in contexts where people are less willing or less able to commit to them. Those already involved in the work of running the system become cynical about the amount of effort required to keep the wheels turning, while wary onlookers (both members and potential members) decline to commit themselves to being the next generation to keep the show on the road. This is increasingly where we are in 2017, and it is a dangerous place for any church to be in. Worn out by the demands of the system, people become forgetful of its virtues. Frustrated by the limitations of the institution, people become disdainful of its potential. Overwhelmed by the needs of the denomination, people become ungrateful for its gifts.

21 There is no quote in relation to Scotland which corresponds to the famous remark that 'the Labour Party owes more to Methodism than it does to Marxism', but that's the thought I have in mind here.

The role and figure of 'The meenister'

The figure of the minister looms large within Scottish culture. In his 1990 Christian vision of Scottish identity, Will Storrar spoke of the 'hindering icon' of the minister, standing between the Scottish people and their view of Christ.[22] The black-coated, black-gowned presbyterian minister is a more complex cultural character than is often allowed by critics. Historically, the authority of the pulpit was offset by the expectation of visiting any house in the parish, the aura of disciplinary severity was offset by the practice of pastoral care, the insistence on elite education was offset by traditions of lad o'pairts access to the vocation, the suspicion of the middle-class incomer could be overcome by their record as local advocate, and the right to live in the big house was offset by the relatively modest stipend. From the earliest days of the Scottish Reformation, the role has been performed in a variety of ways, some monstrous, some saintly, most somewhere in between. Perhaps most significantly of all, since 1968 the maleness of the role has been offset by the introduction of women as ministers of word and sacrament.

Cultural critic Tom Nairn (paraphrasing Diderot) famously quipped, 'Scotland will be reborn when the last Church of Scotland minister is strangled with the last copy of the *Sunday Post*.'[23] As I noted above, the sting of that is as reduced today as the power and status of its target. Would-be revolutionaries today are more likely to simply ignore ministers rather than engage in comic fantasies about eliminating them. The institutional role of the minister within the Church of Scotland continues to be structurally vital and significantly loadbearing in much the same way as it has been since the seventeenth century. The General Assembly is still made up of equal numbers of ministers and elders, but at presbytery level elders now far outnumber ministers. Alongside this change, theological imagination about ministry has not been static. While there was little explicit change or challenge to the role of the minister for the first 400 years of the

---

22 From the video made to accompany Storrar's 1990 book.
23 Tom Nairn, 'Three Dreams of Scottish Nationalism' in Miller, 1970, pp. 34–54, at p. 54.

Kirk's history, there were intimations of change in the theological thinking associated with the ecumenical movement in Europe from the 1920s onwards. Although it is not a term which sits comfortably within Reformed theology or ecclesiology, the idea of the 'laity' grew in importance as a theological theme through the three ecumenical strands of Life and Work, Faith and Order and the World Mission Conference, as well as through the work of the Student Christian Movement. The growth of Baptist and Pentecostal churches, the rising influence of evangelicalism and the work of CSSM/Scripture Union and the InterVarsity Christian Fellowship also played a part in developing and equipping those in non-ordained roles to play an active part in the ministry of the church. The Scottish presbyterian missionary, ecumenical activist and theologian J. H. Oldham was a key figure in developing ecumenical debates about the laity. Significant publications here included Hendrik Kraemer's *A Theology of the Laity*[24] and Oldham's colleague, Kathleen Bliss's *We the People : A Theology of the Laity*.[25] From the 1960s, the influence of the charismatic renewal gave fresh impetus to this, with an emphasis on 'gifts' rather than roles or offices, as the key factors marking and equipping individuals for ministry. This agenda has been shared across theological traditions within the Church of Scotland, with the gifts, contributions and voices of 'every member' within worship being championed both by evangelical and charismatic groups and leaders and by the Iona Community. However, almost a century after this became a talking point, 70 years after the formation of the Iona Community and the first WCC study programmes on the role of 'the laity' and more than 50 years after the arrival of charismatic renewal, patterns of relationship between ministers and members in the casting and choreography of worship and pastoral care remain very varied and uneven. Worship in many places still remains very minister-centred with its content solely or mainly determined by the gifts and attitudes of the ministers. Pastoral care may be shared across a team of members and elders, but old lore about it not being a 'proper' visit unless done by the

---

24 Kraemer, 1958.
25 Bliss, 1963.

minister herself can still be tenacious in its hold on mindsets in congregation and parish.

At the same time, there is a common perception that the cultural and social status of kirk ministers is now much changed and much diminished. This needs to be read against a backdrop of a decline in deference towards middle-class professions across the board, and I would argue it is as welcome in the church as it is more generally. But even if we wish good riddance to deference, we might be concerned about a role on which so much weight is still being placed appearing to be less valued. Research into how ministers feel about their own work and status points in two different directions. While there has rightly been concern about clergy stress and burnout, surveys also show relatively high levels of satisfaction among ministers.[26]

What has heightened concerns and focused minds in the past five years has been the decline in Scotland in the numbers of candidates for full-time, stipendiary ministry of word and sacrament. Over the next decade, many more ministers will retire than are predicted to enter training. An already high level of vacant charges is rising towards levels which will make traditional patterns of ministry increasingly unsustainable as we move towards 2030. The broad explanation for the declining number of ministry candidates is the overall decline of the church and its ageing demographic. Within this overall picture, however, there are further questions to be asked about whether the supply of potential ministers has shrunk faster than might have been expected, if so, why, and what can be done about it.

Certainly the minister's role and duties are changing. The shortage of ministers has led to many churches being united, but perhaps even more significantly to many more being linked.[27] While this is particularly prevalent in rural areas, it is a pattern which has been spreading into towns and cities. Ministry in a linked charge brings distinctive challenges and stresses. The attention

---

26 Multiple surveys in North America and in the UK, including work by Francis, Brewster, Archbishops' Council Report of 2001; US Congregational Life Survey, www.uscongregations.org.

27 Linkage is when congregations in different locations share a minister, but remain constitutionally distinct. This is the norm in most rural areas of Scotland.

and concerns of the minister are stretched beyond one parish, such that more effort has to go into covering the basics in each location, with less time available for innovation. A focus on pastoral work and an increased workload in this area may make it hard for ministers to respond to the call for a more 'missional' approach to the witness of the church within its parish.

The Kirk has responded to this, like other denominations, by looking to top-up the supply of stipendiary ministers with non-stipendiary Ordained Local Ministers. This programme, in operation since 2011, was a rebranding of the longstanding Auxiliary Ministry programme. At its introduction, many of the Kirk's remaining 'Readers'[28] were encouraged to transfer to the OLM programme. Ordinations under OLM have been a trickle rather than a flood and the programme remains less popular than a similar scheme within the Church of England.

'Tomorrow's Calling'

With not a little whiff of panic in the air, the Ministries Council has since 2013 begun to take the work of supporting and enabling vocations much more seriously and has become more intentional about reaching out to those who are sensing a calling, including women and men under 30.[29] The 'Tomorrow's Calling' initiative, backed by well-made short-form videos and a well-designed social media campaign has certainly been successful in attracting attention in and beyond the church, including from younger people. This kind of initiative will need to be resourced and sustained into the future.

---

28 Trained, but non-ordained women and men who preached and led non-sacramental worship.

29 Over the decade from the late 1990s, the average age of candidates entering education for ministry had begun to rise, with a particular lack of candidates under 30. This contrasted with patterns throughout the twentieth century, when many had entered the ministry straight from university after studying MA and BD Min. in succession. Those entering the ministry in their 40s or 50s were clearly going to offer fewer years of service and need to be replaced more quickly than younger candidates.

At the 2013 General Assembly, I successfully moved a motion calling for the church to set higher targets and also encouraging them to follow the example of the Methodist Church and the Church of England in creating a new 'pioneer' track for ordained ministry. As just noted, progress has been made on the first of these, but no progress has yet been made on the second.[30] I will return to the church's response to this below, but before that we need to reflect on another key bulwark of presbyterian polity.

The session

The consistories of early reformed churches in mainland Europe, which in Geneva had both civil/municipal and ecclesiastical functions, were given a more narrowly ecclesiastical form in Scotland as Kirk Sessions. In Session meetings, the elders elected (and at first elected only annually and not ordained for life) by the congregation sat with ministers to oversee the governance of the church and the moral and spiritual discipline of the parish. From 1560 to 1966, the office of eldership in the Church of Scotland was open only to men.

The historical origins of the eldership lie in a series of powerful acts of theological imagination, through which Bucer and Calvin, Knox and Melville moved towards reconceiving *episcope* in corporate and conciliar terms through a graded system of councils or 'courts' in which ordained ministers and elected elders sat together on equal terms. This turn away from a hierarchical system of pope, (arch)bishops and priests, in which *episcope* was exercised personally by various ranks of 'clergy', was a striking innovation in church governance and polity. It had effects and implications in two directions, both relativising the power and prerogative of the ordained minister and promoting the influence

---

30 Ministries Council responded to the 'pioneer' dimension by supporting the creation of five new Pioneer posts across the country, which presbyteries could bid for in 2015–16. While this is welcome, it has simply drawn existing ministers out of the already diminished pool and not properly addressed my concern, which was to create a distinctive pathway into ministry for those called to plant new congregations or fresh expressions of church.

and status of the non-minister, the initially non-ordained elder. While Knox and the *First Book of Discipline* initially envisaged annual election of elders, the move to *ordain* elders and make the office lifelong came within a generation, along with the heightened emphasis in the *Second Book of Discipline* (1578) on the 'spiritual' character of the eldership.[31]

Margo Todd, in her groundbreaking history of the Kirk in early modern Scotland, helps us to see with great clarity that there is not and cannot be a single story about elders within the church. Todd argues that in early modern Scotland 'the real power lay in the hands of lay elders – each, however mundane his occupation, had the same vote on session as the minister and together they considerably outnumbered the clergy'.[32]

Even when Kirk Sessions were at their harshest, Todd's forensic research into early Session minutes demonstrates that alongside the examples of harshness and prurience there were many examples of Sessions showing care and compassion, responding to issues such as domestic violence within their parish and generally contributing to social peace and a reduction in crime and violence across the country.[33]

By the nineteenth century, few Kirk Sessions were any longer the enforcers or investigators of public morals that some zealous sessions had been in previous centuries.[34] Increasingly it was managerial and administrative roles which loomed large alongside pastoral and spiritual duties. Elders' continuing disciplinary roles in 'fencing the table' through the distribution and potential rationing of Communion tokens could be performed in coldly mean-spirited or gently pastoral ways. The growth of congregations, the construction of many new buildings, the creation of a parallel system of sessions within the Free Church after 1843 – all

---

31 On the history of the eldership within the Church of Scotland, see the fine, recent paper by Alexander Forsyth at www.resourcingmission.org.uk/sites/default/files/downloads/History%20%26%20Theology%20of%20the%20Eldership%20Paper%20Dec2015_0.pdf; see also Todd, 2002, pp. 370–1.

32 Todd, 2002, 37.

33 Todd 2002, pp. 406–9.

34 Although Todd argues that this was often done flexibly and co-operatively and that it restrained evils such as domestic violence as well as the sexual misdemeanours which are often cited. See Todd, 2002, p. 403.

of these challenges shaped the eldership in the Victorian era. In this period of accelerating economic and industrial development, urbanisation and burgeoning municipalism, the Kirk elder became closely associated with social standing, bourgeois respectability, honesty and, not uncommonly, temperance. As larger congregations did more, developing a wide range of associated activities and societies, from Sunday schools, Bible classes and Boys'/Girls' Brigade companies, to literary and dramatic societies and Savings and Loan Clubs; as more buildings acquired pipe organs, first gas then electric lighting, as well as more elaborate heating systems; and as budgets grew alongside this, the eldership acquired an increasing roster of institutional and administrative responsibilities. Within some congregational constitutions, these more 'practical' or 'temporal' concerns were the business of 'Managers' or of a 'Congregational Board', which perhaps made for greater clarity. Nonetheless, a number of tensions within the identity of eldership were gathering force by the beginning of the twentieth century. The first was that the prestige attached to the role meant that some men sought it, expected it, or even reluctantly accepted it, because it was seen to fit with another role they had in the community: doctor or lawyer, head teacher or local businessman or member of a prominent local farming family. That such social considerations seem often to have weighed as heavily as more spiritual considerations would come to feed concern about how willing some elders were to live into the 'spiritual' office they had been ordained to. Certainly from the eighteenth century, but perhaps even from Melville's time, the eldership was seen to have clear associations with social status in Scotland. This has been steadily declining since the 1960s, as the social status and importance of the Kirk declines. The role to which women were finally admitted in 1967 was one whose social importance was already waning.

The theological story around eldership is also tangled and confusing. As noted above, government by presbyters had become a key ecclesiological distinctive of Church of Scotland polity. Over time it also became a key social and cultural feature of the Kirk's identity. There was a problem however. The exegetical and hermeneutical methods used by Calvin, Knox and Melville to justify this new polity did not wear particularly well. Already by the Westminster Assembly in the 1640s, there had been questions raised by others in the Reformed tradition about appropriate scriptural warrant for the eldership and these have never either gone away nor been adequately answered.[35]

Until the twentieth century, presbyterianism was so dominant in Scotland that doubts from other denominations about the theological and scriptural basis of eldership made relatively little impact. From the 1920s onwards, a rise in ecumenical awareness and contact introduced a new era of comparative ecclesiology, in which ecclesial traditions had to become more self-conscious about explaining their identity and its rationale(s), their 'faith and order', to their ecumenical neighbours. In 1948, Lesslie Newbigin, who was still then working in India as a Presbyterian minister and Church of Scotland missionary, published *The Reunion of the Church: A Defence of the South India Scheme*.[36] It appeared a year after the creation of the Church of South India, following complex and contested negotiations. Ecclesiological debates around the birth of the Church of South India were intense, with enormous condescension and haughtiness shown by some Anglican critics and commentators to those churches born on the wrong side of the episcopal blanket, which their congregations in South India were planning to unite with.

Newbigin's approach remains interesting today. It combines some pragmatic accommodations to episcopacy with powerful deconstruction of exclusionary narratives of apostolic succession. For Newbigin, two things were crucially important. One was that the church, like individual believers, lived out of the doctrine of justification by faith alone, through grace alone. In theological and spiritual terms, he saw attempts to secure the church's own status and position via arguments about polity as a resort to 'law'. The second conviction was that the church was a pilgrim people and that the ecumenical movement represented the call of God for the church to keep moving forward on that pilgrimage, in ways which served the *missio Dei*.

---

35 'The majority of the Westminster divines did not support the Scottish contention that the office of eldership was derived directly from Scripture.' Forsyth, 2015, p. 22.

36 Newbigin, 1960, p. ix.

Newbigin never turned his back on his presbyterian roots or disavowed presbyterian ordination and polity, but he did move on from them. In *The Reunion of the Church* he quoted Robert Rainy's judgement with approval:

In particular we are Scottish Presbyterians; we value the life and the traditions we inherit, though we refuse, and we need to refuse, to place them in the room of our living Head or of His Word. We own some benignant purpose of God in the genealogy of Church life in which He has cast our lot and in the peculiar influences which are derived to us from past history, We are not insensible to this, we are not tired of it, but it must not run into idolatry.[37]

G. D. Henderson's book on the eldership was blunt about the decline in the status of the office.[38] In the post-war period, leaving aside the perennial issue of presbyterians having to explain and justify the eldership within ecumenical 'Faith and Order' circles, there was awareness of the need within the Kirk to renew the understanding and undertaking of the eldership. The wartime Baillie Commission had raised the issue of admitting women to the eldership, and this rumbled on for two more decades before progress was finally made. Iona Community members, George Wilkie and Ian Fraser, contributed to these debates about the renewal of the eldership, Wilkie more directly through his 1958 Iona Community pamphlet on *The Eldership Today* and Fraser indirectly in his lively and illuminating 1959 reflection on parish ministry, *Bible, Congregation and Community*.[39]

Sandy Forsyth quotes Stewart Matthew's verdict, writing in 1990,

that the functions of elders by the 1950s and 1960s, whilst sometimes onerous in a business sense for the internal affairs

---

37 Principal Rainy, speaking at the 1904 General Assembly of the United Free Church after the House of Lords judgement had handed the entire property of the United Free Church of Scotland, quoted in Simpson, 1909, pp. 365–6.

38 Henderson, 1935.

39 See Forsyth 2015, p. 27, and Fraser, 1959.

of the Church, had become emasculated in their public face to 'The Doorman' (at Sunday worship), 'The Spiritual Postman' (delivering communion cards), and 'The Royal Cup-Bearer' (at communion).[40]

He also notes Matthew's judgement that Wilkie's pamphlet in 1959 represented a turning-point, with its argument that 'the current appreciation of the eldership was redolent of the central community position of the Church in the Christendom era, and that now in post-Christendom the eldership must become the lay vanguard of mission in the parish'.[41]

The thinking of Wilkie and Fraser reflects the theological ferment around mission and evangelism which characterised the 1940s and 1950s. The prospects for such a new 'lay vanguard' leading mission in the parish were being explored in the work of the Iona Community, in the missionary efforts of 'Tell Scotland', and in the missions led by D. P. Thompson. Forsyth's review offers an illuminating survey of reports on the eldership since the 1960s,[42] noting the major theological influence of T. F. Torrance on the 1964 and 1989 reports of the Panel on Doctrine.[43] Torrance's opinion, unchanged over the 25 years, was that there was no direct scriptural support for the office and that it was best understood as an expression of the church's call and commitment to *diakonia*.

Perhaps unsurprisingly, given his theological authority within the Kirk in the 1980s, Torrance's view of the elder-deacon (which identified him clearly with the 'lay-presbyter' side of the debate) convinced many of those seeking to lead theological opinion and change church law. The Committee of Forty in the 1970s, the Panel of Doctrine in the 1980s/1990s and the Assembly Council in the year 2000 – all tried to lead the Kirk towards significant changes in how eldership was understood and practised – through limiting terms of service, introducing compulsory sabbaticals and

---

40 Matthew, 1990, pp. iv–v, quoted in Forsyth, 2015, p. 26.
41 Quoted in Forsyth, 2015.
42 He pays tribute to Nigel Robb's prior work which informed his own.
43 Torrance published a key article in the *Scottish Journal of Theology* on 'The Eldership in the Reformed Church' in 1984.

replacing ordination with commissioning. All of them largely failed.

Forsyth's account of this offers a fascinating case study in the concerns of this book: how to approach institutional reform within the Church of Scotland. Tracking the debates between what has come to be called 'lay' theories of eldership, in opposition to 'presbyter' theories, can feel like a journey into a private museum of presbyterian mania, whose concerns seem increasingly abstruse and opaque. What we need today and what his work helps us towards, is a new ability to read some of these past debates in context and to assess how we negotiate them in our own context.

As someone working within the field of practical theology, I often tell my students that what people *do* is always interesting to us (not just what they think or say they think or what they feel they should or shouldn't do – but what they *do* do), and why. So it is interesting for us, as we try to make sense of the history and practice of eldership, to think what people have done by rejecting change. Alongside that, when we follow the debates around eldership (and this is clearly visible in Forsyth's account) we can see that elders were not only fending off challenges to their 'terms and conditions'; many of them, from the 1970s onwards, have also increasingly been taking on duties which had been reserved to their brother and sister 'teaching elders' – the *ministers* of word and sacrament. Read through the reports of the Panel on (Worship &) Doctrine and the Assembly Council, and this concern surfaces repeatedly.

Demarcation of the minister/elder boundary had been a concern even as the role of the elder was being enhanced in *The Second Book of Discipline*, which was careful to point out that 'Such as are commonly called Elders labour not in Word and Doctrine'.[44] However, it was, I think, wholly understandable that this hybrid office, poised between what other traditions called clergy and laity, would be affected by the rethinking of the role of laity which gathered pace from the 1950s onwards and was given a new impetus by the global charismatic renewal from the 1960s.

---

44 Forsyth, 2015, p. 57.

Given that the role of clergy/ministers was affected by this, as we have already noted above, how much more that of elders?

We can now see that in the past 50 years there have been two dynamics which might have pulled the eldership in opposite directions. On the one hand, the attempts at a robust intellectual take-down of the overstated theological and scriptural claims for the office of eldership have been unsuccessful in practical terms. They have been more persuasive for theologians and ministers who have sat on church councils, but less persuasive for the wider community of elders who have voted in presbyteries and in General Assembly. Not only have the proposed changes been resisted by those whose status and role they seemed to threaten, but the second dynamic at work is that there has simultaneously and unofficially been a steady expansion of elder activity into what was traditionally the minister's domain. This has been driven by a number of factors. Theologically, many elders and ministers now embrace a theology which sees ministerial monop-olies within worship as mistaken, unbiblical and unhelpful. There are more liberal variants of this (for example the drive of the Iona Community towards multi-voiced worship, with rich involvement from lay people) as well as those more associated with charis-matic (and non-charismatic) evangelicalism. Those who have been involved in highly participative Iona or Wild Goose wor-ship, those who have been active in Scripture Union, Christian Union or in renewal networks, are very unlikely to want to return to being 'pew fodder' and passive laity. They are used to leading prayers, leading worship times, reading scripture, bringing words of challenge, testimony or encouragement, leading Bible studies or reflections and in some cases teaching and preaching regularly. Church law has barely kept pace with this. Every Sunday, 'lay' people lead worship and preach in kirks across Scotland, as often without presbytery permissions as with them.

So far I have only referred to what has been happening because of theological enthusiasm for it, from across the theological spectrum. In other cases, the involvement and leadership of elders and members is being driven by necessity. As the number of vacant charges increases, it is becoming harder to find cover by ministers, deacons or readers. In some cases, congregations are keen to have younger people leading worship in preference to the retired minister or authorised (but often elderly) reader options available to them. As I said, what people *do* is always interesting.

What also needs to be understood about what I have just been describing, is that it is not simply and perhaps not even mostly about elders: it is about a steady revolution in expectations about who can and should be active in leading worship and other 'spiritual' gatherings in the life of the congregation. The eldership are caught up in that broader movement. Giving a tweak to a well-known and much-discussed paper on 'the people formerly known as the audience', someone has written of 'the people formerly known as the congregation' highlighting similar dynamics towards forms of co-production as opposed to mere 'reception'.

I suggested above that intra-presbyterian debates about lay or presbyter understandings of eldership were outmoded and that this is because the life of the church, the practice of congregations, has flowed on beyond those debates to ask and answer new questions. Interpreting these new currents is a speculative task, because there is hardly any research to work from, but my judgement is that resistance to changing the terms and conditions of the eldership has been rooted in a complex and uneven set of motivations. Some of it has been about nostalgia and traditionalism. Some of it has activated longstanding defensive instincts in the culture of presbyterian eldership about ministers liking to have their own way and wanting sessions to know their place. Some of it has been animated by the trends I have been describing – moves towards a more visible and active role for members in key areas of spiritual and liturgical practice. If that has been happening both by conviction and by necessity, and elders have been borne along by those currents, why would they support moves which seemed to be diluting their role and status?

Debates and dilemmas over the theology and practice of eldership within the Church of Scotland in the past 50 years have been hard to resolve, because they have involved the church getting a number of its wires crossed. The first two generations of reform in the sixteenth century saw an eldership which had been invented for pragmatic reasons and justified by creative hermeneutical means undergo a strange evolutionary ascent between the two books of discipline, into a new and unprecedented kind of ecclesiastical species.

Margo Todd, with Durkheim sitting on her shoulder, has given us an eloquent and persuasive account of the social function of Kirk Sessions in early modern Scotland. They filled a gap, met a need, did a job and created a role for themselves. They made themselves indispensable within Scottish society and were such for some 300 years, from 1560 to 1860. Over the next century, they remained powerful in some respects, but shed many of their previous functions. Over the past half-century they have seen their social status and cultural visibility steadily reduce. To be a kirk elder no longer has the same cultural meaning in 2017 that it had in 1917 or 1967. Of the significant numbers of women who have so strengthened and enriched sessions with their intelligence, faith and activism, most have had to wrestle with protracted decline and debilitation. Many of them joined ageing and shrinking sessions watching over ageing and shrinking congregations, in ageing and leaking buildings.

Scottish society today neither understands nor values this role in the way it used to. It now only really has meaning within church culture – and here, too, it is in trouble. The missional turn within the contemporary church means that a premium is now placed on missional leadership. If in the past institutional survival had become the operative goal of many congregations and this could be enabled by sound administration and effective pastoral care, this is true for a diminishing number of parish churches. Increasingly, institutional survival will come only through missional renewal. The tide is going out too fast for it to be otherwise. Sessions which had functioned reasonably well as administrative or pastoral bodies are experiencing new and unsettling challenges as urgent questions about missional leadership are put to them.

Of Stewart Matthew's three roles, 'Doorman/woman' still survives (although I know of one church which now refuses to let elders do door duty unless they undergo 'welcome training'). 'Spiritual Postman/woman' is a disappearing role, as Communion cards disappear from most parishes; and 'Royal Cup-bearer' is also changing, as Communion practice moves from being infrequent and formal (penguin suits and funereal hush) to frequent, participative and (even) celebratory.

Congregations which have been pummelled by decades of relentless decline are being confronted with sobering and intimidating adapt-or-die scenarios. While faithful administration and wise governance are still needed, they are not enough without a new capacity for leadership. Here, in my experience, is where a number of concerns surface:

- Many Sessions are too big and there can be suspicion of attempts to create smaller groups tasked with vision, strategy and innovation; so Sessions struggle to lead and leadership struggles to emerge.
- There is significant loss of hope and faith, many elders no longer believe that congregational growth is returning and are reluctant to embark on exhausting and apparently pointless initiatives.
- Many Sessions are struggling to call and ordain new elders; the combination of reduced status, a challenging context, a dwindling number of folk shouldering the responsibility and the concept of ordination to a lifelong role is making what is anyway a much reduced number of younger members more wary of taking on this ministry.
- Imagined as a structure between minister, congregation and parish, eldership needs to be renegotiated both in relation to ministry of word and sacrament and in relation to church members.[45]

The members

In asking about presbyterianism, having asked about ministers and elders, we need to also ask about members – those who I called 'the people formerly known as the congregation'. We noted G. D. Henderson's verdict that Calvin's legacy in terms of polity had an 'aristocratic' quality to it. The flip-side to this is of course that it also relegated some to the status of the *demos*, to be ecclesial *plebs*. The Reformed tradition has not generally been

---

45 At the 2013 General Assembly, the conservative evangelical minister Rev. Louis Kinsey unsuccessfully moved an amendment allowing elders to be authorised to 'preside' at Communion.

keen to speak of 'the laity'. Its own internal division into congregationalist and presbyterian streams has tended in the past to
harden positions which did not deserve to be set in stone. In the
Church of Scotland today we still implement and still valorise,
a system which offers far too meagre a role to the congregation,
as the whole company of church members. They are enlisted and
empowered in the call of a minister, when they are asked to vote
and sign the call. Similarly, in the election of elders, they may have
a role as electorate, although in many places this may be only
consultative. Thereafter, their only formal involvement is at the
Annual Stated Meeting, when they receive the accounts. Under
the new Model Constitution, provision is expressly made for those
who are not elders to be co-opted to various sub-committees of
the Kirk Session, but this is a concession, not a requirement.

I believe the Kirk has been unwise to so minimise the formal
role of the congregation within its polity. An alternative model
which lies close to hand is the example of the United Reformed
Church, formed from unions between the Presbyterian Church of
England and the Congregational Church in England and Wales
in 1972, augmented by further unions with the Church of Christ
(1981) and the Congregational Union of Scotland (2000). The
URC is an example I will return to later in the book and it is certainly not without its troubles and problems as a denomination.
In this respect, however, I think it offers a useful model to the
Church of Scotland. We can learn from its tradition of valuing
and honouring 'the church meeting' and of giving it a key role in
discerning God's purposes, known through the work of the Holy
Spirit. Our theological understanding of the church meeting could
be enriched by looking to the work of Mennonite theologian John
Howard Yoder on 'the rule of Paul' and to similar points made
by Anglican political theologian and ethicist Oliver O'Donovan.[46]
Their work reminds us that here too we see an example of church
polity offering an influential model to secular political culture,
that of an open deliberative assembly in which all voices should
be valued, since as O'Donovan stresses, God might speak through
'the least of these'. This example has perhaps most famously been

---

46 Yoder, 1992, pp. 60 ff; O'Donovan, 1996, pp. 281–82.

influential upon the 'town meetings' of New England, in the USA. If we brought the debate closer to home, we might be moved to reflect on this not only as an area in which the Kirk's practice had been deficient, but one in which Scotland's wider political culture had as well. If the General Assembly functioned for centuries as a surrogate parliament, if it offered a powerful model of political assembly and deliberative governance, it was still one rooted in the more 'aristocratic' traditions of representative democracy.

What the Kirk and Scotland have both lacked are deeper and broader traditions of *participatory* democracy. Here again, we can ask the theological question of how polity responds to the *missio Dei*. What questions does the gospel ask of our political culture, what responses does it invite and invoke? It is time to leave behind the casual accusation that this or that innovation in the life of the Kirk might smack of 'congregationalism' and to ask again about the proper role and rights of church members. We should do this also because, in recent decades, membership is showing signs of becoming a theologically incoherent category, which is poorly understood by congregational adherents and half-heartedly commended by ministers and elders.

There are good reasons and bad reasons why we in the Church of Scotland have been struggling with the idea of 'membership'. Some of those good and bad reasons have to do with how our theology of baptism and Christian initiation has evolved. The older Reformed sequence of infant baptism, nurture, instruction in faith, public profession of faith, admission to the Lord's Table, enrolment as a voting member of the congregation, has been undercut by two things: a reduced appetite and enthusiasm for infant baptism, coinciding with a more open and 'hospitable'[47] practice of Communion. There is a slow tide of warm fuzzy anarchy sweeping through Communion practice, as parents across the land simply opt to pop a piece of Communion bread into the mouth of their curious 'me too' baby or toddler, who may or may not have been baptised. To risk repeating myself, what people *do* is always interesting. If we read the Lord's Supper in the light of stories in the Gospels of kingdom feasts and feedings, the radical

---

47 We could also say less discriminating . . .

hospitality of Jesus seems to many (including many Reformed theologians) to call for a wholesale unfencing of the Table. When the new norm becomes this (apparently) benign anarchy, one consequence is that the classic sequence of initiation doesn't seem to work so well any more. Practice in this area of church life is messy and untidy at the moment, in ways which make what a previous generation called 'joining the church' less and less intelligible to young people.

Insofar as we have a rising generation in the church, this includes parents less sure about paedobaptism, some of whom are opting for services of thanksgiving and blessing, while hoping and praying for a credobaptism in later years.[48] We also have a new sequence of initiation developing unofficially, in which Communion is coming before public profession of faith for many young people and before baptism for some.[49] We certainly have fewer young people going through the traditional sequence. This means there are fewer occasions for the key moments in that sequence to be witnessed by other children and young people. The concept of 'joining the church' is thinning to a vanishing point within the presbyterian imagination in Scotland. In 1950s Scotland, if not as strong an idea as 'making your first Communion' was for Roman Catholic children, it was still a rite of passage for many presbyterian teenagers, just as their infant baptism had been.

I think it would be a mistake to imagine that our response to this could simply be one of greater rigour or strictness. How people behave will sometimes reveal that they are being godless or careless, but it may also be a signal that churches need to look again at a changing context and offer a new articulation of theology and doctrine in response. In this case we have a number of theological questions queuing up to be answered:

---

48 In doing this, reformed parents can claim both Karl Barth and Jürgen Moltmann as theological allies.

49 Wesley described Holy Communion as a 'converting ordinance', an event in which through participation, people encounter Christ. In a sermon on the verse 'Do this in remembrance of me', he wrote: 'But experience shows . . . Ye are the witnesses. For many now present know, the very beginning of your conversion to God (perhaps, in some, the first deep conviction) was wrought at the Lord's Supper.' Wesley, 1826, Vol. 3, pp. 188–9.

- Karl Barth's notorious question about whether baptism in the era of Christendom has been 'irregular' and needs to be reviewed in the light of the church's mission.
- Questions about who Communion is for and whether the Table should be fenced, again to be looked at through the lens of mission.
- The questions about membership and church polity raised by O'Donovan and Yoder.[50]

This last question is one which has exercised me in my own reflections on presbyterian polity; and again, my thinking was shaped by witnessing what people did. When I was minister of a URC in Hackney, in east London, some of the most active, committed and faithful folk who came into the congregation had not previously been members of the URC.[51] They began to give money and to get involved in various kinds of service in the congregation. They were also clear that they were not interested in joining and could not see the point of it. However, when church meetings came around, some of them were unhappy that they were unable to vote. They were baptised (some of them twice!), they could take Communion, they were part of the body of Christ, they felt and acted as if they were part of the congregation – why could they not vote?

My hunch is that such questions were hidden inside the life of the Kirk for most of the twentieth century, their theo-logic concealed by a settled practice. As the practice has begun to unravel, the questions which emerge send us back to theological reflection. In particular, we are sent back to ecclesiology, to our doctrine of the church. There is only one holy catholic and apostolic church, which is God's creation, which is Christ's body. This church, what the Scots Confession of 1560 calls the Universal Kirk, cannot be simply equated with any one body or denomination, nor does it subsist in any one church on earth. It is invisible and known only to God. Its visible face is seen in Particular Kirks, which are

---

50 And in Leeman, 2016.
51 They were a mix of unchurched folk, former Anglicans, and some from independent churches.

identified as true Kirks, by their witness to Christ, in particular their conformity to the *notae ecclesiae* – the notes or marks of the church.

This distinction, which the Scots Confession makes in the terms just used, helps to shed light on our anxieties about membership. Our baptismal liturgies include an explicit declaration of welcome into the one, holy catholic and apostolic church and our baptismal hymns include affirmations of the relationship between Christ the Head and the newly baptised as 'member' of the body. With these affirmations already made, presbyterians are increasingly confused about how to understand a further move into 'membership'. I confess to sharing in this confusion. There are no easy ways through this and it is tempting to suggest that it is a prime topic to be passed to the Kirk's Theological Forum for further reflection.[52] Certainly we need to study and learn from how these issues are being negotiated on the ground by ministers, members and adherents across Scotland.[53] The way forward seems likely to involve a combination of further work on our theology of participation in both baptism and Communion, work on the more rarely discussed topics of confession and profession of faith, and work on a theology of participation in the church as polity.

The brand

Talk of presbyterianism as a 'brand' invokes its cultural meaning and reputation, its cultural currency and the work this brand does when 'presbyterian' is used as an epithet. In historical terms, we could put together a literary litany stretching from the sixteenth to the twentieth centuries, showing how Scottish literature has named the sins of its presbyterian fathers and brethren and

---

52 I was a member of the forum from 2013 to 2016.

53 A recent (2016) Glasgow PhD by Rev. Dr Ruth Bell (now Morrison) and one still in progress by Rev. John Carswell bring fresh light to the topic of baptism and initiation.

their effects on Scotland's children.[54] In early twentieth-century Scotland, in keeping with the cultural power of the Kirk and its aspirations to control and police cultural and ethical mores, there was a good deal of bitterly critical pushback from writers, artists and critics. The Scottish literary renaissance of the 1920s and 1930s produced a number of memorably unflattering portraits of the Kirk and its ministers. The themes don't change much over the centuries: cruel, loveless, judgemental, exclusive, joyless, culturally Philistine, sexually repressive . . . these are the typical accusations levelled at the particular form of Presbyterian/ Calvinist Christianity which we have made in Scotland.[55] Edwin Muir in *Scotland 1941* wrote that 'Knox and Melville clapped their preaching palms/and bundled all the harvesters away'.[56] In the 1960s, Alan Jackson's poem 'Johnny Lad' claimed 'O Knox he was a bad man, he split the Scottish mind/one half he made cruel, the other half unkind'. Dundee songwriter Michael Marra wrote an ode to sabbatarianism called 'Chain Up the Swings'. Liz Lochhead swore that never in a month of Sundays would she go back.

Although I hope and believe that these are fading, the Kirk and its ministers continue to carry lingering associations of moral severity and aesthetic austerity. This also seems to depend on the persistence of a gendered stereotype of 'the minister' which

---

54 See the chapter by Alison Jack on 'Worship in Scottish Literature' in Forrester and Gay 2009.

55 It is interesting that the Church of England, whose seventeenth- and eighteenth-century record contains more than its fair share of torture, mutilation, execution, cruelty and coercion, does not seem to have carried over the same reputation for severity that the Kirk has. This is despite the fact that on some key issues, which the wider Scottish and British culture is highly sensitised to, the Kirk has moved towards convergence with the mainstream liberal conscience much quicker than the Church of England has. The ordination of women and the accommodation of people in same-sex partnerships are two key examples, where the Kirk has moved much sooner than the Church of England. Despite that, the Church of England does not carry the same cultural burdens or attract the same kind of cultural animus which the Kirk does. People speak of 'the archetypal, handwringing Anglican clergyman', of which *Pride and Prejudice*'s Mr William Collins is one of the classic studies. Even 'Rev.' is some kind of sympathetic update of this – hapless, bumbling, doubting, benign. The archetypes and stereotypes of Anglican clergy and kirk ministers are still very different, even today.

56 www.poemhunter.com/poem/scotland-1941/.

has not yet been shifted for the Kirk (despite the record of three women as Moderators of the General Assembly in the past ten years) in the way that a pop culture mass media portrayal of the Vicar of Dibley has shifted it for the Church of England.[57] It remains true that the adjective 'presbyterian' is rarely used as a positive cultural descriptor: 'joyless presbyterian' is a more likely association than 'presbyterian party planner'.

Without simply becoming craven or descending into self-loathing, it can be therapeutic for an institution (as for an individual) to see itself as others see it. Precisely because presbyterianism has shaped important cultural institutions in Scotland, it has generated significant amounts of cultural critique across various art forms. Such critique offers the Kirk a mirror to its life, through which it can reflect on its record. For an institution which places such a high value on corporate confession of sin, I am not sure that it has often faced, named and acknowledged the sins which its literary critics accuse it of. On the other hand, the current vitality of Scottish studies and the rise of a more developed critical appreciation of Scotland's past may also bring with it a more nuanced and appreciative sense of the Kirk's contributions to Scottish culture. There has been an element of 'what did the Calvinists/Presbyterians ever do for us?' about some of the critique. Craig Beveridge and Ronald Turnbull presaged a more positive account of Calvinism in the 1980s and 1990s,[58] of which the literary output of Marilynne Robinson has since given a powerful exemplification. If we are moving beyond the Scottish 'cultural cringe', we may also find some reasons to move beyond a presbyterian 'cultural cringe'.

---

57 Or more recently, Rev. Kate Bottley's presence on Gogglebox.
58 Beveridge and Turnbull, 1997.

The future

So what future does presbyterianism have within Scotland? What does it have to offer Scotland? If in the past it has asked too much and given too little, how might that change in the future? How can a presbyterian church serve the mission of God?

Before I suggest some answers, two caveats. First, a reminder of my argument that there are multiple 'presbyterianisms' and that it is by definition an evolving and reforming tradition, as well as one which is always contextualised. Second, while I have my own views and positions on the most divisive issues facing the church today, the proposals I make here are intended to be habitable for folk who occupy a range of theological positions. They are about how we adapt and reform institutions with vision and wisdom, not about partisan positioning.

Presbyterianism is primarily a polity – a way of ordering and organising the church as institution. As a polity, it has some gifts which I believe can keep giving.

Freedom to reform

The title of Douglas Murray's 1993 book captures something vital about the Reformed tradition of ecclesiology and our branch of it. In recent theology, Roman Catholic theologian Nicholas Healy has offered an influential critique of 'blueprint ecclesiology'.[59]

Ian Hazlett, in his discussion of the Scots Confession of 1560, characterises the approach of Reformed theology in this way:

> While the Reformers were in no doubt that they stood in an Age of Enlightenment (perceived as divine rather than human), they were also aware that the Word of God in Scripture did not contain categorically prescriptive imperatives on all facets of doctrine and praxis. When the gradations of biblical authority faded out, human speculation, ingenuity and experiment took

---

59 Healy, 2000.

over. It followed that it was essential to the self-understanding everywhere of Reformed doctrinal statements and practical schemes that being fallibly human compositions, their status was only ad hoc, provisional and interim. They were not an object of faith and had no equivalence to the divine authority and holy status of Scripture as legitimately interpreted, despite the tendencies of captious traditionalists at various points to seem to claim otherwise. Such subordinate standards could therefore be changed, supplemented, modified or replaced, as happened in the end.[60]

Healy's argument has been that Roman Catholic ecclesiology has been too idealised, too 'theoretical', insufficiently attentive to the messiness and fallibility of church practice and to the particularity of social and cultural context. While Hazlett's account of Reformed theology might seem to avoid those pitfalls, it is salutary to note that the Kirk is still waiting for its Vatican II moment in relation to the Westminster Confession. Reformed ecclesiology recognises that the church is both revealed and constructed, both authorised and improvised, both constrained and free. For Scottish presbyterians the polity they have constructed is an inspired but flawed attempt to be faithful to the gospel in a particular context. Its openness to reform is expressed well by Jürgen Moltmann's concept of 'apostolic procession', which affirms the eschatological nature of ecclesiology.[61] Jesus Christ is building his church, but is building it through the ministry of his disciples,[62] who are seeking to build it on him and through him and with him, in the power of the Holy Spirit. Our freedom to Reform is a freedom to keep listening and learning, a freedom to keep on discipling our polity-making. This is something we need for the future. It is also something which continues to have wider political implications.

If this is true of the church, how much more of the nation, the state, the commonwealth, the res publica. Presbyterian political imagination should be marked by humility and a restless dynamism,

---

60 Hazlett, 2010, pp. 33–41.
61 Moltmann, 1977, p. 312.
62 1 Corinthians 3.10–15.

because it sees the institutional structures of the Church of God in a dynamic relationship to the mission of God. The *ekklesia* lives within a relation of call and response. The structures we build, the lines we draw around presbytery or parish, the division of our work between councils and presbyteries, the division of responsibilities between national, regional and local church; these are always being offered to God as a response to the call to come to Christ and be built into the *oikos pneumatikos* – the spiritual house of 1 Peter 2.5. Perhaps, in cultural terms, this is what Charles Taylor perceives about the reforming zeal of Calvinism in early modern Europe and what has been too little seen by cultural critics in Scotland, who have been too preoccupied with fatalist tendencies in the Kirk and its theology to do justice to the restless ambition of the Reformed project of disciplining and improving society: of re-forming it.[63] It is interesting to read the logo of the Kirk, Moses' burning bush with the motto *nec tamen consumebatur* in the (fire)light of 1 Corinthians 3.[64] The Kirk finds in its life, both that which cannot be consumed and that which must be.

Representation and deliberation

Also among the gifts of presbyterianism have been its twin stresses on representation and deliberation. These features of its polity reflect a particular understanding of how the Holy Spirit is in and with the church. Paul writes, 'You are the body of Christ and individually members of it' (1 Corinthians 12.27). Even in its liturgical gatherings, the church is a deliberative assembly, where as one speaks, the others weigh what is said (1 Corinthians 14.26–33) – an ecclesiology and polity which stresses representation, implicitly honours and values those who are represented. This is 'body' theology, in which the composition of courts and councils is called to reflect how God has

---

63 Taylor, 2007, p. 121.

64 1 Corinthians 3.13: 'the work of each builder will become visible, for the Day will disclose it, because it will be revealed with fire, and the fire will test what sort of work each has done. If what has been built on the foundation survives, the builder will receive a reward. If the work is burned, the builder will suffer loss; the builder will be saved, but only as through fire.'

'composed' the body (1 Corinthians 12.24). The shape of our polity reveals how we value one another, what steps we have taken to listen to one another, how we are empowering and restraining one another. As with civil law, church law always expresses an implicit anthropology, a vision of who we are in relation to one another and to God. If it silences or disenfranchises women, if it restricts the roles they can play and the offices they can hold, it is bearing witness to a view of their place within the body and within the divine economy. This is true not just of church law, but of church practice. If women could be heard, but are not; if minorities could be ordained, but are not; such silences and absences bear their own testimony to the health of the body. If a meal in which members of the body will not 'wait for one another' cannot be the Lord's Supper (1 Corinthians 11.20), can a church in which they will not wait for one another truly be the body of Christ? In that sense, the informal motto of the Poverty Truth Commission, often used by those within the Kirk's Priority Areas, is very presbyterian: 'Nothing about us, without us [or our representatives], is for us'.

The often-made suggestion that between 1707 and 1999 the General Assembly acted as a surrogate parliament for Scotland, needs, I think, to be subject to many qualifications, but there is something to it. For all of its limitations, exclusions and flaws, there have been many worse examples of parliamentary deliberation. Convenors, clerks and moderators have their place, but there is something powerful in the way any commissioner to the General Assembly can get up, stand in line and take their turn to speak. The process stands in contrast to the House of Commons where scores of backbenchers rise during debates, trying to catch the eye of the Speaker, with many never being called. The sight of a Rev. Professor, Principal of Christ's, New or Trinity College, waiting in line behind a farmer from Cromarty or a teacher from Carluke is also a testimony to how this body politic works. The adjournment of an Assembly with the intention that (God willing) it be reconvened in a year's time, when representatives from parishes throughout Scotland will again be called to attend, to represent, to deliberate and decide by voting; this is also a testimony to the understanding of the body which operates within the Kirk. The relegation of the monarch or their representative to a place outwith the bounds of the Assembly itself, where they cannot speak or vote, is a political testimony to the fact that they are not the king or queen, the ruler or governor of the Kirk.

Finally, it is always worth making the point, as Churchill once said, that 'jaw, jaw is better than war, war'.[65] While this might seem obvious to us, presbyterian assemblies in Scotland emerged in a historical context in which people were used to killing and torturing one another over differences in religion. The commitment to deliberation and to accepting the outcomes of lawful voting in a representative Assembly are also, in important ways, commitments to resolving differences peacefully. While some General Assemblies down through the centuries displayed violent and hateful rhetoric and sought the punishment and death of opponents, the model of representative, deliberative and authoritative Assemblies remains important for a theology of peacemaking.

If this seems like a rather romantic account of presbyterianism, perhaps that is no bad thing. If we have no love for our institutions, we will not value and maintain them and we will not have the patience or heart to do the work of reforming them.

Subsidiarity and 'federalism'

Another key feature of presbyterianism in Scotland is the example it offers of a division of powers between the local, regional and national levels of church government, an example of 'subsidiarity' and of 'federalism'. American legal scholar Marci Hamilton has written a fascinating account of the role of the Scot John Witherspoon in the framing of the US Constitution, arguing that Witherspoon's presbyterian convictions shaped his advocacy of the federal settlement which prevailed.[66] In polity terms, this is the counterpoint and counterbalance to a localism which lacks capacity to unite and integrate the interests and concerns of diverse and geographically separated groups into a single whole.

---

65 The phrase works best in a plummy RP English accent – this brings out the 'rhyme' of the word-play.

66 In Feldman, 2000.

The guarantee of representation underwrites an institutional contract which puts in place a tiered hierarchy of courts. The General
Assembly has final authority, but church law codifies a balance of
powers and functions between congregation/Kirk Session, presbytery [synod], and General Assembly.

In theological, ecclesiological terms, the binding together of distant and disparate congregations and parishes into a single whole,
is a provisional witness to the unity of the one Kirk.[67] Decisions
about the distribution of powers and functions between the different tiers or levels of the system pose real dilemmas. Hamilton
quotes Witherspoon's conviction that 'good government must be
complex' and involves wisdom in creating the right mix of governance across the different levels of the system.[68] Here we see
a Reformed and Presbyterian stress on polity/political tasks, the
goals of which cannot be simply read off from revelation,[69] but
have to be devised and agreed through the exercise of (God-given)
human reason, informed by scripture, guided by the Holy Spirit
and deployed in community.

Corporate oversight/episcope

Finally, and perhaps disappointingly for some both within and
beyond the Kirk, I believe that aspects of our historic theological
resistance to personal *episcope* remain a valuable part of the witness of our polity. I want to introduce some nuance here, because
the detailed suggestions for reform to be offered in Chapter 5 may
appear to be pointing in the opposite direction and may be read as
an attempt to promote 'bishops' by sleight of hand. I don't intend
to rehearse all the theological arguments here, but I stand with the
mainstream of Reformed theology and ecclesiology in believing
that on scriptural, theological and sapiential grounds, we should

---

67 The phrase 'One Kirk' occurs in Chapter 16 of the Scots Confession of 1560.
68 Hamilton in Feldman (ed.), 2000, p. 57.
69 Or be taken as self-evident on the basis of a 'primitivist' reading of the New
Testament, which assumed that polity today could simply be a direct copy of polity
then. Cf. the Plymouth Brethren.

affirm corporate rather than personal forms of authoritative over-sight. I hold to a functional rather than an 'ontological' view of ordination and ministry.

Beyond the presbyterian cringe?

A presbyterianism of the future will need to negotiate its iden-tity by way of an audit of its strengths and weaknesses as a denominational and ecclesial tradition. In Scotland, this calls for a conversation between the Kirk and the wider culture, through its members, ministers and theologians. There will be things in our past to hold our hands up to, to express regret and to apologise for. There will be judgements others have made which we may want to contest as simplistic or plain wrong. There will be unrec-ognised virtues and achievements which we may want to lay claim to and draw attention to, not out of pride but out of a concern for truth. The key thing is that a living tradition in good health, an institution with a good memory and a working conscience and, in our case, a church which aspires to be *semper reformanda*, is a church in process, a church on pilgrimage, a church which is 'still being saved', a church which, as Lesslie Newbigin wrote in 1948, is living by the doctrine of justification by faith.

Why be presbyterian?

Without evading guilt, equivocating over the worst sides of pres-byterianism, or trying to deny its historical baggage, there are grounds to defend its record and commend its future potential. In Scotland, there is a case to be made for its inclusion in the canon of *inferiorism*, which has been explored in the past few decades by Craig Beveridge, Ronald Turnbull, Cairns Craig and others. Theories of inferiorism[70] suggest that cultures which are

---

70 Developed originally by the African-Caribbean post-colonial thinker Frantz Fanon.

dominated by other cultures internalise a view of themselves as second-class or 'inferior' and become highly self-deprecating. They tend to over-focus on the downside of institutions, cultural movements and the like. Beveridge and Turnbull explored this in relation to Calvinism (among other things) in their books *Scotland After Enlightenment* and *Eclipse of Scottish Culture*.[71] It would certainly fit with their theory, if many Scots, including those within the Kirk, were to have an overdeveloped sense of criticism and disdain for this historically powerful institution and an underdeveloped appreciation of its positive contributions to national life.[72]

A key argument of this book has been that there is a need to rehabilitate and represent a Reformed presbyterianism as a way of being the Church which people can understand and identify with. Within the Church of England over the past two decades there have been a number of articles, blogs and an entire book of essays addressing the question: 'Why I am (still) an Anglican. . .'[73] With the exception of a few blog posts from the more austere end of the spectrum, there is not much evidence of this kind of discursive pro-presbyterian apologetic here in Scotland. I don't reach for marketing analogies very often, but an appropriate one here may be the diagnosis applied to some well-known High Street 'general' stores by retail analysts: 'People no longer know why they shop at . . . .'[74] My sense is that in Scotland today, fewer and fewer people know why they are a presbyterian, and hardly anyone thinks of reasons why they might want to become one.

On that last point, an interesting comparison could be drawn with the Evangelical Covenant Church in the USA, whose situation I know a little of through a former colleague who works in one of their seminaries. In recent years, a number of independent congregations have approached the ECC (in what could be called an Isaiah 4.1 move) and come into membership of

---

71 Beveridge and Turnbull, 1997.

72 Note the irony of Carol Craig's reading of a Scots crisis of self-confidence reproducing an inferiorist reading of Calvinism.

73 See, among others, Chartres (ed.), 2011.

74 Insert store chain; it has been said about Woolworths, Marks & Spencer, British Home Stores and others.

this historically Swedish Lutheran denomination because of the advantages they perceive to being part of a denomination whose identity they warm to, whose values they trust and whose institutional resources they can benefit from. It is hard to imagine this happening in Scotland today and much easier to imagine traffic in the other direction, with frustrated Church of Scotland congregations seceding to become independents. This is worth reflecting on, given the institutional and financial strength of the Church of Scotland, and it represents another aspect of this crisis of confidence in our own tradition.[75] If presbyterians do not value their own polity and institutions, why would anyone else ever come to join them? If there is to be a way back from this, or better a way forward, it will have to involve renewing the intellectual and theological grip presbyterians have on our own tradition and finding imaginative, affective and effective ways to recatechise members and adherents about 'being presbyterian'. We need to regain confidence in the idea that churches with a presbyterian polity can respond faithfully and effectively to the challenges of mission in twenty-first-century Scotland. Crucial to regaining that confidence will be recognising the ways in which that polity must continue to be reformed and recalibrated for a changing context.

75 It could also be seen as representing an alternative 'left-wing' ecumenism – if traditional 'right-wing' ecumenism is about institutional mergers between old-line denominations, this would focus on a consolidation of institutional identity between independent churches, church plants and the Kirk.

3

Follow the Money

Jesus was clear: 'where your treasure is, your heart's there too'. As Reformed Christians with a sober and realistic understanding of human nature, we understand the wisdom of the Watergate maxim – 'Follow the money' – which is itself something of a paraphrase of Matthew 6.21. Whatever people say their values are, their spending habits tell you much of what you need to know about what their values really are. How money is raised and spent, and who authorises and arranges that spend, acts like a tracer element, like dye or barium, in any institutional body. It offers an indispensable way for us to map power and accountability within our institutions. So there is nothing unspiritual about wanting to talk money: quite the opposite. Like freedom and whisky, money and spirituality 'gang thegither'. If we want to talk about the renewal and reform of the church, we will need to talk and think about what it does with its money. The Church of Scotland raises and spends around £100 million each year[1] and it holds around £150 million in reserves.[2] These are large numbers, but we are a large institution.

There is, then, some good news and some bad news about the Kirk and its money. The good news is that we are not broke. Over the ten years from 2006 to 2016, income has held up well, despite a serious ongoing decline in membership. We might also say that it is good news that we are not fabulously rich, since that would seem to be a dangerously unspiritual condition for a Christian church. We are, you could say, comfortably off. Thanks

---

1 Around £70 million of this comes through offerings in local congregations.

2 Many of the reserved funds are, however, restricted in what they can be used for.

to the diligent work of the Council of Assembly and Stewardship and Finance, as well as individual councils, there appear to be no financial scandals or wipe-outs looming. Some concerns remain over pensions, in a way common to many similar large institutions across society, but it feels as though a close and prudent eye is being kept on the difficult challenges and choices around these.

The bad news is that future prospects look very challenging. There has only ever been one significant large-scale piece of academic research done in this area, Wolfe and Pickford's economic survey of the Church of Scotland, commissioned by the Kirk and published in 1980, based on field work undertaken between 1973 and 1977.[3] Their conclusions still carry the same deadly simplicity they had then: that once the general economic climate is accounted for, the key factor affecting income is membership.[4] A future in which we predict falling membership must therefore include predictions of falling income and prospects of a downward spiral setting in.

In my judgement, our financial managers and administrators have been doing well at what we as a church have asked them to do until now. The key question for the decade 2020–30 is, what will we ask them to do in future? Which is also a way of saying, what will the church ask of itself?

Reports to the 2014 General Assembly breathed a sense of relief that the church's finances and those of individual councils were under better control, that financial monitoring had been tightened and financial reporting improved.[5] The Council of Assembly's report to the 2014 General Assembly described as 'understandable' the fact that 'challenges to the current system of Ministries and Mission contributions' had emerged, in the face of the pressures being felt by individual congregations.[6] Its response was to establish a 'thorough review of strategic funding and resource allocation'[7] to report to the 2015 General Assembly before a likely further phase of consultation.

3 Wolfe and Pickford, 1980.
4 Wolfe and Pickford, 1980, p. 107.
5 RGA, 2014, 1/7.
6 RGA, 2014, 1/3.
7 RGA, 2014, 1/3.

I will admit to being disappointed at General Assembly 2016, that the high-level working group reviewing the Kirk's financial systems for the Council of Assembly recommended virtually no change to present arrangements. The Council of Assembly report was clear as to why this was done: because until now income was still holding up well and to embark on change seemed to be to introduce too much risk.[8] The danger is that this is a missed opportunity. No one yet knows what effect the introduction of many more ministerial vacancies will have on congregational giving, but there is good reason to fear it will not be positive. There is a danger that the looming cliff-edge of ministerial retirements could also become a cliff-edge for congregational giving. We need a persuasive vision for the future of the system, as well as a sober assessment of its present. In order to explore that in this chapter, I want to look back at how we came to have the financial system we have now, at what it was designed to do, and whether it is still fit for purpose. I then want to consider the potential benefits and pitfalls of some possible alternatives.

Financing the Kirk

In a helpful historical overview at the beginning of their work, Wolfe and Pickford note that for seven centuries, from the middle of the eleventh to the middle of the eighteenth, the main source of subsidy for priests' and then ministers' stipends were the parish 'teinds'.[9] These funding streams, known as 'spiritualities', were supplemented by offerings and other revenue streams, known as 'temporalities', which came from the church's own land holdings.[10]

Within the Reformed tradition, while there was a 'jealousy' for the Kirk's spiritual independence, there was also a deep

---

8 RGA, 2016.

9 Wolfe and Pickford, 1980, pp. 5–6; 'teind' is the Scots term for tithe or tenth.

10 For details of how church landholdings played a part in the Reformation and what happened to them, see Andy Wightman's powerful book *The Poor Had No Lawyers*.

commitment to the principle of 'establishment', which included the belief that the 'state'/civil magistrate/local landowners/prosperous burghers/town councils had an obligation to give financial support to local kirks.[11] This was a basic 'Christendom' belief, that the church had a claim on wider society, even as it baptised and educated their children, joined women and men in marriage, supervised their morals and buried them at their (mortal) end. It belonged to the struggle to be recognised as the monopoly religious body in a particular territory, to be accepted as The Church of Scotland. This is the tradition that in some European countries has evolved into a still continuing system of 'church taxes'. In Scotland, although 'teinds' are a form of this, the trajectory has been different.

These topics are well covered elsewhere for those who want the full historical picture,[12] so I will offer only a sketch of the main developments. At a local level, the Christendom bargain (or covenant?) in Scotland was given a new and controversial exemplification by the 1711 Patronage Act, which was passed in response to the demands from local landowners to have, as they saw it, rights to nominate a minister to the parish church, commensurate with their responsibilities to support it. While the tensions introduced by this Act would take more than a century to fully gather steam, the eighteenth century also saw other developments which would, in the long term, be momentous for church funding. The founding of the Secession Church in 1733 marks the real beginning of 'the voluntary principle' in Scottish church life. This is the conviction, as opposed to establishment's sense of entitlement to support from the state, that a congregation or denomination should be supported by the free will[13] offerings of its members. Once secessions take place, those who are funding churches on the voluntary principle tend to become highly resistant to the establishment principle, not least because if establishment is effective in financial

---

11 Until the nineteenth century there was no central administration to speak of, so funding was really only needed by and directed to local kirks and for instruction in divinity at universities.

12 See Gibson, 1961.

13 Hence the term 'voluntary' from the Latin *voluntas*/will.

terms, seceders are paying twice – for the church they go to and the one they don't.

With the establishment of one and then a series of secession churches, as well as the presence of a small number of Baptist and Methodist churches and Quaker meetings, by the end of the eighteenth century the voluntary principle was there to stay in Scottish church life. The Ten Years Conflict, which led to the Disruption of 1843, was driven by a cluster of issues and concerns, which included both a rebellion against patronage and a deep frustration at the refusal of the 'state' to fulfil its side of the establishment bargain, to perform its covenantal duties and rise to the challenge of financing the building of new churches, in particular for Scotland's burgeoning urban population.

When Thomas Chalmers led the departing ministers and elders out of the Auld Kirk's General Assembly and into the inaugural assembly of the Free Church, he and others insisted they were departing what he called 'a vitiated establishment', but were not deserting the establishment principle. That may have been so, but in practice the only way to fund the new denomination was through the voluntary offerings of its faithful. As Wolfe and Pickford observed: 'The task set the new Church was an enormous one – nothing less than that of producing a complete and exact replica of the Established Church they had left, relying on the resources which the members could supply.'[14] Significant amounts of Victorian Scotland's considerable share in the profits of the Industrial Revolution and the British Empire were to be directed into the coffers of the new Free Church by both its better heeled benefactors and its supporters of more modest means. The vehicle through which they were channelled was Thomas Chalmers' famous sustentation fund, established and open for business on 18 May 1843, in anticipation of the Disruption, but before the final denouement of the schism had been played out. By Disruption Day, upwards of £223,000 had already been secured for the Building and Sustentation Funds.

The story of the rise of the Free Church, and indeed the subsequent parallel recovery of the Auld Kirk, is covered in many other

---

14 Wolfe and Pickford, 1980, p. 23.

places. My specific concern here is with two key developments which proved to be decisive for the future of the Kirk's finances: the enormous boost the Disruption gave to the voluntary principle, and the way in which Chalmers' new fund and those who administered it introduced a new kind of bureaucratic centralism into denominational life in Scotland, albeit initially in a fairly lean and mean form.

After the great schism of the Disruption, the second half of the nineteenth century witnessed a new dynamic towards consolidation of presbyterian identity, as most of the Secession churches came together to form the United Presbyterian Church in 1847, and most of the UP Church then united with most of the Free Church in 1900 to form the United Free Church. In financial terms, the 1900 union brought together two different systems: the UP Church had operated an *augmentation* fund while the Free Church had established a *sustentation* fund – the first topped up local funds from a central pot, the second gathered funds locally to a central pot and redistributed them to local congregations.[15]

The last stage of this consolidating process, the union of the United Free Church and the Auld Kirk in 1929, had to wait for a series of negotiations and developments to take place, which were both delayed and then in certain respects impelled by the First World War. Douglas Murray notes that for the UF Church, stunned by the impact of the 1905 Free Church Case in the House of Lords,[16] 'A union with the Church of Scotland, in which the freedom of the church to change its constitution and unite with other churches would be recognized by parliament, became an attractive possibility.'[17] The formulas which expressed that freedom were enshrined in the Articles Declaratory of 1919, recognised in the Church of Scotland Act of 1921. For the Church of Scotland, the 1905 case had been a warning about the need to formally gain control over its property and endowments and this

---

15 Gibson, 1961, p. 43.

16 When the House of Lords awarded the entire assets of the Free Church to the small minority which had refused to enter the United Free Church – an outcome subsequently corrected by a settlement reflected in the Churches (Scotland) Act 1905.

17 Murray on 'The Union of 1929' in Lynch (ed.) *Oxford Companion to Scottish History*, 2001, accessed via Oxford Reference Online, 2007 edition.

was finally achieved through the Church of Scotland Act of 1925. Taken together, these two acts paved the way for the 'Glorious Union' of 1929.

While the Church of Scotland had increased the size and reach of its own central bureaucracy in the years between 1843 and 1929, the Union of 1929 strengthened and enhanced this process in at least two ways. First, it led to the creation of a single, much larger denomination which took more work to administer; and second, it grafted the organisational culture of Chalmers' 'built from scratch' Free Church into the old tree, which had grown more organically and less systematically over the centuries.

For the Church of Scotland, this had consequences, which were seen by Gibson in his work *Stipend* as blessed and providential. The constitutional reframing which made the 1929 union possible neither definitively espoused nor finally foreswore the establishment principle, but it came with a realisation that the future funding of the Kirk was going to rest predominantly on the liberality of its own members. Union brought the voluntarist instincts of the UP and Free traditions and the centralised processes of the Free/UF tradition into the culture and organisation of the Kirk.

Gibson's 1961 book is a paean of praise to the happy consequences of this synergy. He comments about Chalmers' fund: 'Clearly it had to be a fund that gripped the imagination of ordinary men and women and would keep its hold.'[18] This is an important insight, and while he goes on to recognise the part played by assiduous house-to-house collection by the Free Church's reinstated 'diaconate', he is surely right that how people perceived and imagined the workings of a fund was crucial to their continuing support for it. This is a point I will return to below when I consider options for the future.

In understanding the history of financial systems within the Church of Scotland, we have to pay attention to both the technical and the cultural aspects. The decline of the establishment principle reflected very real changes in the relationship between church and state: broadly speaking, the state expected less from the church (in the provision of services for education, health and

---

18 Gibson, 1961, p. 46.

welfare), the church expected less from the state (in terms of funding church 'extension' and maintaining church buildings) and the church expected more from itself. These trends, which were already evident in the latter half of the nineteenth century, continued into the twentieth. They were at work through the union of 1929, would intensify with the onset of post-war decline and are continuing trends as we move further into an increasingly secularised twenty-first century in Scotland.

From his vantage point in 1961, Gibson had no doubt how crucial the introduction of Chalmers' sustentation principles had been for the survival and adaptation of the Kirk in the three decades since Union. A key question for the Kirk as it considers its own financial future is the issue Gibson raised of the kind of 'fund' which can grip the imagination of its members in the twenty-first century in the same way as Chalmers' fund gripped their imagination in the nineteenth.

The more decentralised approach of the UP tradition had its strengths and its defenders. Wolfe and Pickford quote Gibson's observation that 'The strength of the UP method of payment of stipend direct from the congregation to ministers "lay in impressing upon congregations with limited resources the claim which their own minister had upon them for adequate support".'[19] By way of contrast, Gibson suggested that 'a "hidden import" of the Sustentation Fund was its encouragement of brotherhood amongst the Free Church ministers. It was a financial embodiment of the doctrine of the parity of ministers.' Not only that, but he went on to argue that 'it fostered the view . . . that the ministers are not the servants of the congregations or parishes to which they happen to minister, but servants of the whole Church'.[20]

Our historical survey has already shown us that a variety of financial systems – state support, voluntarist augmentation and voluntarist sustentation – have all been adopted by Scots presbyterians at different points in the past.

To make the same point, we could also compare the systems operated by presbyterian churches today in different parts of

19 Wolfe and Pickford, 1980, p. 25.
20 Gibson, 1961, p. 49.

the world. In the PCUSA,[21] for example, there is much less central control. Congregational discipline is not primarily achieved through a powerful financial centre and there is no attempt to achieve an even spread of ministry across the country through any system of central planning or rationing. The result here is a much more 'Darwinian' approach to congregational survival and to levels of ministerial stipend, which can vary sharply – some posts attracting two or even three times as large a stipend as others, taking account of congregational size, management and supervision responsibilities. The budgeting process is very firmly congregation and presbytery based and weighted, with churches being assessed a per capita amount for each member towards presbytery and national denominational costs and making voluntary contributions for broader national and international mission and relief work.[22]

My point here is not at all to suggest that this is a better system than the one we are working with in Scotland; it is simply to reinforce the earlier point that we live in a world of multiple presbyterianisms. The importance of context means that we cannot read off simple lessons from the relative 'success' or 'failure' of presbyterian churches in different locations. What 'works' in one location or at one period in time may not be effective or helpful somewhere else or in a different historical moment.

We noted above that within a theological 'family' such as the Reformed tradition, and even within a sub-family of presbyterian traditions, polities can be differently calibrated and that the work of calibrating and adjusting them is a task which requires missional wisdom. Presbyterian churches bring resources from their past into new contexts in which they will hear a distinctive call, to which they need to make a faithful response. This applies to their financial systems as well. The type of 'fund' which gripped the imagination of Victorian presbyterians after a damaging national schism, may not similarly grip the imaginations of

---

21 Presbyterian Church (USA).

22 There is also an interesting polity ruling that if a church does not pay their per capita then a presbytery must pay it for them, although this has been unsettled by the recent turbulence in the denomination as churches have withheld contributions due to disaffection with national developments.

twenty-first-century Scottish congregations, demoralised by secularist attrition and unsure about the wisdom of central planning.

Presbyterian (financial) values

So how do and should presbyterians handle money? The 2014 Council of Assembly Report put it like this:

> Each congregation contributes according to its means. Those with the greatest financial resources contribute most and those with the smallest financial resources contribute least. In this way the Church of Scotland is a sharing Church, where the strong support the weak and the redistribution of contributions enables the provision of a territorial ministry throughout Scotland.[23]

To be presbyterian is to have a commitment to financial solidarity between congregations who have different means, within and across presbyteries (and into the world Church). I accept that if it lost that commitment, the Kirk would lose its presbyterian soul. My argument is, however, that as things stand we have prioritised solidarity at the expense of sustainability, flexibility and opportunity.

As well as our traditions of solidarity, there is also a rich history of presbyterians aspiring to be good stewards and cheerful givers, who can create viable and sustainable congregations. There is a healthy aspiration to pay our own way and not to presume upon others, which has often helped to energise and mobilise local churches to do all they can to be self-supporting. There is also an element of pastoral and social psychology, which recognises that people have a different awareness of what is local and near. Loyalty to what is local need not be toxic to wider solidarities. The key is to have effective formulas and systems which offer good institutional ways to negotiate this. Talk of 'too much of our money going to 121' may reflect spiritual selfishness or

---

23 RGA, 2014, 1/8.

miserliness, but it may also be a sign that we need to recalibrate our systems.

Without compromising on generosity and solidarity, we need to reinvigorate local motivations to be sustainable and adventurous. Our current highly centralised systems are strong on pooling and sharing, but they look increasingly less well suited to motivating local giving. The acute missional challenges facing the Kirk over the period to 2030 call for a new financial imagination which will maintain a powerful commitment to smart, creative and empowering expressions of national sharing while incentivising a new era of local responsibility and offering greater local and regional flexibility.

We need to explore new ways to support and incentivise congregations across the spectrum and to pilot these in a variety of locations and situations across Scotland.

Congregations in Scotland's poorest and most remote parishes

As both a national and a presbyterian church, the Church of Scotland must continue to show solidarity with its congregations in Scotland's poorest places and should be adamant about its desire to share with them and to invest in them. This financial commitment has been expressed most recently through giving increased weighting to congregations in the poorest 'priority' areas and most remote rural areas of Scotland, within the Presbytery Planning process of rationing supply of ministers. Since these posts are centrally funded, an increased allocation represents a higher level of investment in these congregations. Determining the level of investment made in these parishes is a challenging task for the church. When done through a national system of rationing ministers, there is a danger of a counterproductive effect developing in the institution as a whole, because the weighted allocation to some areas competes with allocation to other areas and inevitably deprives churches in these areas of access to ministry. In this way a well-intentioned mechanism can have vexatious unintended effects: if it weakens the investor/subsidising/aid-providing congregations,[24] contributing to their decline and loss of membership and income, it can fuel a downward spiral in the level of resource available to pool and share.

There are no easy answers to this issue of levels of investment. It will have to be determined in relationship, through an honest and respectful dialogue across the church. However, one option which will be important is to continue to stir the imagination and the felt solidarity of the national church through the existence of one or more dedicated funds to which congregations and individuals make voluntary contributions for the support of mission in priority areas and in remote rural areas. Currently this role is being carried by the brashly named 'Go For It'[25] fund, whose scope, remit and procedures I have significant reservations about. I am not persuaded that this fund in its existing form will inspire and attract voluntary giving of the kind I think is necessary in the future, nor that it is yet guided by the holistic missional thinking which can support congregational growth and church planting in Scotland's poorest areas. The danger with instead allocating some of the responsibility for presbyterian solidarity to a voluntary fund would be that churches failed to support it adequately; but if that were to happen, the national church would need to be called to account for it. The advantage of such an additional fund could be that, when combined with a significant baseline level of investment within the system, an emphasis on grace and freedom could inspire positive attachment to the cause.

A danger with any system of cross-subsidy is that it removes responsibility and motivation from those who are 'aid-receiving', so that they lose a sense of the value of what they are receiving, of the costs to the wider body of providing it, and of their own agency in securing it. One way to address this is to provide some

---

24 And also potentially weakens their capacity as the major providers of further candidates for ministry of word and sacrament, exacerbating the scarcity of this human resource.

25 The General Assembly of 2012 established the 'Go For It' fund, amalgamating the former Parish Development, Emerging Ministries and Priority Areas Staffing Funds. It, like the funds it replaced, is a mechanism for distributing some of the main Parish Ministries Fund according to alternative criteria.

of the outside investment in the form of match funding, whereby local fundraising triggers and levers additional support from presbytery or the national church. This does not mean only helping those who help themselves, but it does mean creating a clear motivational mechanism for those who can.

A further concern about financing priority area churches has to do with the prevalence of extreme congregational fragility in such areas and the theological and missional instincts and priorities which have been shaping investment. As someone who has lived and worked in urban priority areas in England and Scotland for 16 years, I am deeply committed to a holistic theology of presence and witness and to the church's role in the struggle for social and economic justice in these areas. However, I am less convinced that the Kirk has been as effective as it could have been in supporting evangelism and enabling congregational growth in priority areas. Theologies of 'fragility' have their place and value, but some of those who advocate them have been conspicuously lacking in enthusiasm and advocacy for bold, intentional measures to reseed existing congregations or plant new ones. As someone from an evangelical background who laments that tradition's sins of omission in relation to a political theology of justice and peace, it pains me when some more liberal voices within the church seem in danger of making the opposite omission. I value the strength and clarity of the Five Marks of Mission produced by the Anglican Communion:[26]

- To proclaim the Good News of the kingdom.
- To teach, baptise and nurture new believers.
- To respond to human need by loving service.
- To transform unjust structures of society, to challenge violence of every kind and pursue peace and reconciliation.
- To strive to safeguard the integrity of creation, and sustain and renew the life of the earth.

---

26 www.anglicancommunion.org/identity/marks-of-mission.aspx#navigation – sources given here are *Bonds of Affection* 1984 ACC-6, p. 49; *Mission in a Broken World* 1990 ACC-8, p. 101.

The Kirk's investment in priority areas in Scotland needs to be guided by the Five Marks, and my hope is that future investment will be consciously related to such a full-spectrum theology of mission.

Churches, ministers and money

The provision of a body of educated and accredited ministers of word and sacrament, whose stipends (and pensions) are fully covered from central funds, continues to be the main financial call on the Kirk as a national institution. At the end of 2016, the church's 1,331 parishes were being served by around 890 ministers of word and sacrament at an annual cost of some £37 million. While the church's finances have been impressively resilient despite falling membership, we must return here to questions raised in Chapter 1. The Kirk is a demographic time-bomb in terms of members, ministers and finance.

The statistics presented to the General Assembly in 2017 will show that there are around 200 vacancies across Scotland's parishes, and expectations are that this situation will have worsened dramatically by 2030, unless there is a significant and sustained increase in the number of candidates for ministry. At present there are four ministers retiring each year for every one being ordained. Membership shows no sign of stabilising, if indeed there is something close to a 'floor' which it is likely to hit. It would be wise for the Kirk to brace itself for membership figures around 280,000 in 2020 and for a further fall to 150,000 by 2030.[27]

Two things seem likely to happen to the Kirk's finances in the period leading up to 2030: income will decline significantly, perhaps more slowly than membership, but in a more or less direct relation to membership decline; legacy income will also begin to decline significantly as the generations most likely to bequeath money to churches die off. What is not yet clear is what effect the increasing shortage of ministers will have in terms of how

---

27 These estimates are confirmed by the results of the 2016 Scottish Church Census, which were just beginning to be disseminated as I was finishing this book.

members and adherents perceive their giving to the Kirk. Since the voluntarism of the Chalmers' model became the norm for the church, contributions to 'the maintenance of the ministry'[28] have been presented as the first call on members' giving. The financial imaginary of Scottish presbyterians has had at its heart the model of the parish minister – of 'our' minister. Members gave (and probably in this order of priority) to maintain the ministry, through provision of stipend (centrally) and manse (locally); to maintain the church building; to fund local mission activities in the parish; and to support the wider polity and work of the Kirk. As things stand, the system makes some concessions in how it assesses parishes which are 'in vacancy'. Official guidance states:

When vacant, a congregation's Ministries and Mission contribution is reduced by a vacancy allowance of (as at 2016) £910 per month, and £980 per month for linked charges, so that the congregation may pay for a Locum or for other cover arrangements. The 2016 fee for a Locum is £315 per month for each day of pastoral cover a week plus a fee for pulpit supply. The vacancy allowance is sufficient to cover two days of pastoral work plus the associated pulpit supply.[29]

Until now, the system has continued to assume that during a vacancy, congregations will pay their full Ministries and Mission assessment, minus the 'vacancy allowance'/locum allowance.

For the congregation I have been working with in Glasgow for the past three years, that means out of an annual income of £72,000 they will pay £46,000 – £10,900 = £35,100. They have now been in vacancy for nine years, so over that period they have paid in some £250,000 in Ministries and Mission contributions after their vacancy allowance was deducted. They have paid that money, while being told they would not get 'a minister of their own' and being encouraged to link or unite with a neighbouring congregation.

---

28 Gibson, 1961, pp. 1–2.

29 www.churchofscotland.org.uk/__data/assets/pdf_file/0016/35026/Vacancy_guidelines_for_kirk_sessions_and_interim_moderators.pdf.

Now I am aware that hard cases make bad laws, but I think this is an interesting example for a number of reasons. This is an ageing and declining congregation, with a challenging building which enjoys a very good location, but is expensive to maintain and would be very hard to sell on or adapt for another use.

For the past nine years they have been consistently subsidising other congregations across the Kirk, and doing this to a degree which has made it hard for them to invest more in local mission. The congregation are relatively well heeled, stubbornly attached to their building and a good many of them[30] would not adhere to a union[31] so while the capital asset of their manse would accrue to a united charge, it is very unlikely that anything close to the existing level of giving would. The challenge which emerges from their situation is, without losing sight of their presbyterian identity, their capacity and their desire to share resources with other congregations: how can they best be enabled and empowered to reach out in five-mark holistic mission to their parish? It does not seem in the church's best interests to keep calling congregations like this to be significantly aid-giving until they simply give out and fold themselves. Not only that, but for the system as a whole, every congregation like this which closes is one less to pool and share with others in the future.

The parable which comes to mind here is found in Luke 16.1–9, where a shrewd manager writes down the amounts owed by his master's debtors. The application I am suggesting is this. In a situation where between 2020 and 2030 there seem likely to be unprecedented numbers of ministerial vacancies across Scotland, the imaginative bond which connects givers to the Kirk will be stretched as never before. Left without 'a minister of their own', members and adherents will be less willing to give or to give as much. If during their vacancies they are significant net contributors to the wider church while struggling and declining themselves, they are likely to become more resentful about the disparity

---

30 Perhaps 50 per cent of the membership?

31 Some for reasons I would not defend, some because they travel back to this parish for family/historical/social reasons and if leaving it would relocate local to where they live.

between the 'allowance' they are granted and the contributions they are sending away.

Taking the Presbytery of Glasgow as an example, ratios of Ministries and Mission assessment to overall income vary from 48 per cent to 64 per cent, with the example noted above sitting at 61 per cent before the vacancy allowance is applied, and still remaining just above 50 per cent after it is applied. This is not a sustainable formula.

Devising new formulas for congregational assessment is a process fraught with difficulty. It is essential but not interesting, vital but not enlivening, strategic but not sexy. As with income tax and other forms of taxation, fixing the rates requires an alchemy of technical skills, psychological understanding, theological/ ethical integrity and creative instinct. This process calls for complex 'design' skills, to build the formulas around memorable images and ideas, to reach a compromise between simplicity and adaptability and to strike a balance between positing ideals and anticipating behaviours. It has to minimise the resentments of the poorest and the richest. And it has to work. The formulas have to raise enough money to meet existing commitments, to pay salaries and provide for pensions. They have to maintain responsibility and incentivise liberality. Small wonder, when the system seems to have been coping remarkably well under pressure, that we have been cautious about changing it. That said, I believe it must change if it is to serve the future of the church and adapt to the huge challenges we are about to face.

My suggestion is that reforms to Church of Scotland funding formulas should be carried out on the basis of the following principles:

1 We provide generous but reviewable support for our poorest congregations, which includes elements of match funding as part of a package – I suggest we call these Investment Congregations or Solidarity Congregations.
2 The funding formula should have a nominal *floor* and *ceiling* to it.
    a The floor should relate to the basic cost of parish ministry, currently around £50,000 for a full-time post and should

represent a healthy aspiration for congregations to become self-supporting.

b The ceiling should act as a maximum figure for assessed contributions from wealthier congregations and might be set at £100,000. The decision to leave more money with these congregations would reflect a judgement that the Kirk would benefit from encouraging some congregations to grow further. It would be part of a deliberate institutional strategy to support the development of a greater number of larger churches.

c A ceiling would have the effect of reducing the funds available for subsidy, so it would be necessary to draw more congregations towards being self-sustaining.

3 The system should both support those congregations which cannot become self-sustaining and reward those which can. In addition to Investment Congregations four other categories might be useful here:

a *Development Congregations* could work on a match-funding basis to move the total to the floor level, with a tranche of money beyond that retained locally and income beyond that split between local and national church.

b *Self-Sustaining Congregations* would pay the floor level to central funds and retain all additional money raised locally, subject to a 20 per cent sharing levy.

c *Contributor Congregations* would pay the floor level + £30,000[32] to central funds and retain all additional money raised locally, subject to a 10 per cent sharing levy.

d *Invester Congregations* would pay the floor level + £50,000 to central funds and retain all additional money raised locally, subject to a 2 per cent sharing levy.

The categories suggested above would be subject to income limits. The system would offer limited but significant incentives for

---

32 These are indicative and illustrative figures – the work of resetting such formulas involves a combination of technical and political factors which need to be worked on within the councils of the Church.

congregations to move into the next category. In particular, limited increases in contributions to denominational funds would unlock greater local control over spending. The reforms proposed reflect the following assumptions:

1 The current system lacks incentives at all levels.
2 Its simplicity has some merits, but acts as a drag on giving and encourages congregations to shelter money from central assessment.
3 Smart 'gearing' of incentives can release significant additional resources for local mission while maintaining adequate funds for pooling and sharing and for denominational support.
4 The lack of a ceiling is holding back the expansion and growth of stronger churches with unhelpful consequences.
5 The failure to adequately promote an aspiration to be self-sufficient is intended to destigmatise being 'aid-receiving', but also limits responsibility and aspiration and contributes to disempowerment.
6 Promoting local control and limiting central 'take' on rising income is key to boosting local income.

Special cases?

It may be that a reform of funding formulas along the lines advocated here would create enough flexibility to address these situations, but I do want to note the special financial needs of two particular cases.

The first concerns congregations which are at risk of dissolution or of feeling forced to enter unions which a presbytery does not believe are in the best interests of the parishes concerned. I know of a number of situations where congregations have in reality, if not in legality, entered what we in the Kirk call 'an unsatisfactory state'. Reasons for this are usually complex and often painful. They can include ministerial health, ministerial ineffectiveness, congregational division, poor leadership. A spiral of decline sets in, sometimes under a tenured minister who refuses to leave a charge. At present, we do not have good enough choices to offer to such congregations and presbyteries move to dissolve or unite them because they don't see what else to do. I believe we need to work out creative ways of giving them 'last chances' by offering them reset/restart 'grace' periods. While that sounds like a good thing, there will often be local opposition.[33] In some cases, presbyteries need to gird their loins for the 'tough love' option of declaring that, for reasons of missional ineffectiveness and congregational fragility, a local church is indeed 'in an unsatisfactory state'. But they also need to be able to reach for presbyterian carrots as well as presbyterian sticks. The Kirk can learn from the better examples of how this has been done in some English education authorities, where schools have been put on 'special measures' or gone through a full 'restart'. Sometimes providing a carrot will be enough to persuade a session or congregation to vote for change. Crafting options for appropriate financial support is crucial to what is variously termed 'restarting', 'reseeding' or bringing in 'turnaround teams'.

This may take the form of a package of support, consultancy and coaching such as we have seen in the Kirk's 'Chance to Thrive' programme for priority areas;[34] it may involve the creation of a grant regime to support a new phase of work in the parish concerned, but it could also involve offering a congregation the challenge and opportunity of opting out of the standard financial arrangements and working on some intense, local strategies for fundraising and investing in mission, which are not solely dependent on making grant applications to central funds. Particularly for vacant congregations, including some which are becoming non-viable in terms of numbers attending but are not entirely broke, an alternative to saying they must close or unite could be to see whether, given more financial freedom and

---

33 In my experience some congregations would rather die than change. Some flat out refuse to contemplate changes to the fabric of their buildings, only to see them sold and immediately radically remodelled by the new owner to enable the new use. This kind of intransigence is, I believe, a form of spiritual and intellectual cowardice, which is both self-indulgent and negligent in relation to parish mission.

34 www.churchofscotland.org.uk/__data/assets/pdf_file/0007/26746/Chance_to_Thrive_Report_2014.pdf though see above for my own concerns about the theological priorities of recent work in priority areas.

discretion, some could find new ways to add capacity and grow towards sustainability, for example by employing family workers or youth workers alongside OLMs and active elders, or by hiring a 50 per cent minister, if they could find and pay one. These 'grace periods' would be time-limited and could involve a congregation walking back towards one of the standard financial formulas over a five-, seven- or ten- year period.[35] The Luke 16 principle reckons with the reality that unless drastic action is taken, if the congregation folds, its income largely folds with it. It suggests that in some cases a refusal to compromise will lead to greater losses in the end.

The second special case, which is related but distinct, has to do with the financial provisions made to support church planting within the denomination. Unhappiness with the operation of the Emerging Ministries Fund (2008–12) led to it being assimilated into the new 'Go For It' fund (2012–). I have never been convinced this was wise, and continue to believe the Kirk needs separate streams of funding for church planting and a separate national unit to support it.

In the period to 2030, the church faces the challenge of having to do five things simultaneously: close unviable churches, manage declining churches, support declining churches to grow again, support growing churches and plant new churches. In terms of church planting, the Kirk is still on a steep learning curve. Our structures, systems and culture are still largely organised around a maintenance model of parish ministry. We lack vision, skills and a dedicated resource stream for church planting. We have no recognised ministry path specifically associated with this and we have no bespoke provision for pioneers and church planters within our education for ministry pathways. Some may wonder why we need to plant new churches if we are closing others, but there is no contradiction here. Some congregations will have to close because their internal culture is toxic and they have invited their own end through a mix of pettiness, rancour and banal conservatism. Some

---

35 For example, a 100 per cent reduction in Ministries and Mission could be reinstated over ten years at 10 per cent a year; a 50 per cent reduction could be reinstated at the same rate over five years; or held for two years and then reinstated 10, 20, 20 in the final three years.

will close because they are tied to inappropriate sites or unsuitable buildings and lack the desire or capacity to reinvent or relocate themselves. Where the Victorians planted or built churches, especially during the competitive fever of the post-Disruption decades, was not always where a parish church would be built today. Some new churches will not be linked to a geographical area, but to a network, or subculture.

We lack detailed research into needs and prospects, so these figures are based on broad judgements, but my best guess would be that the Kirk should be readying itself to close around 200 churches and to plant or reseed around 100 in the decade 2020–30. The example of the PCUSA in committing to establish 1,001 New Worshipping Communities in ten years is a powerful sign of a sister church investing in mission and growth, and in fresh expressions of church.[36] If we aimed at 101 in 10, we would need to invest boldly, as they have. We would need a financial regime, from seed grants to development funds, which enables new congregations to be planted, and charts a financial 'pathway' towards their acquiring full status and making their own contributions to the work of the denomination. We would need additional funding to develop a 'pioneer' pathway into ministry of word and sacrament.

Surpluses and reserves

There is another thing which has come along with the high rate of retirals and the rising number of vacancies. The Kirk no longer has as many ministers to pay as it had hoped, and the giving of its members has held up better than it had feared. The relevant officials and convenors speak of this in hushed tones if they speak of it at all. No charity likes to be seen as being in any way flush, and experienced trustees realise that relatively comfortable balance sheets can lose their balance all too quickly. But in an independent study like this, candour requires the observation that there now seems likely to be a window during the next five years

---

36 www.presbyterianmission.org/ministries/1001-2.

in which the resources of the church may be declining less rapidly than its liabilities.[37]

Alongside that we might position a different but not unrelated question about levels of reserves. I am not going to tackle the technical issues around reserves in this book, beyond saying that when an institution faces the level of challenge and crisis which the Kirk is facing, it needs to think hard about its reserves. The dilemma faced by rapidly declining institutions is when to accept greater financial risk and invest more in new and adaptive responses. Run your reserves down unwisely or prematurely, squander them in panic or in blind enthusiasm, and the church of 2030 is unlikely to rise and bless you for doing do. On the other hand, hoard them fearfully, guard them doggedly, ration them grimly on the grounds although today is rainy, there are likely to be worse floods coming – do these things and you may end up, as Alice observed, having a smile without a cat; or, to use an image closer to home, walls without church.

Questions of the use and abuse of surpluses and reserves will need to be determined in the proper forums. Here I simply want to draw attention to some worthy causes, should some additional sums of money be found down the back of certain presbyterian sofas in 121 George Street in the next five years:

1 The first is a simple acknowledgement of the importance of protecting pensions for workers and ensuring they are properly funded.
2 Staying with the same theme, the salaries of ministers and deacons are neither meagre nor generous – they should be the subject of gentle improvement rather than benign neglect.
3 One part of addressing the critical shortage of ministry candidates is the provision of a proper training stipend for all candidates within Initial Ministerial Education (IME). Many of my students have moved from earning £30,000 a year to bringing

---

37 Cf. the observations made in the 2016 Ministries Council Report at 1.3.1.8. As long as giving continues to stay at somewhere near current levels, the reduced number of Parish Ministers (Hub leaders) will free up money to pay for other forms of ministry. (Tell-tale signs in any organisation that belts are not unduly tight include the more liberal use of consultants.)

in less than £10,000 a year. This has put strain on them and their families. I am sure the prospect of such financial stress has also deterred some from becoming candidates.

4 While we are on initial ministerial education, I will discuss some of the key issues in the next chapter[38] but the future of IME (and CME)[39] is going to be more expensive than its past. We are in the twilight of the Christendom model of training ministers in Scottish Divinity faculties, in which the state footed much of the bill for both grants and the provision of lecturers, libraries and learning facilities. In the future, the provision of appropriate, bespoke, relevant forms of IME will have to be driven and funded by the Kirk and its ecumenical partners. Even if, as I hope, the Christendom patterns can evolve and adapt, they will need investment to reform and supplement them for the future.

5 Invest more in research and statistics. The Kirk owes a great deal to the goodwill and generosity of Rev. Dr Fiona Tweedie, but it should take inspiration from her example and from the fine example of the Church of England's Research and Statistics Unit.[40] Whatever the years to 2030 hold, it will be easier to respond wisely if we are clearer about what is happening to the Kirk on the ground across Scotland.

Conclusions

I have held over some other questions about financial reform, pending a discussion of further structural reforms in Chapter 5. The key issues here have to do with devolving much greater levels of financial responsibility to a smaller number of more powerful presbyteries. This is an area where the legacy and methodology of Chalmers does loom large. The language of recent debates and reviews has left the core principles and structures of the system

---

38 page 121ff.
39 Continuing Ministerial Education.
40 www.churchofengland.org/about-us/facts-stats/research-statistics.aspx.

untouched, focusing on tweaking 'allowances' which are given back to the regional church by the national church.

This is not surprising given both the theory and actuality of current patterns of governance, of the kind of presbyterianism we currently have within the Church of Scotland. With the exception of a small amount of presbytery 'dues', money moves in large part from the local church to the central/national church, where the key budgeting determinations and decisions are made at a national level for the whole of Scotland and national distributions are made accordingly. It seems uncontroversial to say that different values and priorities may be ranked and positioned differently within differing financial regimes and these may function more or less effectively depending on the needs of the institution and the features of the context. The nineteenth-century Chalmers/sustentation model created a strong strategic centre in order to sustain and develop a new national institution. This system, which we inherit, is strong on national solidarity but weaker on regional and local responsibility. It has now become so familiar to us in the Church of Scotland that our current version of financial federalism has become associated in many people's minds with a 'presbyterian' as opposed to a 'congregationalist' ecclesiology. This is the assumption I want to question and explore here.

We need to talk more candidly and creatively about money and we need a more radical conversation than we have so far been prepared to have. We need to look at the financial habits of other presbyterianisms, including that of the PCUSA, as a way of seeing ourselves with new eyes. We need to consider the specific values and priorities we are aiming to promote within our systems and how these relate to the needs and context of the Kirk in the period leading up to 2030.

I understand institutional reluctance to change a system which still seems to be working, so this conversation around money will be one of the most difficult of all. If we can have it well, then it might help the spirit in which necessary reforms are introduced. It will also help if we can agree on the principles which should underpin a reform of the system. It might be easy to agree on these first four:

- *Simplicity* – it should be clear and easy to understand and not too complex to administer.
- *Responsibility* – it should encourage all members, as they are able, to share the burden.
- *Equity* – it needs to be fair and seen to be fair.
- *Solidarity* – it needs to share with the poorer and poorest.

The current system does a reasonable job of conforming to these principles. There are three additional principles which it does less well with:

- *Liberality* – motivating and incentivising giving.
- *Flexibility* – recognising the different needs of Drumchapel, St Giles Cathedral and Gatehouse linked with Anwoth and Borgue.
- *Subsidiarity* – devolving appriate degrees of financial control.

Even if we secure a broad agreement on principles, a formidable technical challenge remains in designing a revised system which achieves them. I say technical, but as with questions of national and local taxation, there are also crucial psychological, metaphorical and emotional issues in play. How do people perceive the system? How do they feel about it? These are also key questions when designing a financial regime for an institutional church and when naming and describing its operations to church members. Another important caveat is the need for humility on the part of its designers, because in a complex system where perceptions affect behaviour, reforms may have (negative) unintended consequences. We could, with the best of intentions, make things worse.

Inevitably, this is one of the key chapters in the book and it is also one of the most complex. It would be foolish to pretend that there are easy answers to the financial challenges and dilemmas facing the Church of Scotland, but it would also be unwise not to take the opportunity to subject the current systems to radical questioning. Given the rumbles of discontent that have been around for many years, if the outcome of the analysis here and of other conversations it may support and inform is that we are already close to an optimal system, then the work of revalidating that system will have its own value. If the conclusions here point to potential benefits from more radical reforms, then the hope is that the analysis here can inform and encourage such reforms.

Underlying this discussion of money and resource has been another of the key assumptions of this book: that the renewal of the Kirk can be enabled, facilitated and resourced by its central bodies and officials in crucial and indispensable ways, but it cannot be driven or directed from above or from the centre. The call of this book is for an adjustment in our polity, a recalibration of our systems, a redistribution of powers and functions. This kind of adjustment only ever takes place when money begins to flow in new channels and when spend is authorised and audited by new actors. Follow the money. If the money has not moved, the power has not moved either. If the power has not moved, we have not reformed the Kirk.

4

Changing Ministry

Although I have already referred a number of times to the challenges facing the Kirk in relation to declining numbers of ministers, the question of the future of 'ministry' deserves a chapter in its own right. This is an area where practical theology needs to assert and assume some responsibility.

When I successfully encouraged the 2014 General Assembly to adopt the proposal to mark 'A Decade for Ministry', my main hope was that the timescale would help the whole church to understand the scale of the task which was facing us. There was work to be done which could not be done quickly or painlessly. To take just the immediate presenting problem of declining numbers of ministers of word and sacrament, as retirals outstripped ordinations it would take at least five years to see the fruits of any new initiatives in the area of vocations. Ministries Council had already begun to address the issue of vocations with renewed urgency and were making some use of council employee Catherine Skinner's 2013 MBA Project *Facing the Future: How Can the Church of Scotland Increase Its Number of Ministers In Order to Remain Viable as an Institution in the 21st Century?*[1]

In *Facing the Future*, Skinner noted the significant challenges facing the Kirk, with around 70 per cent of its ministers due to retire in the next 15 years (2013–28). Although she suggested that from the 1950s to the 1980s there was some level of central focus on initiatives to maintain recruitment, she offered the disturbing conclusion that 'the Church as an organization has not undertaken any active recruitment of ministers for the last fifteen

---

1 I am grateful to Catherine for letting me see a copy of this unpublished study.

years'[2] (1998–2013). Her analysis of the Blue Books[3] showed that between 1999 and 2012 'no reference is made regarding recruitment other than publishing numbers presenting for training, until the report to the GA of 2012 which notes the "pressing need" [RGC 2012:4/19] to encourage more vocations'.[4] Her conclusion was devastatingly simple: 'The Church of Scotland needs considerable focus on the recruitment of ministers over the next five to ten years otherwise the Church in its current form will cease to have a large enough workforce to cover its requirements.'[5]

She illustrates this conclusion by noting that in 2013, 69 per cent of the ministerial workforce was aged over 50, and in that year alone, 34 were due to retire while just seven were to be ordained.[6] The projections were that if 2013 recruitment levels were not increased, the Kirk would have a shortfall of around 250 ministers by 2025. Skinner further notes that, while in 1978 the most common age of applicants was 22, with three over the age of 45 accepted, in 2013 the average minister began ministry at the age of 48.[7] The obvious consequence is that each older minister will serve for a shorter period of time and there will be a swifter retirement cycle than had previously been the case.

Skinner argued that the dramatic fall in recruitment in the 1990s reflected a change in approach by the central church and a reduction in their work on this issue. While she was not sure this reduction in effort had been intentional, she also noted a change in language from 'recruitment' to 'call' and an assumption developing that encouragement of call would take place at 'local' levels, without active intervention from central administration.[8]

In 2012, the church used its website and mailing list to advertise Vocations Conferences, as well as introducing an optional 'Vocations Sunday' in which ministers were encouraged to use one

---

2 Skinner, 2013, p. 8.
3 The colloquial term for the bound collections of General Assembly papers produced each year.
4 Skinner, 2013, p. 35.
5 Skinner, 2013, p. 8.
6 Skinner, 2013, p. 9.
7 Skinner, 2013, p. 32.
8 Skinner, 2013, p. 36.

Sunday service to discuss vocations. Skinner noted: 'This is all the Church currently does in relation to recruitment to Ministry' and characterised this as a 'passive rather than a proactive stance'.[9]

A further issue emerging from Skinner's research was a decline in key institutions which had emerged as 'incubators' for ministry candidates, in particular of activities for youth within the church, which had performed a bridging function.

While Skinner's work is extremely useful and it was clearly supported and encouraged by Ministries Council, for whom she works, it is troubling to note that this significant (though relatively brief) piece of work was only undertaken at her own initiative as a component of her independent MBA study. It was not commissioned by the church itself and might never have happened. That the church has had to rely on this type of self-initiated and self-funded research is not encouraging and begs some questions about strategic awareness and planning at such a critical point in its life.

My understanding is that the conclusions and recommendations contained in Skinner's work have gone on to inform the development and implementation of the 'Tomorrow's Calling' initiative.[10] The 'Decade for Ministry' initiative was also something developed outside the formal activity of Ministries Council, which was not initially welcomed by them, although it was swiftly accepted as an expression of the General Assembly's intent and concern, which was potentially helpful to the Council in developing a new phase of work around vocations. It is hard not to agree with her conclusion that the 14-year period from 1999 to 2012 represented a time when perceptions of the problem were not well honed and opportunities to begin to address it were missed.

One of the lessons of her research is that the church's own research into recruitment and monitoring of work around vocations needs to be improved and developed. We need to develop a better understanding of trends, of triggers, of incubating and bridging factors and of inhibiting factors. We also need to develop a richer understanding of how ministers feel about their work,

9 Skinner, 2013, p. 37.
10 www.tomorrowscalling.org.

about levels of satisfaction and fulfilment, and about areas in which they need more or different support, more or different education and training. There should be a regular, recurring, comprehensive survey of ministers, deacons and other parish workers, conducted every five years by the central church, with input from academic practical theologians and human resource academics into the design and analysis of the research. Surveys of this kind conducted in 2020, 2025 and 2030 will help to build up a fuller picture of experience of paid ministry within the Church of Scotland, which can inform the encouragement of vocations, initial ministerial education and ongoing support for those working for the church.

Of course, research alone will not address the crisis of vocations. A number of other practical initiatives are needed, but before I reflect on what those might be, I want to reflect on our understandings of ministry in a changing church and a changing Scotland.

Mission and ministry

The 1999 report *Ministers of the Gospel* prepared by the then Board of Ministry, followed the broad currents of an ecumenical theology of ministry which had been developing through the World Council of Churches Faith and Order process, in particular the understandings which had been developing in dialogue with the influential 1982 report on *Baptism, Eucharist and Ministry* as well as the responses to that report, and the 1998 Faith and Order Paper on *The Nature and Purpose of the Church*.[11]

Two broad ecumenical affirmations were developing, which the Church of Scotland was echoing. The first was that ministry belonged to the whole church, that it was an expression of the prior, primary and exemplary ministry of Jesus Christ, and that it belonged within the wider context of the church's mission, which was itself an expression of and outworking of the *missio Dei* or mission of God. In *Ministers of the Gospel* the German Reformed theologian Jürgen

---

11 All key documents are downloadable from www.Oikoumene.org/en/resources /documents/commissions/faith-and-order.

Moltmann is quoted, 'It is not the Church that has a mission of salvation to fulfil in the world; it is the mission of the Son and the Spirit through the Father that includes the Church.'[12] The second affirmation was that within this broader understanding of ministry there remained a crucial and honoured place for 'the particular ministry of Word and Sacrament' which was a gift of Christ to the Church.[13]

Looking back on *Ministers of the Gospel* a number of dynamics can be detected. On the one hand there is an affirmation and acceptance of the 'turn to mission' which was already growing within global ecumenical theology in the 1990s and which has continued to strengthen in the years since then. Alongside the much-quoted words from Moltmann which the report cites, Tim Dearborn's succinct observation is now very often quoted: 'It is not the Church of God which has a mission, but the God of mission who has a Church.'[14] *Missio Dei* thinking or what we could call 'new missiological thinking'[15] has been hugely influential within the global, ecumenical Church and within the global evangelical movement for two reasons. First, it expresses what we can call a 'post-colonial' understanding of church and mission. It moves mission from being something done *by* largely European, white, Christendom churches of the global North, and done *to* the global South. It makes all Christians, all churches everywhere, the objects of the mission of the triune God before they become, even in a secondary way, its subjects. The second reason for its embrace by those former 'sending' churches is that in Europe and North America, many of them are facing a rising tide of secularisation and a disorientating experience of decline. The South African missiologist David Bosch, in his classic work *Transforming Mission*, famously reflected on how questions of mission had been understood by the Reformed tradition as it had emerged within early modern Europe.[16] The focus on reforming and purifying churches with the support of Protestant authorities

---

12 Quoting from Moltmann, 1977, p. 64.

13 *Ministers of the Gospel*, 2.2.2.

14 Dearborn, 1998.

15 *Missio Dei* has its theological critics, e.g. http://themelios.thegospelcoalition.org /article/mission-a-problem-of-definition.

16 Bosch, 1991.

drove a strong emphasis on being ministers of the gospel, but was initially less engaged with the prior Roman Catholic tradition of external *missions* to non-Christian territories. While this would change with the growth of the Protestant missionary societies from the late eighteenth century onwards, the tendency to focus on *ministry* within Christendom and conceive of *missions* beyond it exercised a long-lasting hold on the imagination of churches such as the Church of Scotland. The nineteenth century saw the development of a parallel language of home mission and foreign missions, but it was only from the 1920s onwards[17] in the wake of the Russian revolution that concerns about Western secularisation began to radically reshape the relationship between ecclesiology and missiology and to move European churches from what Stephen Neill called the age of missions to the age of mission.[18]

As the world emerged from the horrors of the Second World War, the 1950s saw new attention given to mission and the theology of mission. In Scotland, this was exemplified by the work of the 'Tell Scotland' movement (1953–66), an ecumenical initiative which was developed with the intention of engaging in well-rounded mission initiatives to reach what had since the 1920s been dubbed 'the churchless million'. My colleague Sandy Forsyth has written an important missiological study of this period in Scotland.[19] The work of Lesslie Newbigin and Stephen Neill reveals that in the 1950s and 1960s there was real optimism from them and others about a theological consensus developing around an ecumenical theology of mission. In Scotland, as elsewhere, that broad consensus proved very difficult to maintain and to develop. It was pulled apart from both sides of the spectrum. Liberals who became infatuated with secular theology and 'religionless Christianity' disdained the language of mission (and as Newbigin notes, the language of 'church') in favour of Christian participation in broad social movements for humanisation, progress, justice and peace.[20] Conservatives, meanwhile, eschewed the

---

17 The 1928 Jerusalem Conference of the International Missionary Council witnessed rising concerns about secularism.

18 Neill, quoted in Bosch, 1991, p. 391.

19 Forsyth, 2017.

20 See the powerful account in Newbigin, 2009, p. 165.

consensus to work within organisations which had a more clearly defined evangelical confession and which offered a tighter focus on evangelism and individual salvation. This polarisation which began in the 1960s would be continued through the 1970s and 1980s, with evangelical Lausanne offering a theological counterpoint to the more liberal World Council of Churches and evangelical IVF/UCCF doing the same in relation to the Student Christian Movement (SCM). With the polarisation came stereotypical oppositions and denunciations of the other side: liberals didn't care about evangelism, evangelicals didn't care about social justice, etc. However, while Protestants were dividing noisily on these points, the Roman Catholic Second Vatican Council (1962–65) had produced important new work on mission and evangelisation, which began to exercise influence within and beyond the Roman Catholic communion.

David Bosch's 1991 book *Transforming Mission* is often identified as a key marker on the journey towards a new era of missional theology, although Lesslie Newbigin's work and publications in the 1980s following his return to England also made a crucial contribution.

If the previous consensus had been pulled apart from both sides, other developments across European, Northern and global Christianity opened up routes to a new era of convergence in missional theology from the 1980s onwards:

- A revival and renewal of evangelical social ethics took place under the influence of John Stott and others in the Lausanne movement, with Latin American, African and Asian evangelicals bringing new perspectives to the mix, which were less in thrall to Western individualism and more sensitised to political and economic struggles in the global South.
- The international advance of the charismatic renewal from the 1960s both crossed denominational boundaries and made the identity of evangelicalism more flexible and fluid.
- There was a cooling of enthusiasm for 'the secular', a sense that 'death of God' theology would not deliver the energy, passion or community that its advocates had hoped for; if some then made the post-Christian move and left the Church for good,

others rowed back towards a post-liberal version of the centre ground. Radical a/theistic liberal theology went into retreat and became a minority pastime.

Alongside this theological convergence, mainline Christian denominations across Europe had begun to move into a serious and sustained decline from the 1960s onwards. It is impossible to determine this with much precision, because definitive statistics don't exist, but the perception on both sides was that more liberal congregations in the Church of England, Church of Scotland, Methodist Church and United Reformed Church declined more quickly and grew more slowly than more evangelical congregations. There were still plenty of liberal Protestants and liberal Protestant ministers and they continued to press the churches in particular over issues of inclusion and exclusion, but there was little sense apart from these issues that they had the theological winds filling their sails. While the Iona Community was broadly identified with a more liberal theological stance, impelled by the poetic and musical genius of John Bell, its liturgical output mostly remained stubbornly orthodox, Trinitarian and Christocentric. It embraced inclusive language, but like its French cousin in Taizé, it valued the classic, catholic shape of the liturgy, and its literary character was richly shaped by the direct use of scripture. It continued to demonstrate a deep commitment to seeking justice and peace, but such commitments could now be positively appreciated by its growing constituency of broadly orthodox and open evangelical supporters.

The mainstream churches in Scotland and England were shrinking and they were changing. Acceptance of women's ministry came decades later in the Church of England than it had for the Kirk, with the Anglicans also proving more cautious in their recognition of same-sex relationships than the Church of Scotland would be. But as both practice and tone gradually changed, it was clear that both churches were gradually adapting to social changes across British society. While some of the most conservative figures on both Evangelical and Anglo-Catholic wings were quick to protest this as concessions to worldliness, or even as apostasy, they were unable to lead significant schisms or secessions.

So how has the Kirk changed over the past 30 years? The tentative thesis, which I have sketched here, is broadly that evangelicals have become more open and liberals have become more orthodox. One way to view this is that there has been convergence upon the centre ground, but my judgement is that the balance of numbers and of influence, certainly across the ordained ministry of the church, has been shifting towards a broad evangelicalism or what might be called in Brian McLaren's nicely turned phrase, 'generous orthodoxy'.[21]

Again, it is my judgement, although there are no statistics to prove or disprove this, that this gradual change in the theological centre of gravity of the Kirk has been driven by a number of material factors. In general, the more evangelical congregations have grown faster or declined more slowly; their children's, youth and student ministries have held up better; they have produced more candidates for ministry and there has been an increasing presence within academic theology departments of evangelical scholars who identify with them.

This steady but significant shift has been offset by the journey which a new centrist coalition within the church has made in relation to issues around gender and sexuality. This has, ironically, led the most conservative evangelical forces in the Kirk to understand what might otherwise be recognised on a range of indicators as their ships coming in, as instead an experience of defeat, betrayal and apostasy. With many of them still not willing to accept the ordination of women, the limited accommodations made over the ordination of women and men in same-sex relationships became for those conservatives, the hill which all 'true evangelicals' were expected to die on.

I am trying to stay in descriptive mode here, to reflect on how the church has been changing. I do think it is possible, because of the vehemence with which those two ethical and hermeneutical issues have been contested, to miss how, across a range of core doctrines, the Kirk as a whole has quietly become more theologically conservative in its doctrine of God, its Christology, its theology and spirituality of salvation, its understanding of the

---

21 McLaren, 2004.

work of the Holy Spirit and, whisper it, its general doctrine of scripture. That same central two-thirds of the Kirk,[22] have also become more open to a thoughtful and exploratory relationship with culture and the arts and have become more committed to the idea that seeking social justice, at home and globally, is an integral part of the gospel. They have reached a settled, hermeneutical judgement about women belonging within ordained ministry and church leadership on equal terms alongside men, and although many of them are still on a journey of dialogue and debate around same-sex relationships, they have moved beyond overt homophobia and are repelled by cruelly judgemental attitudes towards LGBTQ people.

This attempt to sketch changes in the dominant theological ethos of the Kirk, and of its ministers in particular, seems to me to lead back naturally to the conversation about mission. What I see now shaping the missional consciousness of the church is the interaction between this theological pilgrimage, the accelerating decline of the institutional church and the journey of Scottish culture and society into a broader and deeper condition of secularisation. These are being experienced simultaneously by those of us within the church and we are having to process them personally, theologically, spiritually and institutionally.

Perhaps more than at any other time since the era of 'Tell Scotland', the Kirk is realising that it must mobilise for mission, that it must understand and plan its future through a missional lens. One thing which gives me cause for hope is that there are signs once again of a developing ecumenical consensus about a theology of mission. Key aspects of this were articulated by Newbigin in the 1980s, and the first major programmatic statement came in 1991, with David Bosch's 'emerging, ecumenical, missionary paradigm'.[23] More recently, we can set alongside one another the Lausanne Movement's 2011 Cape Town Commitment[24] and the World Council of Churches' 2013 statement on Mission

22 I am offering informed 'guesstimates' here.
23 Bosch, 1991, pp. 368ff.
24 For the text of this (agreed by the 2010 Cape Town conference) see www .lausanne.org/content/ctc/ctcommitment.

and Evangelism, *Together Towards Life*.[25] There are still some significant differences of emphasis between the two documents, but there is also a significant overlapping consensus, an important degree of common ground. The most important form of that common ground is the human form it takes in the mainstream of ministers and members within our churches, who are ready to affirm and express such a consensus. A shorthand version of this and one we can work with across the length and breadth of the church, as a popular tool for catechism and a focus for planning, is the already mentioned Five Marks of Mission.

Ministry in a missional church[26]

The mission of God has a church. Missiology frames ecclesiology which frames ministry. We begin with the *missio Dei* as an overarching vision of the work of God in creation and redemption, of the world called to be reconciled to God, in Christ, through the renewing and life-giving work of the Spirit. Move to the *ekklesia*, the called-out people, the called-to-follow people and we find, in words attributed to Karl Barth, the Church as 'the world already turning to God'. As they are called, turn and gather, so the Church hears the word of the risen Christ in John 20.21: 'As the Father has sent me, so I send you'. This is the word which incorporates disciples into the *missio Dei*, which confirms and anoints the Church as the church apostolic.[27]

Ministry within the apostolic church is ministry which 'imitates' the apostles and their imitation of Christ. Like the ministry and mission of Jesus Christ, it is rooted in love: 'there is mission because God loves people'[28] and in love it repeats the call to repent

---

25 www.churchofscotland.org.uk/_data/assets/pdf_file/0008/20699 /Mission_statement.pdf.

26 See especially Chapter 4 in Faith and Order Advisory Group of the Church of England, 2007; see also this PCUSA paper by Paul Hooker on missional ecclesiology. www.pcusa.org/resource/what-missional-ecclesiology/.

27 See also Flett, 2016.

28 Bosch, 1991, p. 390.

and believe the gospel and to follow Christ.[29] Ministry does the work of the one who has sent the Church[30] and, like the kingdom of God, whose coming the Church seeks and prays for, this work aims to be therapeutic,[31] because, in part at least, 'the kingdom is creation healed'.[32] The ministry of Jesus Christ, as imitated in the ministry of the Church, is all that the Church does as it seeks to do the will of the one who has sent it. It is work done in the name of Christ, in obedience to God, in the power of the Holy Spirit.

The presence of the kingdom calls for the renewal of all human work within a renewed creation mandate. At its most expansive, ministry describes all human work done in the service of God. Ministry is the work of the whole Church and encompasses the work of the Church both when it is gathered in worship and learning and when it is sent and dispersed. The 'Five Marks' offer a summary of key areas of that work of ministry, which identify it as work shaped by the *missio Dei*. If we zoom in from the *notae missionis*[33] to consider the tradition of *notae ecclesiae*,[34] we find in the Scots Confession of 1560 that there are three: 'the true preaching of the Word of God; the sacraments rightly administered and ecclesiastical discipline uprightly administered'.[35]

Agreement about the notes or marks of mission and church is easier to achieve than agreement about who is called and authorised to do which parts of the work of ministry. We noted above that the second affirmation of *Ministers of the Gospel* was of a crucial and honoured place for 'the particular ministry of Word and Sacrament'.[36]

---

29 Mark 1.15, 17.

30 John 9.4.

31 On the therapeutic relevance of Christology, see Moltmann, 1990, p. 44, where he works with Bonhoeffer's question: 'Who is Jesus Christ for us today?'

32 Küng, 1977, p. 231.

33 'Marks of mission'. For a fascinating discussion of this term, see Kärkkäinen, 2009, Chapter 5, pp. 66ff.

34 'Marks of the church'.

35 Chapter 18 of the Scots Confession (1560); in the Church of England 2007 *Mission and Ministry* report these three are related to the Great Commission and to Christ's *munus triplex* or threefold office of being prophet, priest and king.

36 *Ministry of the Gospel*, 2.2.2.

I am not ready or willing to dissent from that conclusion, for reasons which I will explain. However, I think there are reasons to apply some theological pressure to it. If we come to believe with Miroslav Volf that ordination belongs not to the *esse* or being of the Church, but to its *bene esse* or well-being,[37] then that may free us to show more flexibility and creativity in our approach to changing ministry.

In his book *The Church in the Power of the Spirit*, Jürgen Moltmann made a distinction which I find helpful, between the *charge* given to the community and the *assignments* within the community.[38] The charge here means what is given to the Church in the Great Commission and involves, in our case, the Church of Scotland being charged to continue to display the marks of the Church, to manifest *kerygma, koinonia, diakonia*.[39] Moltmann argues that while the charge to the Church is constant, the *assignments* made within the Church in order to fulfil that charge can exhibit a more varied form.[40] While he argues this with conviction, he nonetheless refers to 'the difficult relationship between the common commissioning of all believers and special assignments within the community'.[41]

It is fair to say that Moltmann's position here is radical in relation to the mainstream of reformed ecclesiology and that it has been more popular with 'Free Church'/Baptist/ Independent commentators (such as Moltmann's doctoral student Miroslav Volf) than with Reformed theologians. It is also important to note how questions of ordination relate to broader questions of ecumenical relationships between churches of different traditions. Volf's book *After Our Likeness* was written to explore this last question and to defend the 'ecclesiality' of churches in the Baptist and Anabaptist tradition, as well as the growing number of Pentecostal and Congregationalist churches within the global Christian community. If we looked back to Newbigin's 1948 book on the formation of the Church of South India (CSI), we would see the

---

37 I.e., that it can be seen as desirable, but it is not essential; see Volf, 1998, p. 248.
38 Moltmann, 1977, pp. 300ff.
39 Proclamation, communion, service.
40 Moltmann, 1977, pp. 306, 307.
41 Moltmann, 1977, pp. 199, 302.

ecumenical anguish experienced around the question of ordination. Theologians and churchpeople who were committed to the cause of ecumenism in the twentieth century made huge efforts to overcome historic divisions and reach common ground on this question. In relation to the Kirk, we could mention the ecumenical conversations, inspired by the CSI union and formation of the WCC, which from 1949 brought together the Church of England and Church of Scotland, and from 1954 also involved the Scottish Episcopal Church and the Presbyterian Church of England. This period saw leading Kirk theologian, T. F. Torrance, publish his book *Royal Priesthood* in 1955, in which he proposed the idea of 'bishops in presbytery'. The report of the Joint Conversations (known colloquially as 'The Bishops Report') went to the General Assembly in 1957 and was rejected in 1959 on the grounds that it implied a denial of the catholicity of the Church of Scotland and of the regularity and validity of its ministry. The same issues would resurface a generation later in the Scottish Churches Initiative for Union (SCIFU) which would also be rejected by the General Assembly in 2003, on very similar grounds.[42]

Since 2003, it is fair to say that this kind of official institutional ecumenism has been 'quiet' in Scotland. There are few grand schemes under consideration, at least that I know of. But more than a decade on, this may be a good time to reflect on the 2003 vote and to look back to the 1959 vote. One thing the two episodes shared in common, which is a central concern of this book, is the relationship between church and mission – and indeed, between ecumenism and mission.

In 1957, the dream was of a new era of ecumenical relationship between the Church of England and the Church of Scotland,[43] which would offer a powerful testimony of Christian unity to British society. In this first wave of ecumenical theology, after the slaughter and enmity of two world wars, Christian unity was seen by many as vital to Christian witness. After all, how could Christians work for reconciliation in the world if they could not be reconciled to one another? In 2003, the SCIFU proposals

---

42 Kesting, 2014.
43 And English Presbyterians, Scottish Episcopalians.

coincided with a new beginning for Scotland, with the arrival of the Scottish Parliament in 1999. They were also prepared at a time when it was already very clear that the mainline denominations were all in trouble, with established and accelerating patterns of decline. Surely, it was argued, it was time to put aside the 'competition' for churchgoers, the wasteful duplication of resources and unite in a new initiative to be a church *for* Scotland.

I was not living in Scotland when SCIFU was being developed and I have no desire to engage in any kind of blame game, so I will simply observe that for some people this was a tragedy of presbyterian intransigence, for others a tragedy of episcopalian intransigence, and for still others a matter of some indifference. Despite the theoretical connections between mission and ecumenism, for many on the evangelical wing of the churches, ecumenism is seen as primarily a 'liberal' passion and its champions are seen to lack the instincts for mission and evangelism which would be required to make an interdenominational union, organised in 'maxi parishes', into a potent vehicle for mission to Scotland.

Since SCIFU is no more and shows no signs of resurrection or reincarnation, I wonder whether, in the second decade of the twenty-first century, with decline even more advanced, the Church of Scotland might be ready to consider two issues in a new light.

The first is the question of ordination, both to the ministry of word and sacrament and to the eldership. The second is the question of regional superintendence.

By my understanding, the Kirk's commitment to ecumenism, which I endorse and share, has had the accompanying effect of reinforcing conservative theological instincts[44] about ordination. So long as ecumenical activists and diplomats are trying with great patience and care to mark out common ground, more radical approaches such as Moltmann's are likely to be seen as a threat, just as the ordination of women was in the past and the ordination of those in same-sex relationships is in the present. Ecumenism therefore tends to reinforce conservatism in relation to doctrines of ministry, because it continually reminds a particular church that a decision for a more radical option will increase

---

44 Here I do not specifically mean 'conservative evangelical'.

the distance between it and those with whom it is trying to forge ecumenical relationships. In this respect, the fact of ecumenism having gone quiet and settled back into the friend zone as opposed to hoping for a church wedding, may mean that this is a moment in which the Kirk might allow itself to think more creatively and flexibly about the relationships between ordination, ministers, elders and sacraments.

On the second point, more scope for creativity and flexibility might allow us the freedom to move in the opposite direction. Freed from the pressure of negotiating with Episcopalians/ Anglicans over mutual recognition of ministries, we might consider allowing ourselves an experiment or three with more long-term regional leadership of a distinctively presbyterian kind. It would be a way of 'unbundling' the bishop role and removing the parts we don't like.[45] It could be temporary, experimental, provisional and, even potentially, reversible.

In both these cases, my motivation for wanting to explore options for change is missional. My suggestions about regional leadership will make more sense when seen in the light of the proposals for structural reform in the next chapter, so here I want to reflect further on locating ministry within mission.

Changing ministry – intentionally missional

Early in the book I noted theological reservations about 'pelagian' approaches to church growth, accepting they had some validity but also suggesting they could be overstated. 1 Corinthians 3 is a key passage here, allowing us to talk in active terms about ministry as human work, while also emphasising what only God can do. Paul's embrace of the master-builder/architect metaphor helps to support an active account of what some presbyteries call 'mission strategy', while remembering that, as the 1662 Anglican Book of Common Prayer puts it, 'We do not presume'.

With that as warrant, my key concerns here may seem simplistic, obvious and ineffectual, but there is some grounding for them

---

45 On the metaphor of 'unbundling', see my discussion in Gay, 2011, Chapter 3.

in recent Anglican research into church growth.[46] The simple claim is that it seems to make a difference when congregations, elders and ministers become more intentional about mission, evangelism and church growth. Churches which show little interest in growing, for the most part, seem not to grow.

Here I will claim to have had most of the predictable conversations and heard most of the objections, often accompanied by ringing declarations that 'it is not about bums on seats' and I remain mostly unconvinced when people deploy that kind of argument. There is the basic issue of consistency and non-hypocrisy, where those who deplore numbers which mean bad news, become sudden converts to their value when they indicate success. But there is also the substantive question of why, if the gospel is good news, we would not want to see more and more people believe it and respond to it? I hold my hand up and confess to being someone who believes that bums on seats matter. They're not the only thing that matters and they don't matter most – but they matter, and let's not pretend they don't.

Here as before, until someone offers a better one, I am willing to rest on the 'Five Marks' as a guide to missional intentionality. I confess to being hugely disappointed by the report of the Kirk's 'Mission Forum' to the 2014 General Assembly, which seemed to me to offer a rambling, unfocused and ultimately unusable set of definitions of mission.[47] I am convinced of the value of working with a clear, brief, focused, memorable and balanced statement of missional intentions. I am persuaded it makes a difference when ministers and congregations adopt and own this kind of intentionality and use it to focus their planning, their deployment of resources, their Christian education.

---

46 www.churchgrowthresearch.org.uk/UserFiles/File/Reports/From AnecdoteToEvidence1.0.pdf; some aspects of this research are problematic in correlation – causation terms.

47 See Appendix II: www.churchofscotland.org.uk/__data/assets/pdf_file/0008 /20060/Mission-And-Discipleship-Council-report.pdf – the appendix reads like an unprocessed and unredacted transcription of flip-charts which had been hung around the walls of the forum meetings.

Missional presbyteries

So far, I have been considering the congregational level, but I also believe that same focus on missional intentionality needs to be a transformative focus for presbyteries in the period 2020–30. There are some significant things to be learned from the example of Fresh Expressions in the Church of England over the past decade. One of them is the importance of diocesan leadership and support and, within that, of the particular role which can be played by individual bishops. One of the concerns of this book is that in key respects our Church of Scotland presbyteries are not fit for purpose. There are exceptional individuals, giving faithful and imaginative service, and there are examples of committees and working groups working creatively and taking initiatives. I mean no disrespect to them by suggesting that we remain in urgent need of a missional re-imagining of the Kirk and by positing that reformed and restructured presbyteries have a crucial role to play in leading and shaping this.

The reform and re-imagining which I believe is needed involves a review of the language and conceptuality which is basic to how we understand presbyterianism. In particular, we need to take another look at the judicial and administrative language of 'courts' and 'clerks', which currently looms too large in our ecclesiology. My concern is not to replace the judicial notes, but to supplement them and reframe them. Here, despite other ongoing problems and issues facing the PCUSA,[48] I do think the work they did in the years leading up to the adoption of their *New Form of Government* in 2011 deserves serious consideration by the Church of Scotland.[49] In essence, what this work did was to offer a new articulation of the theological basis of presbyterian governance in the light of the *missio Dei*. In the new section G-3.0101 it says this of councils of the church: 'The reason councils (sessions, presbyteries, synods and the General Assembly) exist is to help

---

48 For a sobering comparison between the Kirk and the PCUSA, see renowned Presbyterian blogger Steve Salyers ('GA Junkie'): http://blog.gajunkie.com/?p=1567.

49 www.pcusa.org/site_media/media/uploads/oga/pdf/nfog-missional -church.pdf.

congregations and the whole church be more faithful participants in Christ's mission.'[50]

Earlier in this chapter, I anticipated that some of the points I would make might seem to be beside the point. This is an example. Would it really make a difference to do this? Has it saved the PCUSA or been a silver bullet for their problems? The answer to the latter question is of course no. The answer to the first 'Would it make a difference' question is more complex. The work of reforming the Kirk, as I understand it, calls for a complex mix of institutional and cultural change. None of the individual changes we may make, for example to the rubric of church law or the structure of governance, may mean much on their own – and in this, as in all things, unless the Lord builds . . . That said, the attempt to work through and to work out such issues has the potential to be part of necessary cultural change within the Kirk. Work on these issues represents a form of institutional 'repentance', *metanoia*, a renewal of the mind of the institution, which can contribute to the transformation of its practice. To agree that without the quickening of the Holy Spirit, none of these initiatives will be enough, is not to agree that they are unnecessary or pointless.

In the case of presbyteries, we need a new articulation of what they are *for*, which identifies and even 'confesses' the missional as the frame within which the judicial and the administrative functions of presbytery find their meaning and value. The process of making that missional affirmation will, I believe, help to focus our minds on what they should be doing, as well as the other 'wisdom' calls involved in the *kybérnēsis* or governance and administration of the church.[51]

Changing ministry – options for change

In the final part of this chapter, I want to set out some practical options for change which reflect the issues raised above.

---

50 https://fpccolumbia.org/Websites/fpccolumbia/images/BookOfOrder.pdf.

51 1 Corinthians 12.28. The focal metaphor associated with the etymology here is of steering a ship.

Moltmann talked of 'the difficult relationship between the common commissioning of all believers and special assignments within the community'.[52] He regards the formative historical examples of how that relationship was negotiated as flawed and problematic, whether in the form of consecration to Ignatius's monarchical episcopate or co-option to Calvin's aristocratic '*venérable compagnie des pasteurs*'.[53] He wants to move our thinking towards a more fluid and flexible understanding of the *commissioning* and *assigning* aspects of ministry, which reflects the messianic rule of Christ and the charismatic gifting of the Spirit.[54] The key thing is for the community to remain centred on the *essential charges* of word and sacrament, discipline and care (prophetic and ecological witness) while exercising the freedom it has in Christ, through the Spirit, to make *variable assignments*.

I noted that Moltmann's work in this area had not gone down a storm with Reformed churches around the world.[55] There is a certain romanticism to its radicalism, which in part reflects the decade he was writing in. A generation later, I am going back to it because I believe it can speak to our situation, but I also want to set against that a recognition of the ongoing difficulty of negotiating the relationship between the common ministry of all the baptised and the special ministry of the ordained. The problem with Calvin's ordinary offices of pastor/teacher, elder, deacon[56] – which is the main theological understanding of ministry we inherit in the Kirk – is that in their maintaining for the pastor/teachers a monopoly on the ministry of word and sacrament, they effectively perpetuate a 'clerical caste' who have too much of the work of ministry loaded into this single composite role. The virtue of that model having become normative for many Reformed churches is that it has often proved itself to be fruitful and popular in practice

---

52 Moltmann, 1977, p. 302.
53 Moltmann, 1977, pp. 303–6.
54 Moltmann, 1977, pp. 303–6.
55 Although, when delivering the Chalmers Lectures, the venerable Scottish practical theologian Chris Wigglesworth expressed his enthusiasm for the book.
56 He also makes room for doctors – who teach and write theology for the church.

and it has been reasonably effective in maintaining institutional stability and unity.[57]

What we have to face currently, however, which might send us back to listen to Moltmann again, are two significant problems with the ordained ministry in the Church of Scotland today. The first is a set of concerns about how well this model is working, both in relation to allowing the ministry of the whole people to flourish and in respect of its ability to respond to church decline. The second is the deadly simple problem of supply. If we make this model of ministry effectively indispensable to our ecclesiology; in Moltmann's terms, if we make this particular form of the *assignments* inflexibly essential to the *charge* given to the church, then we have nowhere left to go. This is the devastating problem facing the Roman Catholic Church in Scotland today, which is drawing out some creative solutions in the form of 'extraordinary ministers of Holy Communion'[58] but is also being forced to resort to a drastic programme of merging parishes to ensure they can be served by a shrinking community of ageing priests.

It is also being faced by the Church of England, who have the advantage over the Roman Catholic Church of having opened their ministry to women, but who have also managed to develop the non-stipendiary ministry to a far greater degree than the Church of Scotland has.[59]

---

57 J. T. McNeill, in a classic 1943 article (McNeill, 1943, p. 78), argued that in Reformed theology the doctrine of the ministry was an essential part of the doctrine of the church: 'In the teaching of the Reformed churches the "notes" of the true church – those things by which it may be known – are the pure preaching of the Word, the right administration of the sacraments, and proper discipline. The Word does not preach itself, the sacraments and discipline do not administer themselves. It follows from the nature of the church that certain persons must be vested with responsibility for the maintenance of these means of grace. A ministry of the Word and sacraments thus becomes a necessity in the economy of the church. But the ministry is not for our theologians a matter of economy alone, with no principle of authority beyond worldly prudence and expediency. Instead the position of the Reformed doctors without exception has been that the ministry is a gift of God to the catholic visible church.'

58 On this, see Owen Dudley Edwards, Chapter 13, in Forrester and Gay (eds), 2009.

59 This involves both non-stipendiary ministers (NSMs) and Ordained Local Ministers (OLMs).

Essentially, there are only four ways to address the problem. The first (or 'Tomorrow's Calling' option) is to recruit more ministers. The second (or Roman Catholic option) is to merge parishes and make them share ministers. The third (or Church of England option) is to broaden the scope of ordination and increase supply through a supplementary stream of NSMs/OLMs. The fourth (the Moltmann option?) is to fulfil the charges through embracing a more flexible approach to the assignment of ministries within the church. I am convinced that no one of these will be enough on its own – we will need all four.

The Church of Scotland is facing complex challenges in the work of changing ministry between now and 2030. We already noted the five tasks to be tackled simultaneously: closing unviable churches, managing decline, reversing decline, supporting growth and planting new congregations. We now need to reflect on the kinds of ministry and 'ministers' needed to address this fivefold challenge and on our approach to education, training and formation for such ministry.

Closing unviable churches

This is something we have had a lot of practice at over the past 50 years. The structural issue of oversupply as a legacy of the Disruption has since the 1960s been augmented by the forces of decline. The situation on the ground, however, is complicated by uneven patterns of growth and decline, by diverse forms of ministerial tenure and by the way in which relationships between neighbouring churches are sometimes marked by theological difference or 'bad blood'. This complexity means that a presbytery cannot simply implement a rational programme of planned closures. An area may seem 'overchurched' but may have relatively thriving congregations operating within a stone's throw of one another. A struggling church may resist union with a neighbouring congregation whose theology or spirituality it mistrusts or detests. A congregation where the minister has unrestricted tenure and the fabric fund is healthy may be able to hold out for years until it becomes a zombie, with huge consequences for missional work within its parish.

This makes the process of presbytery planning as much of an art as it is a science. In the period between now and 2030 we will need to approach the closure of congregations in as artful and creative a way as we can. We will need to seize opportunities strategically without simply being opportunistic. We will need to find new ways to practise 'tough love', where a building and location have great missional potential which can be fulfilled only 'under new management'. This will require presbyteries to develop new combinations of carrot and stick, so that restart or reset options can be implemented in places where renewal is impossible for the existing congregation and leadership.

In some though not all areas, ecumenical solutions will have an obvious appeal and should be pursued if they can be developed with a missional ethos.

Managing decline

The management of decline is often used in a derogatory sense (i.e. 'We're not just in the business of managing decline') but need not be. Where there is decline, it needs to be managed. Some of the decline will be irreversible. Some congregations are never going to grow again and will have to be linked or united or dissolved. Where that happens, we need to care for those affected, attend to their pastoral needs and walk with them through the pain and disappointment of loss. We will need the new interim ministers and transition ministers who have become a valued part of the Church's life in the past decade. We will also need the kind of peacemaking, mediation and conflict resolution skills which are being developed in the impressive 'Place for Hope' initiative, because changes which people experience as cuts, closure and rejection will generate anger and conflict.[60]

Enabling renewal and supporting growth

We also need ministries which can enable renewal and growth. Here we meet an area in which I think the Kirk is poorly served

---

60 www.placeforhope.org.uk.

by the current bifurcation between Mission and Discipleship and Ministries Councils, which I return to in the next chapter. New initiatives such as the Priority Areas/General Trustees 'Chance to Thrive' and the Panel on Review and Reform's 'Path of Renewal' programmes are placing an emphasis on coaching and accompanying ministers and congregations through change.

Aberdeen's Centre for Ministry Studies has produced some innovative programming since its establishment in 2017 and represents a creative use of the endowments of Christ's College. In some areas, however, there are serious gaps in provision. With the closure of Glasgow's International Christian College, Scotland's only established and academically rigorous training centre for youth ministry and children's ministry was lost and it remains to be seen how effectively the 'phoenix' body, the Scottish School of Christian Mission, will replace this provision or if it can even survive. Here we find another side-effect of the Kirk recognising five centres for Initial Ministerial Education – that it does not have enough capacity or investment at any of them to develop its own courses in these areas. The most recent research into church growth in the Church of England indicated connections between investment in youth and children's work and congregational growth. The Kirk has hard questions to ask itself here about why it has failed over the past 20 years to support and invest in the training infrastructure needed to produce a pool of workers trained in youth and children's ministry, both paid and voluntary, who can add ministry capacity to congregations seeking growth and renewal.[61]

There are tough questions, too, to be addressed to those like myself who work in Initial Ministerial Education. As I write, a major review of IME is being initiated by Ministries Council and I am happy to agree that this is overdue. We are in the twilight of a Christendom model of educating ministers through the ancient Divinity faculties, and the church has so far baulked at confronting the difficult dilemmas which are arising from a changing landscape. On the one hand, the Kirk holds dear its commitment to 'an educated ministry' and to the location of that education within public universities. The story of Scotland's ancient universities is

---

61 Again, was this a Ministries Council issue or one for Mission and Discipleship?

inseparable from the story of the Church of Scotland and their statutory duty to provide a curriculum for educating Kirk ministers, reflects a Reformed vision of the role of the university in Scottish public life. The road not taken here is the road to establishing separate seminaries. While this did happen after the Disruption, and was taken forward with great energy and distinction, the United Free (UF) Colleges returned to the bosom of the universities after 1929. Like the Church of Scotland's role in public education, strategic decisions about the structure of provision and the nature of church involvement were taken up until the 1950s, with a presumption of continuing presbyterian hegemony within Scotland's educational institutions. This presumption has been wearing progressively thinner for a generation now, eroded from one side by the secularisation of Scottish society, including unsurprisingly its schools and universities and from the other by the relentless decline of the Kirk. This has led us to our current dilemmas and to key structural problems with the current provision in education for ministry.

1 The Kirk's institutional power and influence within the four ancient universities has been steadily eroded and we are now marginal to the operation of the Schools of Divinity and Departments of Theology and Religious Studies. Those who pay pipers call tunes. Our current system costs the Kirk very little and we pay very little to the universities who educate our ministers.[62] One consequence is that, aside from statutory duties, there is very little *de jure* specification in place about what will be taught in these centres and who will teach it. There are no posts left which have to be filled by Presbyterians, or by Protestants and few which have to be filled by Christians. We are now reliant on a de facto situation in which universities happen to have appointed Presbyterians, Protestants and

---

62 The point within a Reformed Christendom vision of Scotland was of course that the Scottish people paid for this 'public good' out of their general taxes.

Christians.[63] This could change very rapidly and we would have no way of formally contesting that.

2 Our marginality has been increased by the collapse in the number of candidates we are sending for IME and our dilemmas about reducing the number of recognised centres. When we have fewer than 30 candidates a year entering IME as candidates (in some recent years this has dipped below 15) and we spread them randomly over five centres, the system begins to crash. Some centres have no candidates and most do not have healthy or viable cohorts any more. Universities, understandably, insist on minimum numbers in order for courses to be viable. This means that specialist courses for the formation of ministry candidates are becoming almost impossible to run, unless they can attract additional students. All new courses have to be approved by university Senates and it is also the case, within secularising universities, that courses on prayer, spirituality, preaching, mission, etc. are looking increasingly exotic to colleagues scrutinising their academic credentials. Meanwhile, we want universities to keep employing suitable people who can run such courses, even though we are not endowing the posts or even sending them students to take the courses. The situation – again I stress the de facto situation across Scottish universities in 2017 – remains relatively strong in terms of gifted staff in core areas, but the absence of guarantees for the future is unsettling. There are also significant weaknesses developing in key areas for ministry development, such as homiletics, liturgy, missiology and pastoral care. It is clear that we have a thinning of provision and the inability to create extra capacity where it might be needed. Connect this to the development of unsustainably small cohorts of ministry students across the five centres and we have some kind of crisis. The old model of IME is effectively broken, although folk in my position across the four ancient universities are still

---

63 I welcome richly ecumenical and plural staff groups in these departments – my point is that it is ridiculous to contemplate a system in which there were no Church of Scotland academics involved in IME and there are almost no formal guarantees of that left in the system.

finding ways to make it work for students as well as we can. However, if the case for reform seems unassailable, the options for reform are all problematic.

3 Over the past three decades, the church has responded to the growing problems with the university-based model of IME by supplementing university provision with its own conference-based programme of formation. It has, I suggest, felt itself to have little option; given that it now has almost no formal influence within the universities, the parallel conference stream represented an area over which it could exercise control. In this period, the system of placing candidates within congregations has also come to be organised and assessed by the church, independent of the universities. Finally, in the past five years, a further layer has been added (unwisely in my view) through the creation of the Ministries Training Network. The effect of this has been to divide the IME/formation process into four parallel streams, which lack any overall coherence, design or integration. I am Principal of Trinity College, but I have no involvement in the selection of candidates, no part in the design or oversight of conferences, no role in the choice, support or assessment of candidate placements in local churches or chaplaincies and no role in the Ministries Training Network. In a seminary context, such as in the USA, the topics we have to tackle in candidate conferences would be tackled in seminary, the placements would be subject to shared planning and oversight from field education staff, and the seminary would be employing appropriate staff with denominational awareness and connections, in core areas of ministerial formation. I am not aware that there has ever been a proper strategic cost–benefit analysis of creating these four parallel streams or that until now Ministries Council have even done the auditing work to identify how much the current system costs the church. In their defence, the wider Kirk has seemed completely unwilling to face the problem. Any suggestion of closing one centre would, until now, have seen its irate alumni on their feet in General Assembly objecting vigorously to this act of barbarism (in the case of the ancients) or theological victimisation (in the case of Highland Theological College). There are also

tricky questions about historic reserved funds and endowments associated with the various colleges and the complex ways in which their institutional identities have been woven together with their respective universities since 1929. New College is by far the wealthiest, with around £3.5 million in endowments, although much if not most of this sum is restricted in various ways. It is generally seen to have had its connection to the Kirk well protected through the particular agreements made with Edinburgh University and the Church of Scotland over the ownership, use and upkeep of its world-famous buildings on the Mound. Trinity College has around £400,000 and no special claim on any buildings or property other than its very valuable library, which is permanently lodged with the University of Glasgow. St Andrews is in a unique situation since there is no former Free/UF Church College associated with it and therefore no separate charity independent of the university and I lack the information to comment on its financial connections (if any) to the Kirk. Christ's College Aberdeen has no buildings, but around £1 million in investments, some of which are also restricted, which it has used since 2014 among other things to support the Centre for Ministry Studies.[64]

All of this means that routes to reform are not straightforward. Some home truths do need to be acknowledged.

- Even if numbers doubled overnight, the Kirk could train all of its candidates at one centre, which could also be funded to develop a state of the art distance learning facility for all those who could not move to that centre during semester time.
- The current dis-integrated model of four parallel streams needs to be reformed and integrated within a new holistic learning contract.
- A new, built from scratch, free-standing seminary is likely to be too expensive and too inflexible.

---

64 Financial information is available for the three colleges and for Highland Theological College and its associated trust through OSCR: www.oscr.org.uk.

- The church needs to develop a clearer specification of what it wants IME to consist of in future and it needs to invest in creating capacity to deliver elements of formation which are not well covered at present.
- The future will be more expensive than the past as the state will not deliver all that the church wants through the existing university system.
- It cannot possibly add the necessary new capacity at all five centres.
- Consolidation to just one centre is likely to be politically impossible and might leave historic assets intended for IME stranded and of limited use to the Kirk in one or more historic centres.
- Detaching the system of IME from all of the historic universities is likely to be politically impossible and would weaken provision in key respects.
- Future provision for IME should take advantage of the financial assets of the existing church colleges.
- A prerequisite for reform should be an audit of the costs of the existing system of conferences, placements, Ministries Council support staff and Ministries Training Network.

Not all of the above home truths point in one direction. There are difficult choices to be made if a new system is to be in place by 2020. I am going to be more reticent on this than on some other issues as I am directly involved, but let me offer some pointers to the kind of solution which I think may be most feasible and desirable.

1 The future will involve one or two recognised 'gateways' to IME, for example a northern and southern option, with an enhanced distance learning capacity.
2 Future provision should be built on top of the historic colleges, once issues of governance have been reviewed and clarified to the church's satisfaction. Colleges will need to merge or collaborate to be part of a 'gateway'. Gateway status will attract significant additional investment from the church to be used in synergy with historic assets as part of a ten-year development plan for the period 2020–30.

3 A new BD Min. 2.0 specification should be agreed between the Church of Scotland, other interested member denominations of ACTS (Action of Churches Together in Scotland) and the relevant universities. Consideration should also be given to enabling specialist qualifications in youth ministry, children's ministry, community development, chaplaincy, pioneer ministry, which would share modules with the BD Min.

4 IME should be overseen by a virtual Church of Scotland 'College', with a national co-ordinating and oversight function. This would direct the church's investment in IME and could directly employ staff to offer additional support to the IME centre(s).[65] It would operate as a distinct unit within the central structures of the church and would replace/incorporate existing Ministries Council posts supporting IME.[66]

5 The new vehicle(s) for IME should from the outset be designed to also support Continuing Ministerial Education (CME) and a broader Education for Ministries (EFM) programme for all congregations and members. It would take over national responsibility for the latter from Mission and Discipleship and would co-ordinate support for congregational learning and education for ministries across presbyteries.

Planting new congregations

I have argued for more than a decade that the Church of Scotland needed to become more strategic and intentional about planting new congregations. I recognise that this asks a lot of a denomination which is already struggling to manage decline and enable renewal, but I think it is a vital part of the ecology of the Kirk's mission effort in Scotland. Some of these plants will be 'phoenix', restart or reseeded congregations which are commissioned to make a new beginning where something old has had to be

---

65 Christ's currently employs staff who are recognised as Honorary Lecturers by Aberdeen University.

66 Within Ministries Council or a revised structure such as the one proposed in Chapter 6.

dissolved and replaced. Some will operate across geographical parish boundaries in relation to specific communities, subcultures or networks, will be authorised by a Presbytery Mission Order[67] and overseen by special presbytery arrangements to ensure that their technical 'intrusion' is not in harmful competition with other congregations. Some will be church plants in neglected or hard-to-reach areas of existing parishes or in areas of new housing.

There is widespread recognition across mainline denominations in Europe, England and North America that these kind of church planting or pioneering ministries, which are being undertaken in both 'lay' and ordained forms, call for a distinctive skill set, customised training and tailored support.

There are also signs, from within the Church of England and Methodist Church programmes, as well as from existing Scottish programmes like Forge and the Scottish School of Mission, that pioneer pathways into ministry connect with the felt vocations of a distinctive set of people, many of them under 40, who might not candidate for conventional parish ministry.

I therefore believe that the Kirk needs to be strategic and intentional about a programme of church planting. As a very rough indicator, my own judgement is that it should consider a goal of planting 100 new congregations by 2030 and should budget accordingly, as well as creating a distinctive vocations pathway for candidates and a customised BD Min. (Pioneer) option within IME.

Having explored the threefold challenge, I now return to the question originally raised alongside it, of ways to address the crisis in the supply of ministers.

Supply of ministers: four options

The 2016 Report of Ministries Council offered an update to the figures already quoted from Catherine Skinner's thesis, which if anything, offered an even grimmer picture of the future:

---

67 In the same way as the Church of England deploys Bishop's Mission Orders.

By the beginning of 2010 . . . the numbers [of candidates] had slowed to a trickle, barely reaching double figures in some years. An almost complete lack of candidates under the age of 30, and very few even under 40 began to point to an approaching crisis. By 2010, well over 80% of Church of Scotland Parish ministers were over the age of 50, with more than 600 due to retire by 2025.

Although the efforts of the Tomorrow's Calling initiative may well increase the numbers engaging in ministerial formation, the Church of Scotland has to face the fact that by the early-2020s the number of full-time Parish ministers will have fallen to around 600. This is so far short of the number anticipated in current Presbytery Plans (850 Parish ministers + 150 other ministries) as to make the inherited model of a single minister in a single (albeit linked in many cases) Parish (with a single set of buildings) essentially unworkable.[68]

The four options noted above as options to address this 'approaching crisis' were more candidates, fewer parishes, new forms of ordination and greater flexibility about ministerial assignments. I want to consider these in turn.

More candidates

Numbers of candidates are at historically and critically low levels. I am a wholehearted supporter of 'Tomorrow's Calling' and recognise the expertise which those tasked with this are now developing in this area. I also welcome the 'Volunteering Vocations' programme, recognising that the PCUSA programme on which ours is modelled has been a pathway towards ministry for a significant number of participants.[69]

---

68 Ministries Council Report in RGA 2016 1.2.2.2 and 1.2.2.3.

69 It is interesting to note that the Church of England is facing similar challenges and has committed itself to a 50 per cent increase in the number of ordinands entering the system by 2020, with a particular concern to increase the number of women and of candidates from BME backgrounds: https://churchofengland.org/media/2521876/commentary.pdf.

Building on these initiatives, I want to add some further suggestions to the mix.

Give us ten: early retirement cohort + fund

Recognising that the ageing demographic of church membership means there is a smaller pool of younger people to draw on, I want to encourage the church to consider a special call to ministry linked to early retirement and to back it with a sum of money from our reserves which will underwrite any pension shortfall caused by taking early retirement. It would need Council of Assembly approval of an appropriate capped sum of money to underwrite the scheme, capped both in terms of numbers eligible and eligible pension levels.

My suggestion is we could call it 'Give us ten', the ten being two years to train and eight to serve. We are already exploring reshaping the BD Min. to a two-year option for graduates. The scheme would be open to people aged between 50 and 55 and we would issue a call to the Church for 50 people to come forward under this scheme by 2020.[70]

Give us five – come over and help us

The second proposal looks in a different direction. Our sister church, the PCUSA, is currently in a more comfortable place in terms of supply of ministers. It is also a wealthy church in a developed country, so we would not be weakening or depleting numbers from another sister church which was facing supply problems of its own. If the PCUSA were willing to give this their blessing, I suggest we seek approval from the Home Office, with the support of the Scottish Government, to operate a managed and supported scheme for PCUSA ministers, perhaps those awaiting their first call, to 'give us five'. We would provide an orientation course and a support structure, which would include access to advice

---

70 The numbers would depend on what was affordable, given likely costs.

and mentoring from PCUSA or former PCUSA ministers already serving in Scotland, as well as regular gatherings for support and training. They would take on vacant parishes on a reviewable tenure basis and serve for five years, under standard Church of Scotland terms and conditions, with any special arrangements regarding pensions, etc. made in advance as part of the scheme. In terms of status, they would be PCUSA ministers serving in another church unless for some reason they wanted to make an application to transfer and stay for a longer period. I suggest we might think about the possibility of up to 40 coming, given the levels of vacancy which are predicted.[71] There are close historic ties between our churches, with many PCUSA churches conscious of their Scottish roots. Something of the cultural confidence and positivity of younger North American ministers might be just the kind of 'leaven' which some of our congregations would rise to.

A woman's place

We should make a fresh appeal within 'Tomorrow's Calling' to women, who are still under-represented in our ministry, emphasising how much their gifts and experience are needed and welcomed in the ministry – as they say these days, a woman's place is in the White House, is in the resistance and is in the ministry.

Pioneer

I have already advertised my strong support for pioneer ministry. While I welcome the five Pioneer Ministry posts which have been funded since 2015, my concern is that they simply draw from the existing, shrinking pool of already called and ordained ministers. I would like to see the church create a new route into ministry, along the lines of the Church of England's Pioneer Ministry

---

71 Numbers would depend on PCUSA judgements and Home Office permissions.

scheme[72] with planned cohorts of up to ten being accepted every year up to 2030. It could be helpful to stipulate that at least 50 per cent of the maximum cohort size accepted had to be under the age of 40. I am aware of some reservations about whether there would be jobs for those who were accepted and trained. That depends of course on the existence of a wider appropriately funded strategy for church planting and on the church demonstrating joined-up thinking and planning here. However, it is also the case that the Church of England scheme works on the basis of assessing a distinctive call and providing bespoke training. In the end, the ordination of pioneers is ordination to ministry of word and sacrament. There is a recognition that those trained as pioneers may not work as pioneers for ever. I don't see how that vocational journey would damage us.[73] I believe, and I think others with considerable experience in this area, like Alan McWilliam of Forge Scotland/Whiteinch Parish Church, would agree that there are 'suppressed vocations' out there in the church, which a scheme like this would help to set free.

There are doubtless other possibilities which are already being explored and these three may come to nothing. I want to stress however, that even if all four of these initiatives were adopted and were maximally successful, we would still be facing a significant shortfall of ministers as we moved towards 2030.

Fewer parishes

The second line of response to a crisis in the supply of ministers is the one already most familiar to us as a church: the use of unions, linkages, guardianships and dissolutions to reduce the number of parishes eligible to call a minister.

---

72 www.churchofengland.org/clergy-office-holders/ministry/selection/pioneer-ministry.aspx.

73 I accept it would be frustrating if we trained 20 people and there were no funded posts open to them, but that would be mainly to do with choices the church was making or not making.

Here, it is again frustrating that we do not have a stronger base of research evidence from which to evaluate the effects of linkages and unions on church membership. Anyone who knows the Kirk will be familiar with talk for many decades of 'happy unions' or 'difficult unions'. They will also know the received wisdom that in the round, unions tend to lose the church both members and income. When people lose 'their church' they often leave 'the church'. Just how many leave and how many come back we don't know, because no one has done the research.

The Church of Scotland is showing some signs of reaching a pivot-point on this issue, although there are still mixed messages being given. On the one hand, indications from the General Trustees suggest that in the short term up to 200 church buildings may have to be disposed of nationally; on the other hand, the most recent proposals from Ministries Council suggest a realisation that appetite for further unions may be waning. In particular, a key paragraph from the 2016 Council report made this observation:

> Past policy has focused on the formal bringing together (either by union or linkage) of parishes into bigger and bigger units under the care of a single minister. Not only has this meant a much greater workload for the individual (often involving duplicate sets of meetings in a linkage), many such adjustments are born in acrimony and bad feeling. This does not lend itself to a flourishing ministry.[74]

The key idea currently under development in this connection is being identified as 'Hub' ministry:

> The Council is exploring a policy of encouraging Presbyteries to group parishes together, without any formal adjustment, under the leadership of a Parish Minister. This involves a shift of mindset in the parishes: understanding that, although there will be, as far as possible, a locally recognised person belonging

---

74 Ministries Council Report in RGA 2016, 1.3.1.1.

to a leadership team across the grouping, there will be a shared minister who leads the team.[75]

The Council is frank about the options, with an element of gallows humour thrown in:

> There simply will not be enough Parish ministers to staff our current patterns. One option would be to go through another round of Presbytery Planning along the lines of the last one, allocating numbers to a base of 600 and leaving it to Presbyteries to work out how to carve this up into 'viable units'. The Council does not believe this is in the interests of the mission of Jesus Christ. As noted above, it will neither create a flourishing ministry nor a focus on mission.[76]

As well as calling for a debate on their Hub option, the Council invites other ideas and options to be brought forward. This, however, is the only one they have brought forward. There is, here, a real sense of constraint to their report, of there being a shrinking range of options for the future. They have already argued that by the early 2020s the shortage of ministers will make the inherited model 'essentially unworkable'. They have further argued in the quotes above that they believe a further round of 'presbytery planning' to the base of 600 is undesirable. It is therefore hard to see where else they have to go.

Nonetheless, it is important to recognise how much the new proposal represents a departure from the 'inherited model' which is basic to how most members imagine their local parish church and may also be integral to their willingness to keep paying their dues. It promises to give with one hand, in that it steps back from a more aggressive and unpopular strategy of closing buildings and merging parishes, but it warns that it will take away with the other, as more parishes lose their own parish minister. The suggestion that each parish will have 'locally recognised people' begs questions which we will consider in the next section. However,

75 Ministries Council Report in RGA 2016, 1.3.1.2.
76 Ministries Council Report in RGA 2016, 1.3.1.2.

two other questions need to be raised now. The first is whether the proposal does not simply represent another way of speaking about linkages. The second is whether it does not in fact represent precisely another round of presbytery planning by another name.

The Hub proposals are in a 'live' stage of development as I write. If they are taken forward, a further challenge will be to enable the role of ministers to change and develop, as many of them move from being a sole practitioner, to being a team leader. There are many more precedents for that within the Church of England and the PCUSA, where multi-person teams are common, than there are in today's Kirk. A Hub minister will need a skill-set, will need aptitudes, management and co-ordination abilities which not all parish ministers are blessed with. There will need to be appropriate training and development opportunities provided. We may need to explore different models for rural and urban hubs. We may need to think creatively about how to support team leaders with different strengths, allowing teams to be formed, some of which may contain higher levels of administrative support for those whose leadership and relational skills are stronger than their organisational capacities.

We will also need to keep a close eye on how this affects recruitment. If the challenges of being a Hub minister make the work less attractive, this will have to be addressed. We will need to consider the implications of a Hub pattern for the historic rights of congregations to 'call' their own minister. We will need ways to evaluate and monitor the work of team leaders, with effective anti-bullying and complaints procedures. We will need to consider issues of authority and oversight. If other churches have found ways to address these issues, there is no reason why we in the Kirk cannot, but we also need to recognise that this route addresses the original problem not by solving it but by making it change shape and by making the role of the minister change shape. The only way Hubs can be effective in addressing the question of shortage is to make more stipendiary ministers into 'team vicars' with charge of a group of parishes. Although Hubs give with one hand, they take away with the other – but this time round, we may want what they can give and be prepared to adjust to what they take away.

New forms of ordination

A third way to address a declining supply of ordained or licensed ministers is to create more of them by other means. This is the route which the Church of England has embraced, reflecting the fact that the pattern of a weekly parish Communion is now normative – unlike the Kirk, in which quarterly Communions remain common.[77] In order for the normal pattern of Anglican worship to continue as clergy numbers fell overall, it has been necessary to provide a new supply of Eucharistic presidents, and this has been achieved through very significant increases in the numbers of Self-Supporting Ministers and Ordained Local Ministers. Of the 28,000 licensed ministers in the Church of England[78] 65 per cent do not receive any stipend and 30 per cent of parish clergy are non-stipendiary.[79]

This stands in stark contrast to the Church of Scotland. Neither the older though still extant scheme of Auxiliary Ministry, nor the newer Ordained Local Ministry programme have been anything like as successful as the Church of England schemes in drawing in new ministers. Within the Kirk, these seem to be suffering the same fate as the stipendiary ministry, in failing to attract enough new candidates.

Greater flexibility about ministerial assignments

The final way to address a crisis in the supply of ministers is to think more flexibly about the nature of ordination itself. This is the option we noted before, which has tended to founder in the face of concerns about ecumenical divergence in the mutual recognition of ministries. However, we also suggested that post-SCIFU, this

---

77 My hunch is again that this is changing and that monthly Communion is the new norm, but I know of no research or reliable statistics which would confirm this.

78 This term covers senior clergy, stipendiary clergy, licensed readers, readers with permission to officiate, self-supporting clergy, chaplains, active retired, lay workers and Church Army evangelists.

79 https://churchofengland.org/media/1868964/ministry%20statistics%20final.pdf.

might be a moment in which, without any cooling of ecumenical affection, the Kirk needed to prioritise missional flexibility over the prospect of a recognition from Rome/Canterbury/Edinburgh which may never come in terms the Kirk finds acceptable.

So, where in particular might the Church of Scotland consider introducing greater flexibility? I want to explore three possibilities:

The ordination of elders

In Chapter 2, we discussed the figure of the presbyterian elder, including the historic lack of support for moves to reform the eldership and the resistance from elders to actions perceived to diminish the role, value and status of the eldership. We also discussed the long-standing anxiety within presbyterianism about the precise scriptural basis for the office in general and for its being an 'ordained' office in particular. The most drastic response here would be to return the office to being filled by annual appointment, as it was envisaged in the *First Book of Discipline* (1560).[80] I think that is unlikely to win support.

I want to suggest a more pragmatic solution, which is based in theological principle, but also seeks to enable a gracious and consensual flow of change.

The key move would be to supplement rather than replace ordained eldership within the Kirk and to understand 'ordination' in this instance in relation to a difference in vocation rather than of status or function. The Kirk would introduce a new form of eldership alongside the old.

Commissioned elders, as I suggest we call them, would be set aside to serve for periods of three years, with that three-year commission capable of being extended indefinitely, subject to concurrence on both sides. The decision to be commissioned or ordained would lie with the prospective elder and they would be asked to make it on the basis of discerning whether they understood their calling to the office in terms of a lifelong consecration or a time-limited assignment. No judgement would be made

---

80 Cf. Louden 1963, 41.

about depth of faith or degree of commitment, the discernment of vocation would be related to what Moltmann describes as the 'charismatic freedom' of the church, recognising that after one or more terms of commissioned eldership, a woman or man might feel called to a different sphere of service. Both forms of elder-ship would be eligible to fulfil exactly the same functions within the courts and councils of the Church of Scotland. The advan-tage of this reform would be that without diminishing, altering or undercutting the status of those already ordained to eldership, or preventing others being ordained in the future, new avenues of ministry could be opened up to church members who have the gifting and calling to serve, but have not felt called to be 'ordained' to this office for life.

Elders and the celebration of Communion

Another area where greater flexibility could be introduced is in relation to elders leading or 'presiding at' the Lord's Supper or Holy Communion. If we compare ourselves to other sections of the Reformed family of churches, this is not such a drastic step to imagine ourselves taking. We would be joining the United Reformed Church and the PCUSA if we enabled presbyteries to authorise suitably trained and experienced elders (who could be commissioned or ordained elders in terms of the suggestion above) to preside at Communion. The question of what to call them I will leave as an open one. The PCUSA call them Commissioned Ruling Elders, having previously called them Commissioned Lay Pastors.[81] I find that terminology on the clunky side, although I agree with moving away from the language of 'lay' which does not belong in the Reformed tradition. The word 'pastor' is a friendlier term, but if we were embracing and developing a more expansive theology of commissioning as part of this more flexible stance, we might opt for Commissioned Local Minister (CLM) to sit along-side OLM. In the PCUSA, they are commissioned for up to three years at a time and can conduct worship, including sacraments,

---

81 http://oga.pcusa.org/section/mid-council-ministries/clp/.

weddings and funerals – working, as OLMs do, under the oversight of an ordained minister. They could work in a vacant charge or alongside an existing minister within their congregation.

A key difference between a CLM and an OLM would be that a CLM could be paid. There would be an agreed route by which a CLM could candidate to become an OLM or, if eligible on grounds of age, a minister of word and sacrament.

Part-time

A final possibility to explore, which builds on the additional possibilities offered by a CLM scheme, is for presbyteries to create more part-time posts in the future or to offer 'house for duty' options, which are relatively common in the Church of England but unusual in the Church of Scotland. Some are already doing this, while others have been more reticent. Greater flexibility about the percentage of FTE (full-time equivalent) might also correlate with some of the more flexible funding options discussed in the previous chapter, or with future challenges for congregations to be self-sustaining, with a percentage of FTE linked to congregational contribution. The point would obviously be to draw more gifted and motivated people into ministry, so it would be counterproductive if stipendiary ministers were not able to get a 100 per cent post if they wanted one. (This option also relates to the proposals for further financial powers for presbyteries, to be discussed in the next chapter.)

When introducing these four ways to respond to a crisis in the supply of ministers, I said that all four would be needed, and I want to reinforce that. The period between now and 2030 is critical for the future of the Kirk and we need to bring all the wisdom and imagination we have to meet the challenges before us. We need, therefore, to engage urgently with all four of these tasks: recruiting more full-time stipendiary ministers, grouping parishes to work more effectively together, recruiting more OLMs, and introducing a more flexible theology of commissioning to allow additional called and gifted women and men to take on the work of ministry.

Equipping the saints and building up the body

I have spent a good deal of time on issues related to ordained ministry, because that is the part of the Church of Scotland's system which is most under threat and where falling numbers are most likely to be the cause of wider disruption and instability within the institution. With the proposal for CLMs, the focus began to move to enabling the diverse ministries of the whole body, and this is an equally vital area for the church. The Kirk of the future, if it is to become more effective in mission, will have to value, develop and support the ministry of many different women and men within its congregations. We noted in Chapter 2 how the movement to awaken and enable 'lay' ministry had received broad support across the theological spectrum. In Scotland, those congregations influenced by the Iona Community and those influenced by the charismatic renewal[82] have both in their different ways sought to move away from minister-centred worship, to worship led by a range of different voices. This has taken many church members on an encouraging and affirming journey in which they have discovered their gifts and found their voices.

This journey of diversifying worship and empowering members has to spread across the whole of the Church of Scotland in the next decade, and it has to spread beyond worship. There are already many ministries within our congregations which are not carried out by ministers; but there are also many members within our congregations who have not discerned their place in the work of ministry. The future of the church has to involve creating more opportunities for people to serve, but also forming more people to take up those opportunities. While I am arguing that some of these opportunities should involve unbundling work which until now has been mostly done by ministers of word and sacrament, I also believe we need to develop a new understanding of how ministries are going to be shared between ministers and non-ministers. This is part of what I believe we need to look for from a new theology of co-missioning: fresh ideas about how we share in the mission of God at congregational level. The future

---

82 A few of which could be the same.

of the Kirk is dependent on finding new ways of *co-ministering*, and we need to explore this in ways which do not discourage ministers or make them feel devalued. We need ministers who understand their role in terms of being mentors and developers of the ministries of folk in their congregations. The work of the Mission Shaped Intro and Mission Shaped Ministry courses, run by Fresh Expressions, in which the Church of Scotland is now a full partner, are good examples of the direction in which we need to travel.[83]

None of this is new. There are already hundreds of examples of good practice all across the Kirk – but it is unfinished business. I believe there will continue to be differentiation within ministry and that the traditional 'professional', highly educated 'General Practitioner' form of stipendiary parish minister will continue to play a key load-bearing role in the work of the Church of Scotland for decades to come. But that role needs to keep evolving. If as Ministries Council predicted in their 2016 report, there are around 600 ministers in five years time who are serving some 1,200 congregations, the role of some of those ministers will have to change quite significantly. If they are working in some kind of hub or parish grouping, they will have to take on more of an oversight role, in relation to multiple colleagues and multiple congregations. They will become more like Anglican 'Team Vicars'. The time spent across multiple parishes, meeting, co-ordinating and supervising other colleagues and others who are co-ministering, is time away from front-line parish work, so they are likely to have a less intimate relationship with any one congregation. This will change the nature of the 'pastoral tie' in ways that some ministers (and congregations) will struggle with.

These changes to ministerial roles will need new forms of training and support, which will need to be built into future provision for IME and CME. A cause for optimism here is the example of how Interim Ministry has been developed since 1997, including the links to Place of Hope forged in recent years. The strong reputation of interim ministry and the high level of trust and confidence associated with it gives reason to hope that a similarly

---

83 www.missionshapedministry.org.

respected cohort of Team Leaders or Hub ministers could be created over the next 20 years.

Ministry is changing, and needs to be changed. Alongside the traditional rubric of ordination, we need to develop a more flexible and dynamic understanding of co-missioning and co-ministering. One further implication of this, for me, is that it adds to my dislike of the current division between Ministries Council and Mission and Discipleship Council. The future, insofar as we can see it, calls for a greater degree of strategic co-ordination and for a more integrated vision of how ministers, elders and members will share in the work of ministry. In the next chapter, I address that problem and aspiration in the light of wider proposals for structural reform.

5

The Architecture of Reform

In this chapter I look at the systems architecture of the Kirk as a presbyterian church, conscious of the metaphor Paul uses in 1 Corinthians 3.10 of being a 'wise architect'.[1] This builds on the discussion of Being Presbyterian in Chapter 2 as well as the discussions of money, mission and ministry in the previous two chapters.

Although we noted that the term 'presbyterian' can point to a culture, an aesthetic, even a spirituality, the tradition is named and known because of the decisions it has taken about how to structure a system of church government. This loads the conversation about reform in interesting ways. Within the international family of presbyterian churches, although there is clear family resemblance, there is a variety of genetic variations, depending on time, place and context. Noting this is important for two reasons. First, it helps to enable conversations about reform to include consideration of a variety of presbyterianisms, as opposed to meeting all proposals for change with an accusation that they represent a 'fall' into either congregationalism or episcopalianism. Second, it encourages reflection on how presbyterianisms have previously adapted to varying historical and cultural contexts and what kinds of adaptation to new contexts and challenges might be called for in contemporary Scotland.

In this chapter, I offer a brief review of how the Church of Scotland is currently structured, before making some proposals for structural reform.

---

1 Often translated 'skilled master builder', but see comments on this passage on p. 385 of Petersen and O'Day (eds), 2009.

Where we are now

The Church of Scotland is currently organised into six councils. The first council is distinctive in being something of a council of councils (The Council of Assembly).The next four represent functional divisions of the work of the church (The Church and Society Council, The Ministries Council, The Mission and Discipleship Council, and The World Mission Council). The sixth council is different in kind from the others: The Social Care Council, known as CrossReach.

The Council of Assembly

The Council of Assembly is the central co-ordinating committee of the Kirk. All other Council Convenors sit on it, along with the Secretaries of those councils, the Principal Clerk, General Treasurer and Church Solicitor. It has a general and strategic remit to supervise and review, to bring budget proposals to the GA, to monitor, evaluate and co-ordinate the work of all agencies of the General Assembly and to attend to the general interests of the church. The Council of Assembly's report to the 2014 General Assembly referred to 'a constructive debate about the real role of the Council of Assembly in a conciliar polity', noting that 'It is clear that Council are accountable directly to the General Assembly and it is less clear what power the Council of Assembly has to set overall objectives.'[2] Discussions on this were described as continuing, while it was noted that the Council's role in oversight, challenge and cross-Council discussion 'remains useful'.[3]

The Church and Society Council

The remit of the Council is to facilitate the Church of Scotland's engagement with and commentary upon national, political and social issues.

---

2 RGA 2014, 1/3.
3 RGA 2014, 1/3.

The Ministries Council

The remit of the Ministries Council is the enabling of ministries in every part of Scotland. It has responsibility for recruitment, training and support of recognised ministries of the church and for assessment and monitoring of how those ministries are deployed. Ministries is the big beast among the current councils. When CrossReach is excluded, its budget represents more than 80 per cent of the church's entire budget.

Mission and Discipleship Council

The Council's remit is to lead the church in developing and maintaining a focus for mission in Scotland, this being understood in terms of the fundamental relationships between mission and worship, service, doctrine, education and nurture. M and D as it is commonly known also oversees the work of The Netherbow: Scottish Storytelling Centre, *Life & Work* (the Church of Scotland's monthly magazine), Saint Andrew Press, CARTA (Committee on Church Art and Architecture) and the Rural Working Group.

World Mission Council

The Council's remit is to develop and oversee the Church of Scotland's participation in global mission partnerships.

Social Care Council

Known since 2005 as CrossReach,[4] this Council provides social care services across Scotland as part of the Christian witness of the church. I will have little to say about its work in this book and it is given its own distinctive place apart within the structural

---

4 Before this, it was the Board of Social Responsibility.

reforms suggested below. This is no way a reflection on its hugely valuable and significant work, but merely reflects its particular role as a service agency of the wider church.

Other administrative bodies

These include the Assembly Arrangements Committee, the Central Properties Department, Chaplains to HM Forces Committee, the national committee of the Church of Scotland Guild, the Church of Scotland Housing and Loan Fund, the Church of Scotland Investors Trust, the Church of Scotland Pension Trustees and the Church of Scotland Trust, the Communications Unit, the Ecumenical Relations Committee, the Facilities Management Department, the Go For It Fund, the Human Resources Department, the IT Department, the Legal Questions Committee, the Nomination Committee, the Panel on Review and Reform and the Church of Scotland Safeguarding Office. Of key strategic importance within the structures are the Department of the General Assembly (which contains the Principal Clerk and Secretary to the Council of Assembly), the General Trustees, the Stewardship and Finance Department and the Law Department.

The Panel on Review and Reform

The panel was created by the General Assembly of 2004 in response to the 2001 *Church Without Walls* report. It was intended to have a sunset clause, but the General Assembly kept issuing new instructions and so the panel has remained in being, its remit being adjusted by the 2013 General Assembly. The revised remit remains very wide ranging, focusing on the 'long-term vision of the church' and 'paths and developments' to implement such a vision at local, regional and national levels. This cross-cutting remit positions it as a kind of internal think-tank for the Kirk, but also creates potential for tension between it and the other councils as well as between it and the Council of Assembly.

Previous structural reforms

Presbytery synod boundaries (1975)

In 1975, there was a major reorganisation of presbytery and synod boundaries which changed these essentially to the boundaries presbyteries still occupy in 2017 and to those which marked out the synods until their abolition in 1993. This reform was linked directly to local government district council areas for presbyteries and regional council areas for synods.[5]

Reform of ministry (1984)

A significant reform took place in 1984, when the Church and Ministry Department became part of a much larger department of Ministry and Mission.

The abolition of synods (1992)

There was a historically significant reform of governance structures in 1992 when the 12 remaining synods were abolished. Synods had existed within the Kirk since the seventeenth century. They were finally abolished because of a consensus that they represented a layer or tier of governance that had become unnecessary.[6] Their powers and functions were distributed both upwards, to the General Assembly, and downwards, to the presbyteries.

Review of General Assembly (1994/1996)

The General Assembly of 1994 gave a remit to the Board of Practice and Procedure to consider the role and operation of the

---

5 This alignment was overtaken in 1995 by further reform of civil boundaries for local and regional government.

6 Abolition of synods was recommended in Wolfe and Pickford, 1980.

General Assembly. The Board brought its report to the 1996 General Assembly, recommending some changes but drawing back from the idea of moving to biennial assemblies.

The Millennial Reform Vision (1999)

The General Assembly of 1999, conscious of the hand of history on its shoulder as the Millennium approached, took two bold decisions to re-imagine its future. It set up a Special Commission anent Review and Reform, which produced a major report to the Assembly of 2001– the report which became widely known by its sub-title: *A Church Without Walls*.[7]

It also commissioned the Board of Practice and Procedure to undertake a study of the future shape of presbyteries, which led to the publication in 2001 of a consultation document called *Tomorrow's Presbyteries*.

Church Without Walls (2001)[8]

The 2001 Report of the Special Commission anent Review and Reform, known ever since as *Church Without Walls*, was a bold, visionary and optimistic report, which offered as close to a review of the whole church as had been attempted since the work of the Committee of Forty in the 1970s. The tenor of its opening words were significant: 'It encourages the Church to return the ministry of the Gospel to the people of God. The aim is to give them the tools and the trust to shape a vision for the church in their own area.' The Commission used the image of turning the church upside down, so that there was a clearer sense that central

---

7 The General Assembly of 1999 appointed the Special Commission 'to re-examine in depth the primary purposes of the Church and the shape of the Church of Scotland as we enter into the next Millennium; to formulate proposals for a process of continuing reform; to consult on such matters with other Scottish Churches; and to report to the General Assembly of 2001'.

8 www.churchofscotland.org.uk/__data/assets/pdf_file/0006/11787/CWW _REPORT_for_website_2Nov2012.pdf.

councils and regional presbyteries existed to serve local congregations. The report was blunt about frustration with institutional structures, speaking of 'structural fundamentalism', alleging that presbyterianism had become a form of 'institutionalized mistrust' which tended to 'legalism' and calling for work to be done on a theology of power. It suggested that most people perceived the church to be over-centralized and 'top down', and that presbyteries were seen as places where duty must be done, but little inspiration or support would be received.[9] It spoke of a breakdown of trust between the church locally and centrally.

Again and again, the report pleaded for greater flexibility and for priority to be given to empowering local congregations, which it affirmed as 'the primary expression of the Church'. It named as the priority for the church 'the renewing, refocusing, relocating and planting of local worshipping congregations for mission across Scotland'.[10]

In a trenchant, verging on brutal, paragraph, it went after the whole institution: Kirk Sessions can be formal and formidable. Presbyteries have become administrative units for servicing the system of committees and regulations rather than a fellowship of mutual encouragement and inspiration. The Central Committees are viewed with suspicion from the parishes and are often impersonal for those who attend. The General Assembly has its moments, but is hardly the best forum for major decision-making.

The report commended a new attention to David Watson's trio of cell, congregation and celebration and a new extrovert spirit of 'friendship'. It urged the release of the gifts of all God's people, more training for elders and more focused terms of service, with regular sabbaticals. Presbyteries came in for particularly strong criticism, with a plea to recover their eroded 'relational heart'[11] accompanied by support for radical reform which would combine informal local area support with larger administrative areas inheriting more powers and resources from the central church:

---

9 Ibid, p. 13.
10 Ibid, p. 20.
11 Ibid, p. 31.

The future shape of the Regional Church will have three functions: relational support for local strategy, regional centres of
worship and inspiration and regions for more comprehensive
oversight and allocation of resources.

The report was relatively silent on issues to do with the central
church, leaving such questions to be tackled in the light of the
coming report on presbytery reform. It did however ask, 'Where is
the leadership within the central administration?' and commented
that, 'The Church is operating with two cultures: the Presbyterian
ethos that resists personal leadership, and a business organisation at the heart of its administration, which requires executive
powers.'

It suggested a new Chief Executive for the central organisation, a change in the date of the General Assembly from May to
September, and a number of changes to allow greater flexibility in
relation to finance. One major initiative called for was the establishment of a Parish Development Fund, with the aim of 'facilitat-
ing congregations to become vibrant worship centres'. Near the
end of the report, it struck a defensive note: 'in our consultations
we have been warned never to underestimate the resistance to
change. One look at our history tempers our optimism.' It named
two barriers to change which lay 'deep in our nature': fear and
power. It closed by reaffirming the call of Christ to the Church:
'Follow Me.'[12]

Tomorrow's Presbyteries (2001)

This consultation document issued by the Board of Practice
and Procedure described the history of changes to presbytery
boundaries since the union of 1929, noting that the logic of the
reorganisation of 1975, to align with local government district
and regional boundaries, had now been overtaken by the further
civil boundary reforms of 1995. Noting that 'we live in an age of
devolution', it set out its reasons for favouring a radical reform

---

12 Ibid, p. 46.

of the system, arguing that, 'Presbyteries need to be allowed to be more active and more responsible than the present set-up of the Church allows' and alluding to this as 'the church being given back to its members'.[13] Advocating a rebalancing of the church's life between councils and presbyteries, it concluded that 'each Presbytery needs to be sufficiently large to ensure a proper basis for such resourcing and executive power'.[14]

The document suggested a radical reduction in the number of presbyteries, creating as few as seven new appropriately resourced presbyteries grouped around regional centres, towns and cities which had good transport and communications links. The new presbytery centres would all be staffed by a mix of full- and part-time workers, and the presbytery areas would be further broken down into Districts, based on 'natural areas', many of them smaller than existing presbyteries. There would be a radical devolution of power, resource and function, with 'many' of the functions of central boards transferred to the new presbyteries.

The work of the Board had been assisted and they stated 'supported' by advice commissioned from the McKinsey Consultancy Group in 2000. In an appendix, three options were set out for a church of seven, ten or twelve presbyteries, with suggestions for how existing presbyteries might be combined in each of the three models. After a period of consultation, none of these options was pursued by the General Assembly of 2002. The mind of the church as expressed here was that it acknowledged the reality of concerns about how presbyteries were functioning and accepted the need for reform, but was unconvinced by the proposals for reform put before it. The term 'super-presbyteries' (not used in the report), which was coined during subsequent debates, was probably not helpful, creating the rhetorical and psychological impression of overly large bodies, looming over local congregations.[15]

---

13 *Tomorrow's Presbyteries*, 2001, p. 6.

14 Ibid.

15 It is possible that the shadow of the SCIFU process was also a factor, with the language of 'maxi-parishes' and 'super-presbyteries' combining to fuel opposition to change.

Table 3. Presbytery and synod numbers, 1929–2017

Year	Presbyteries in Scotland	Presbyteries outwith Scotland	Synods
1929	66	20	
1970	59	5	
1975 (reorganisation)	46	3	12
1992 (abolition of synods)	46	3	0
1995 Local Government Reorganisation			
1999 Creation of Scottish Parliament			
2001	46	3	0
2017	46	3	0

Rejection of SCIFU proposals (2003)

As noted above, the General Assembly of 2003 decided not to support the Scottish Churches Initiative for Union, which would have had major implications for church structure and organisation.

Council reform (2004)

The General Assembly of 2004 approved changes to the central structures of the church, in response to the 2001 Special Commission anent Review and Reform (*Church Without Walls*).

The old boards were reorganised into the renamed councils listed earlier in the chapter. However, the rejection of the *Tomorrow's Presbyteries* report shaped the character of these reforms, since a key dimension of what the Special Commission had called for could not be pursued. The nature of these reforms to central structures was shaped by the absence of regional/presbytery reforms and power was accordingly retained rather than devolved.

Structure and Change Commission (2006)

The 2006 General Assembly appointed an independent Special Commission on Structure and Change to assess the consequences of the post-2001 reforms. Its report commented:

> It has occurred to us that at least some of the disquiet that we have encountered about the centralisation of decision-making may have less to do with changes that have occurred and more to do with changes that have not occurred. Change at the centre has not been paralleled by change at presbytery level.[16]

. . .

> The restructuring undertaken since 2001 has been unevenly implemented. There is unfinished business when it comes to the regional church. At present a considerable degree of power is concentrated at the centre because there is no adequate repository for it elsewhere. Determining the best structure at the regional level will be for the Church as a whole to decide. We do not suggest that it will be simply a matter of putting five or six presbyteries together in a larger grouping in order to do the same old things.[17]

General Assembly Commission to Review and Reform (2008)

In response to the report of the Special Commission on Structure and Change, the GA of 2008 voted to 'Instruct the Panel on Review and Reform to bring to the General Assembly of 2010 proposals for an alternative presbytery structure including, size, devolved powers, staffing, appropriate budgets, along with the resources necessary to facilitate and sustain such changes.'

---

16 Special Commission on Structure and Change report to the 2008 General Assembly, 25/10 s6.1.

17 Ibid, 25/11, s6.2.

General Assembly Commission to review the Third Article Declaratory (2008/2010)

The 2008 General Assembly also established a commission to review the provisions of the Third Article Declaratory and in particular the statement by the Church of Scotland that, 'As a national Church representative of the Christian Faith of the Scottish people it acknowledges its distinctive call and duty to bring the ordinances of religion to the people in every parish of Scotland through a territorial ministry.'[18] The Assembly of 2010 reaffirmed the church's commitment to the Third Article Declaratory, in response to the Commission's report which stated that its consultations had indicated a continuing strong sense of commitment to the vision of the Third Article. For those unhappy with this outcome, it represented an unwillingness by the church to face up to the realities of decline and to re-imagine how the church would engage in mission to twenty-first-century Scotland.

Review and Reform Report to General Assembly (2011)

A substantial consultation exercise was carried out in fulfilment of the panel's 2008 General Assembly remit and a report was brought to the 2011 Assembly, which broadly mirrored the 2001 *Tomorrow's Presbyteries* report in recommending a radical move to a 13 presbytery system. Under their proposals, the new presbyteries would be governed by Presbytery Councils, accountable to bi-annual Presbytery Assemblies, with more informal and relational meetings for support and encouragement taking place through Local Area Groups of around 20 congregations.

Members of the panel had clearly put enormous amounts of thought, effort and time into the proposals, and the decision of the General Assembly not to proceed with their proposals was hugely disappointing. It could be characterised as one of the occasionally[19] 'brutal' effects of presbyterian governance, when

18 www.churchofscotland.org.uk/about_us/church_law/church_constitution.
19 Regularly?

an Assembly sweeps away years of work in a single curt decision. However, it also reflects that other often mentioned notion of communal discernment, 'the mind of the church' and the sense of what 'commends itself' to that collective mind. As it had not been time in 2002, the time for presbytery reform was still not to be in 2011. Assembly's treatment of the panel's proposals was a bitter pill for its members to swallow. For those advocating reform, it smacked of both ingratitude and intransigence. For some of those dismayed by the reaffirmation of the ambitious national vision of the Third Article, it seemed like a further exercise in self-delusion from a church unwilling to face reality. It has been suggested, plausibly, that the reforms became entangled in political calculations around the debate on same-sex relationships and how the Barrier Act would operate in a 13 presbytery system. But there were other factors in play. This represented a massive restructuring for the church as a whole, and despite the extensive consultation undertaken, the implications of the reform were too unsettling for too many people to be embraced in one giant leap.[20] The panel argued in its consultation documents that previous attempts at reform had failed because they were perceived to have been too 'top-down'. Their alternative strategy was to seek to build a bottom-up consensus, through encouraging neighbouring presbyteries to discuss how they could unite into larger groupings.[21]

This was a commendable attempt to understand and respond to the unease they recognised. Their work was also restrained in relation to redesigning the stucture of the church as a whole. While recognising that the reforms they proposed would have major implications for the council structures, they were understandably cautious about overreaching their remit and complicating an already far-reaching proposal by linking it to other major proposals. My judgement, and it is a profoundly sympathetic one, is that ironically their proposals were too restricted and insufficiently comprehensive. Large-scale reform of a complex institution

---

20 Its March 2011 newsletter included the statement: 'The Panel has listened to the diverse opinions about the reform of Presbyteries and recognises the unease within and between Presbyteries about change on the scale that we are suggesting.'

21 PRR STGR-1 13/08/10.

must be undertaken as a systemic process. It is because reform of one area has profound implications for other areas that the architecture of the whole system needs to be considered. My hope in writing this book is that such an unauthorised project, which has no mandate and no authority, in taking the freedom to propose reform of the system as a whole, can serve the mind of the church as it seeks to think through the issues involved. It will be a huge step for a future Assembly to issue a remit for simultaneous reform of both the presbytery system and the council system, but the two areas are so interdependent that there cannot be coherent reform of one without a simultaneous, joined-up reform of the other.

General Assembly: the Moderator's Role and Term (2012)

At the 2012 General Assembly, the Legal Questions Committee, who had been considering the issue, decided to propose no change to the existing one-year term for moderators. This was reaffirmed in the report of the Council of Assembly to the General Assembly in 2016.

The architecture of reform

In this final section of the book, I want to propose a new model for the systems architecture of the Church of Scotland, beginning with a brief sketch of the proposal as a whole, before moving to expand different aspects in more detail. In calling for reforms, we are right to be wary of sweeping judgements about the church being over-governed or having too much bureaucracy. Bill Clinton once said in response to critics of 'big government' in the USA that he was in favour of the country having 'all the government it needed'. While any proposals for reform will have their guiding principles and assumptions, we also need to be flexible and open to nuance. For example, a proposal might consider (as this one does) that the overall numbers of people involved in the central structures of the church were too high, while also recognising that the numbers involved in certain key departments needed to be increased.

The key assumptions which lie behind the proposals made here are as follows:

- Missional leadership needs to be strengthened at regional level.
- Too much power, resource and initiative are held centrally and not enough regionally and locally.
- The church has too many people serving on central councils and committees.
- The current division of councils perpetuates a silo mentality, which includes both competition for resources and defence of council prerogatives, with no adequate management mechanism, other than the General Assembly, for adjudicating between different councils.[22]

It will be obvious from the summary above that most of what I commend has been on the table before at sundry times and in diverse manners. I am not claiming novelty or originality for these proposals, I am simply saying that it seems to me their time has come. I believe that there are five key structural reforms which, if enacted, could help the church to respond more effectively in fulfilling its missional calling to the people of Scotland.

- *Presbytery reform*
  The currently existing 46 Scottish presbyteries should be reduced to 12 regional presbyteries, each of which would have a stipendiary elected Moderator and salaried appointed Clerk, both holding office for a five-year term.
- *Council reform*
  The four main central councils should be merged into one new Church of Scotland Mission Agency, which would work with internal ministry divisions but under a single management structure. There would be a distinctive arrangement for CrossReach

---

22 This with due respect to the Council of Assembly which has made inroads here.

(the fifth council) which would remain as an additional, 'arms length' service agency of the church.[23]

- *Central governance reform*
  The work of the new central agency should be governed by a properly federal Council of Assembly, comprising of elder and minister representatives from each presbytery, which could include the Presbytery Moderators. A Mission Agency Secretary would lead a team of senior managers.
- *General assembly*
  General Assembly should continue to meet annually.
- *Congregations*
  The legal rights and functions of congregations and congregational meetings should be clarified and strengthened within Church Law.

Having sketched an outline of the reform package as a whole, I want to explain the rationale behind these proposals and suggest how some of the operational detail might be filled in.

Presbytery reform

The key reform needed, which will unlock and impel the others, is presbytery reform. This is widely recognised within the church, but so also is the difficulty of producing a new structure which, in the time-honoured phrase, will commend itself to the church. At present we are caught in a Catch 22 in respect of the relationships between the regional church and central structures. It is impossible to effectively devolve power and responsibility, including much greater flexibility in relation to resource allocation, while presbyteries remain so disparate in size and so uneven in capacity. Equally, presbyteries will not be made to work effectively or be

---

23 I have nothing invested in this particular name; for convenience I am following the example of the PCUSA here, who have a single central Presbyterian Mission Agency. CrossReach has a distinctive status and should be treated separately, still under the Assembly and Agency overall, but with its own distinctive pattern of governance suited to its operational needs.

treated by local churches with the seriousness and even enthusi-asm they deserve until they are given more power and respon-sibility. At the heart of this proposal for reform is a vision of presbyteries driving forward the Kirk's mission strategy in their respective areas. The example of the Church of England has been significant here, where it is at diocesan level that strategic leadership and support are being offered to the drive to create a 'mission-shaped church'. I have also found this example per-suasive in relation to the creation of a new full-time stipendiary post of Presbytery Moderator. The Moderator would continue the existing functions of a presbytery moderator, but she or he would be commissioned to offer missional leadership to the pres-bytery. They would emphatically not be a bishop, in the Anglican/ Episcopal sense. They would be subject to the Presbytery Council and to the presbytery. They could propose, but not dispose. They would only ever be *primus inter pares*. They would perform a cru-cial loadbearing, representative, connectional and communicative function within a new federal structure, offering oversight to the central structures of the church, by dint of being voting members on the new Council of Assembly. They would work alongside a Presbytery Clerk, who would typically not be an ordained minis-ter. The Moderator would take a lead in missional and pastoral matters, the Clerk would have primary responsibility for adminis-trative, financial and legal matters.

It will be clear that I believe both the 2001 and 2011 proposals were on the right lines. This proposal echoes both of these, while also drawing from the example of Synod Moderators within the United Reformed Church. The 2011 proposals envisaged a Presbytery Council, bi-annual Presbytery Assemblies meeting for a whole day and more informal Local Area Groups focused on education, training and mutual encouragement.

While 12 is a nicely symbolic number, there is nothing magic about it. The best number might prove to be 7, 11, 13 or 15.[24] The

---

24 In the interview work undertaken for this book, questions about how many presbyteries there should be produced answers which ranged between 12 and 36, with most towards the lower end.

key difference between 46 and 12[25] is that each presbytery can be organised on a scale that will allow it to have the administrative and organisational capacity to take on new powers and responsibilities. No rigid formula of equivalence is needed, but a rough proportionality would be necessary. The size of each presbytery would sit in a range of between 80 and 120 churches.[26]

The reform of presbyteries enables the Kirk to learn from the example of the PCUSA's 'new form of government' and to enshrine a clear missional rationale in the legislation which revises the number, powers and roles of presbyteries. One example of this, linked to my earlier suggestions about the need to plant new churches, would be that the General Assembly could commission each of the new presbyteries to plant or reseed one new congregation a year.[27] If we came close to that, we would be on course for 100 new congregations by 2030.

A key aim of presbytery reform would be to enable more dynamic missional leadership and planning. Overall, it would seek to streamline the administrative demands of participation in presbytery committees, while preserving and even improving internal democracy, representation and participation. It would allow more leadership initiative, and add more management and

---

25 Thought needs to be given to the more distinctive presbyteries, for example Europe/England/Orkney/Shetland, and here I believe the best way forward is to allow them to suggest what structures would best suit their needs. The key thing is that those whose circumstances are non-standard do not feel forgotten or marginalised by the rest of the church, because they do not fit neatly into a square hole. There is no reason why we could not design a structure which has 12 square-ish holes and one or more round ones.

26 While I believe there is considerable support in the church for the idea that the direction of reform must be towards fewer presbyteries with increased powers, one of the dilemmas in considering reform has to do with rationales for the reorganisation of presbytery areas or bounds. Tradition and precedent will always have a loud voice in such conversations – various rationales could be produced: resorting to synod boundaries, but adopting them as presbytery boundaries (12); mapping presbytery boundaries to Scottish local authority boundaries (32); pragmatic reshaping to produce units of optimum scale for the purposes of administration, resourcing, collaboration and governance.

27 The 2013 General Assembly encouraged congregations and presbyteries to develop a Fresh Expression of Church in every parish by 2020. GA 2013, Instructions, section 14, p. 17.

administrative capacity at the regional levels of the church, while still maintaining the prerogatives of presbytery as a court over those who work for it and within it.

Concerns about the merits of this type of reform include the obvious ones of cost: new presbyteries would need an office base and support staff. They would also include the possibility that the new regional tier could feel as remote to local congregations as the national tier sometimes has. Making a reality of more relational, informal structures in local areas might offset and 'warm' the more formal and functional requirements of presbytery assemblies.

Council reform

This section is by far the hardest part of the whole project to write, because it is the most delicate and the one most likely to cause anger or offence. Arguments for increasing capacity at presbytery level are all about increasing budgets, adding staff and adding powers and functions, where for the most part they don't yet exist. Arguments for reforming and refocusing central structures tend to move in the opposite direction. They challenge existing concentrations of power, they will be seen to pass judgement on the effectiveness of existing arrangements and, by implication, of those who are working within them, including a number of people I consider friends. They may even seem to pose a threat to people's livelihoods or to the location of their work, which will be felt in highly personal terms. All I can do is try to tread as lightly as possible, reminding both readers and myself that individual academics wield pens not swords, while accepting due responsibility for this as indeed an attempt to steer and influence outcomes.

Tensions between centre and locale are endemic to the politics of many institutions, not least national churches. These very often develop into an unfair and unfocused animus, in which most things which go wrong somehow become *their* fault. In the case of the Kirk, '121' stands for an institutional persona, authority and culture which has acquired layers of significance and attribution over the years since 1911/1929.[28]

I count myself among those who have been on the receiving end of a major organisational reform within the non-church institution I worked for and can testify to the stress, unhappiness and anger which it provoked in me and many of my colleagues. Institutional reform is a demanding task which tends to be accompanied by unexpected costs, unforeseen complications and unintended consequences. To embark on the wrong kind of institutional reform is a nightmare. It consumes huge amounts of time, effort and emotional energy. When dealing with a large and complex institution, which contains multiple stakeholders with significant emotional and psychological investments in how things are done, it is probably impossible to 'get it right'. It is also always wise to keep in mind the wise phrase credited to organisational theorist Peter Drucker: 'Culture eats strategy',[29] although I also like to add my own less gloomy gloss, that 'culture floats strategy'.[30] Despite the sobering realities of how attempts at reform come undone, it would be a counsel of despair to conclude they should never be attempted.

I accept that the burden of argument is on those who propose change, especially disruptive change, but it is also important when advocating change not to overclaim. Institutional reform will often involve uncertainty. Often it will not be possible to determine its effects in advance. It does make sense to heed the medical advice to 'do no harm' or the homespun, 'If it ain't broke, don't fix it'; but it is also the case that we will almost never get the counter-factual and know how much better or worse it would be if we had or hadn't acted.

A variety of approaches has been taken in the past to commend options for reform. Management consultants McKinsey were

---

28 121 is the shorthand used for the central church in various forms – it derives from the location of the church's central offices at 121 George Street in Edinburgh, where they were built between 1909 and 1911 by the United Free Church. They became the offices of the reunited church after the union of 1929.

29 I first heard this phrase from the theologian Gerard Arbuckle, in a talk about his involvement with Health Service reforms in Australia.

30 I'm claiming this one as Google returns no other results for it!

commissioned to appraise options for restructuring in 2000 and lent their weight to the proposals recommended by the Board, but the wider church was not convinced or reassured. I suggest when Christian people think about the conditions for successful institutional reform, they should have a mix of things in mind. Prayer, providence, the guidance of the Holy Spirit; attentive listening to those directly affected; brave, fearless critical thinking about a range of options, which is willing to challenge the status quo; and cautious, prudent scepticism about claims for what will be delivered. All of these have their place within a wisdom perspective, as does the realisation that how reforms are crafted, named and commended can have a major effect on whether the hidden forces of institutional culture eat or float the strategy.

The suggestion that we should merge the four main councils of the Church of Scotland into a single new Mission Agency is a challenging one. It challenges existing structures of power and participation and posits an untried solution. The reasons for proposing it lie in my perception that despite significant amounts of solid achievement, combined with some outstanding initiatives and outcomes from individuals and teams, the record of both Mission and Discipleship and Ministries Council over the past decade are not so compelling and convincing as to make radical reform obviously unnecessary, given the future challenges facing the Kirk. My central concerns lie with the future effectiveness of these two councils, although aspects of the record of Church and Society and World Mission are also rightly open to question. My proposal is therefore primarily driven by a dissatisfaction with the way in which these first two councils relate structurally within the institution and with the way in which their respective domains and strategic objectives articulate with one another. I am tempted to stop there, but that seems irresponsible and open to the charge that I have insinuated concern, but not clarified in what it consists. The church looks to Mission and Discipleship to resource its life in relation to worship, music, liturgy, church planting, Christian education, prayer and personal devotion, Bible study, mission and evangelism, youth work and children's ministry. My concerns about its performance, during a period when there has been some significant internal turbulence in its operations, relate to a struggle to give the church a strong and clear enough lead around developing a missional agenda and imagination and to a patchy record in producing and supporting courses and curricula for equipping congregations to embrace 'mission-shaped ministry'. I am also not clear it has done enough to support new ways of developing biblical literacy or to use new media and online apps to encourage personal devotions and engage a wider public.

The church looks to Ministries Council to resource its life through the education, formation and support of ministers, readers and deacons, through strategic support for their welfare and strategic concern for their discipline, through encouragement of new and diverse forms of ministry and through a concern that every parish in Scotland should have access to the ministries it needs. I have concerns about its performance, during a period when very significant challenges began to appear in terms of numbers of vocations, when there were long-running concerns about adapting education for ministry and when there were calls for it to engage with missional challenges around church planting, pioneering and congregational renewal. Overall, my concern would be that it has not been prescient enough in anticipating and understanding challenges or timely enough in addressing them. It has felt slow on its feet, a bit lumbering and uncertain about how to give a lead to the church in the face of a developing crisis.

I don't mean those judgements to be unduly harsh, nor am I claiming I could have done better on all or any of them within the system as it stands. But I stand by the claim I made above, that given the scale of the future challenges facing the Kirk, their record is not strong and convincing enough to make radical reform obviously unnecessary.

A number of other concerns about central structures also need to be added. The first again evokes Henderson's comment about presbyterianism asking too much and giving too little. Particularly in the area of populating committees, councils, commissions and working groups, it has been observed by a number of commentators, including former Principal Clerk Finlay MacDonald in his 2004 book on 'a changing church', that the Church of Scotland consumes too much of its members and ministers time and energy in keeping the system going.[31] Our processes and procedures are too expansive, too exhausting and too expensive. We have too many meetings, which consume too many people hours. We pay too many sets of travel expenses and employ too many administrators to clerk and service committees.

In 2016, the Church's Nominations Committee reported that they had been busy preparing to fill 127 vacancies on central committees and councils, to replace those who had moved on in that year, out of a total of some 493 members who comprised those bodies. That is before we add in the hours spent in Kirk Sessions and their sub-committees and the hours spent attending presbytery committees and working groups, and also before our elders and ministers have ventured out to take part in ecumenical forums or community councils.

Not only is this a demanding bureaucratic culture to service, the frustrated tones of sections of the 2001 *Church Without Walls* report indicated 16 years ago that the panel had detected a good deal of alienation and cynicism about aspects of participation in the institution. To be sure, '121' is an easy target and focus, but there have also been some unhappy currents running within it in recent years, witness the signs around the building advising staff where they can get support if they feel they are facing bullying in the workplace.

It is news to no one and certainly should not be to folk who embrace Reformed theology, that the Church of Scotland is a very human institution, which lives only by the grace of God. Sadly, as a minister and member, I bring my faults and weaknesses with me when I take part in its life and work. Perhaps, though, behind some of this demanding regime of meetings and the enormous, endless work of keeping the institutional wheels turning, there may be a summons to refocus, refresh and reform our central structures. As the church declines, there is a danger we more often feel like David in Saul's armour, weighed down by the weight of all the attempts to equip ourselves for action. Certainly, rereading *Church Without Walls* in 2017, alongside the notes of frustration, there are striking and, perhaps, still prophetic calls to find more

---

31 Macdonald, 2004.

grace-notes, to do less, to have fewer business meetings and to recover a greater sense of friendship, relationship and connection.

Again, we need to weigh the cost, remembering the Clinton maxim of ensuring we have all the government we need. We need to be mindful of the ways in which those 493 ministers, elders and members represent points of connection and participation; that when someone flies in from Orkney, or drives up from Kirkcudbright to attend a council meeting, it is also a living practice of solidarity, representation and service.

Devolution

The counterpart to creating fewer, more powerful and responsible presbyteries would be that a reformed central administration, which simplified and streamlined its own operations, would devolve posts, functions and financial responsibilities to the new presbyteries. The intention would be that a unified Mission Agency would involve significantly fewer people in its oversight and governance and would employ significantly fewer people within 121 – I suggest at least a third fewer than at present.[32] The internal ministry divisions would relate to sub-committees of the new Council of Assembly and could also have recourse to reference groups, through gathered and online consultations, as well as maintaining connection and participation by liaising with and relating to presbyteries.

Overall, there would be a renegotiation and recalibration of the federal structure of the Kirk and a reconsideration of how subsidiarity is worked out in its common life.

121 George Street

The most powerful symbol of a structural, cultural and psychological change which the Kirk could make would be to sell 121

---

32 Though as noted above, the new structures might mean some central functions were strengthened, even though numbers working centrally were reduced overall.

George Street and move to new offices. Clearly there would be issues of good stewardship involved here and it would have to be economically and financially plausible. If this were to prove possible, I would argue strongly that the church looks for a new central home which is not merely functional but which makes a powerful ecological, aesthetic and theological statement about its identity and mission within twenty-first-century Scotland. We should aim to find a new home for our national staff which is striking, hospitable, functional and affordable and which is marked by signs that we value art and architecture, that we value our Scottish identity and our connections to the world Church. When we do have to meet in councils and committees, we should aim for something more hospitable and uplifting than we currently experience in the soulless basements of 121 George Street. A building into which the wider membership and public could be welcomed, which contained a foyer or atrium with seating and display areas and a café, would transform the experience of encountering the central structures of the church.

General Assembly

When I first set out on this project, I was very attracted to the idea of following the lead of the PCUSA and moving to biennial assemblies. It is expensive to stage assemblies and so there are savings to be made in halving their frequency. The report cycle is also notoriously and dysfunctionally short, with councils and committees often struggling to pace their work to both give it enough time and meet the deadlines for the Blue Book of Assembly Reports (even in this new world of electronic media). For these reasons, I am still sympathetic to the case for meeting every second year, but in the context of the package of reforms I am supporting here, on balance I favour no change to the annual cycle. In particular, as I reflected on the consequences of reform to the central councils, which would significantly reduce the numbers of people involved in oversight and planning roles, I have come to feel that to also reduce the frequency of assemblies would fuel concerns about too small a group being given too much power. (The new

Council of Assembly and the new senior management/secretary team within a unified agency would indeed be a powerful new core group within the church.) I have come to think that retaining annual assemblies, at least initially, could significantly offset that and continue to offer a valuable opportunity for a national church to show itself in parliamentary mode, asserting that it is one Kirk, seeking to serve and speak to the whole of Scotland. It would be a continuing check and balance on such a stronger manage-rial core.[33] It also offers an important opportunity for the church to experience and to show itself in a more celebratory 'festival' mode, through the successful Heart and Soul gathering in Princes Street gardens.

The Moderator of the General Assembly

Another question which has been revisited regularly since the 1970s is the term of the Moderator of the General Assembly. The role is a strange mix of the honorific, the symbolic and the func-tional. That the person occupying it changes every year means that the Kirk has no regular, familiar, identifiable face in the Scottish public mind. We never really produce a Richard Holloway or a Tom Winning,[34] because we never give the media the continu-ity of focus needed to build a public profile. One sign of this is how rare it has been over the past ten years to see spokesmen and women from the Kirk appearing on current affairs media shows in Scotland. The visible improvements to the Kirk's PR and communications work in the past five years have made some difference, but they can only work with what they have. In terms of the more functional aspects of the role, those who thrive in it comment that they have just worked out how to do it when they hand it on to someone else. One problem about changing the term is that fewer people would get to take on the role and it has

---

33 The core would also have lost some of its functions and power to the new presbyteries, which offsets the 'threat' of a stronger centre.

34 A well-known Primus of the Scottish Episcopal Church and Cardinal of the Roman Catholic Church respectively. Some might of course count this an advantage.

sometimes been seen as a reward for long and conspicuous service. When Finlay Macdonald, himself a former Moderator, commented on this question in 2004, he suggested that 'were this to
be extended beyond one year, then the Church would need to give
the Moderator a more functional leadership role, combined with
a measure of authority' and he also floated the suggestion of them
chairing a 'college' of full-time presbytery moderators.[35] In the
scheme I have sketched in this book, the Moderator would chair
the Council of Assembly, which would contain such full-time
moderators, so the functional leadership role would be strengthened. Moderators could become rarer beasts, changing every two
or three years. They would still only ever be *primus inter pares*
and we would still send them back to the ranks when their time
was up, but they might be able to serve more effectively in the
role while it was their assignment and commission. A potential
disadvantage would be that an extended term might effectively
end their period of ministry in an existing charge.

Congregations

The final area of structural reform I want to discuss may have
been less predictable than some others. It grows out of the discussion of presbyterianism in the second chapter and the observations made there about the growing 'congregationalisation' of the
global Church, as well as reflections on how a theology of ministry has increasingly emphasised the ministries of the whole body.
I believe the role of the congregation is the missing link within
the evolution of Scottish presbyterianism. For too long, 'congregationalism' has been used as a kind of foil against which presbyterians have defined their own polity. In the Church of Scotland,
the 'aristocratic' character of traditional representative presbyterianism has meant that a certain pride is taken in emphasising
that 'The Kirk Session is not answerable to the congregation but

---

35 Macdonald, 2004, p. 73.

only to superior courts.'[36] Even today, on the floor of the General Assembly, a proposal may be effectively resisted on the grounds that it is taking us down the slippery slope to congregationalism. The downside to this way of defining presbyterianism is a failure to see the extent to which it has led to an overly negative construal of the role of the congregation and a reluctance to grant it any additional significant legal or constitutional powers. Here I think the Kirk can learn something from the polity of the United Reformed Church, which was formed as a synthesis of Presbyterian and Congregationalist polities. Within the URC, the Church Meeting is given a status and respect which it does not have within Church of Scotland parishes. It is possible and, I would argue, desirable for the Kirk to adjust its own polity in this direction, without losing the unitive and regulative benefits of having a clear hierarchy of church courts. This form of adjustment would offer a new articulation of the logic of the congregation's role within the system, where it is sometimes very powerful, as when calling a minister, but often entirely marginal or even impotent. It would also help to adjust and relocate the status of the eldership and the Kirk Session, which is in danger of becoming isolated by the reticence of (particularly but not exclusively) younger people to take on a role linked to lifelong ordination, without any formal limits to terms of service.

Fantasy presbyterianism?

This chapter is the one most at risk of the accusation of hubris. Who does he think he is to propose such wholesale reforms to the structure of the Kirk? I may seem to have been indulging in a polity version of fantasy football or a game of Presbyterian Sims,[37] whimsically moving players into new formations, rashly building

36 Cox, J., *Practice and Procedure in the Church of Scotland*, in Wolfe and Pickford, 1980, p. 35.

37 Which is an anagram of presbyterianisms, just as George MacLeod liked to mischievously point out that presbyterian is an anagram of 'best in prayer' (and episcopal of Pepsi Cola).

up virtual possibilities which lack grounding in the realities and complexities of the real world. In my defence, I have tried to make it clear that most if not all of the elements I have assembled here have already been in circulation, some since the 1970s. The 2001 *Tomorrow's Presbyteries* report suggested that the Kirk had become:

a structurally conservative body . . . like many historic institutions facing change, it instinctively looks for the risks and reasons not to act, rather than anticipating the opportunities which open up through change. This may be partly because of the lack of confidence which goes with being a declining body.

Conclusion: What Comes Next?

This book and the lectures which were developed alongside it have offered an extended reflection on some of the key challenges confronting the Church of Scotland today and on the ways in which structural reform of the church's life and work might better enable it to fulfil its calling. As I watch new students coming in to study for ministry at Trinity College in the University of Glasgow, I often think they will have a hard shift to work in the life of the church. Of course, if we set this in the context of church history and the struggles of the Church globally, we can find plenty of salutary reminders of believers facing and enduring much worse. Even so, the period I have been reflecting on, between now and 2030, will hold particular challenges for ministers entering their first charge.

I have only addressed some of the challenges facing the Kirk and I am very conscious of that. As I said in the lectures, someone else will write more insightfully than I could, on a call to spiritual renewal. There will also be a need for further work on liturgical renewal, and I hope to write more on that in future. I am braced for a reaction from some people which scolds me for paying attention to polity and structures when what the church *really* needs is thoroughgoing repentance and renewed devotion to prayer and scripture. I am the last person to discourage either repentance or prayer and I am sure both I and many others are in great need of them. My only plea to such people would be that we do not need to see such prescriptions as alternatives to the kinds of reform I have been considering.

Other people, including some of those whose theological wisdom and judgement I rate very highly, have expressed doubts about the ideas I have presented here. Some have pointed to examples of similar reforms which have been enacted and similar provisions which have been made in other reformed churches, such as the URC and the PCUSA, and reminded me that these churches have continued to decline. Others, including some who have previously been passionate about structural reform, have counselled that the church might never embrace it, that it could become a divisive distraction and that we should return to a focus on coaching and enabling effective ministry practice at a local level. The implication is that the structures will somehow take care of themselves and the work of trying to change them would be too diverting, too draining and too demoralising. My response to the first kind of scepticism is to accept the point, but to also lean on a combination of the wisdom perspective on reform I have been working out in the book and ideas of contextual missiology and ecclesiology. The need to work contextually means that we cannot simply say because something did or did not work somewhere else, in a church with a different history, background, geography and culture, that it is right or wrong for us. A wisdom perspective insists that, in a spirit of prayer and openness to God, you can work on the problems and issues as you perceive them, with the best light you have. Our polity, our structures and processes – these are also part of our witness as the Church. They model ways of our being with one another, hearing one another, sharing with one another, disciplining one another. They also reflect our understanding of God, our discipleship of Jesus Christ, our attentiveness to what the Spirit is saying to our church. I think we are right to be concerned when our life as a church seems to be unfruitful and is marked by decline, and I believe there are ways to respond to these concerns with spiritual and theological integrity, which reflect a longing for the church to grow and flourish, but do not confuse faithfulness and success.

To the second kind of scepticism, I also say a kind of Amen; agreeing that we should not wait on big picture reforms to create pathways to renewal. A wisdom perspective on reform does not trust in the plans of either academic theologians or management consultants, although it does not despise them either. It understands that the peace and unity of the church matter more than its efficiency; and it understands that love is patient, even while it hopes all things.

One question which has haunted the writing of this book is whether God still has a use for the Church of Scotland? While the question may sound extreme, I think there are more and less melodramatic ways of asking it. There have been many examples of faithful witness, loving service and costly sacrifice within the life of the Church of Scotland over the past five decades, while it has been in overall decline. I recognise that, and as I write it, I give thanks to God for it and say that I expect it to continue, God willing, in the same mixed fashion over the next five decades. God will still be active in all of our lives and present to all of our communities. But the question of the Kirk's usefulness to God is a different one, which is hard to frame rightly. It is a question about providence, about blessing and judgement. It has something of the character of lament about it, taking some of the ideas of Psalm 44 which we explored in Chapter 1 and setting them in another liturgical context, which is less feisty and more reflective. The liturgical forms here mix confession and intercession – 'We have lived through some difficult years, Lord; we are very conscious of many failures and disappointments; and much of the news is still bad. Not just for us, but across western Europe, the news is bad for mainline Protestant denominations. What biblical stories should we reach for in this moment? Will there be a return from exile? Or is this the end of "the nation" as we have known it? Are we to be scattered among the other nations/churches?'

To work liturgically and to reflect theologically on a question like this is to set it in a context where we are open to hearing and receiving difficult truths about ourselves. A Reformed understanding of church tradition is predicated on the fact that sometimes God does a new thing as an expression of grace and judgement on the historical forms of the one church. If we believe the creation of the Kirk was in some sense an obedient response to the work of the Holy Spirit, then our origins in the sixteenth-century Reformation represent one such new thing. Similarly, if we believe that the growth of Pentecostalism over the last century into a global family of churches was in some sense a work of God, then it represented a supplement to and renewal of the broader

Protestant (and Roman Catholic) tradition.[1] We could go on: the rise of evangelicalism, the growth of black majority churches in the USA, the development of the modern ecumenical movement, the Second Vatican Council, the charismatic renewal, the growth of feminist, womanist and liberation theology, the rise of post-colonial missiology. Without endorsing all of these currents of renewal, any more than I would claim impeccability for the Kirk, they all to my mind represent attempts at obedient response to the prompting of the Spirit. In some cases, an ancient tradition is renewed in significant continuity with what has gone before. In other cases, a new tradition grows into a distinct historical body politic as a fresh expression of the body of Christ in the world. In certain cases, an existing body reduces to the point of extinction or near extinction.

For those within church bodies which are declining, the liturgical and theological task is not only to ask, as we did in the first chapter, 'What just happened?' It is also to ask, 'What next? Where now?' The work of asking such questions is a work of practical theology in its prospective as well as its reflective mode. It is an act of discipleship, part of our learning to be the church of Jesus Christ.

One thing which I have not said much about, but which has been a major cause of reflection for the Kirk in the past decade, is its commitment under the 3rd Article Declaratory that 'as a national Church representative of the Christian Faith of the Scottish people it acknowledges its distinctive call and duty to bring the ordinances of religion to the people in every parish of Scotland through a territorial ministry'.[2] Looked at through the lens of a systematic theology, the whole question of being a 'national church' does not bear too much theological scrutiny and is, in fact, continually put in question by the central marks of the

---

1 See on this Chapter 3 in Lesslie Newbigin's remarkable 1952 Kerr Lectures, delivered at Trinity College, University of Glasgow, and published as *The Household of God*. Newbigin's focus on pentecostalism was highly prescient and ahead of many other commentators in seeing its significance for the ecumenical movement and for patterns of global mission.

2 www.churchofscotland.org.uk/about_us/church_law/church_constitution#article1.

church: that it is one, holy, catholic and apostolic. A theological account of a 'national church' will have to come by way of a historical, contextual missiology and will understand itself, like the nation it is identified with,[3] as only ever a provisional structure. Yet, like the nation, under God it may discern its calling to a discipling, a catechising into being the church, into being a peculiar people, in a particular place. Since mission is rooted in the loving heart of God, the calling of such a church is to love that place and those who live there. Without compromising its international vision of the church catholic and the global oikumene, it is to realise that its stewardship of creation is to be particularly expressed in cherishing and inhabiting this land, this language, this culture. Who will work to contextualise mission in Scotland if the Kirk[4] will not?

It is possible to read the Kirk's continuing commitment to the parish system as a form of imperialism, a desperate clinging on to the vanity of being a national church as the capacity to inhabit that role ebbs away. Sadly, there may be some truth in that. But there are other ways to live into a territorial imagination. Abraham Kuyper famously said, 'There is not a square inch in the whole domain of our human existence over which Christ, who is Sovereign over all, does not cry: "Mine!"'[5] To be shaped by the logic and discipline of parish is to believe that God loves every square inch of Scotland and every person who lives here. It is to believe with the Puritans that 'every place is immediate unto God'[6] and to reject the logics which marginalise and stigmatise some places as bad areas, as sink estates or junkie-ridden schemes, as 'remote and benighted', the middle of nowhere, or the back of beyond. At its humblest and best, the parish system is an affirmation that God loves Skaw and Skye, Whithorn and Whitfield, Drumchapel and Drumnadrochit, Cumbrae and Cumnock, and it is a prayer for the coming of the kingdom into every corner of

---

3 On this, see my 2014 book, *Honey from the Lion: Christianity and the Ethics of Nationalism*.

4 And the other Scottish churches, together and separately – I mean this inclusively – though I also mean us to hear this as a word to the Kirk.

5 Abraham Kuyper, 'Sphere Sovereignty', in Kuyper, 1998, p. 488.

6 I heard John Stott quote this, but have never found the source.

CONCLUSION

Scotland, that people in every place would know that God's will
for them is life in all its fullness. However the Kirk has to learn
to ration and rationalise its work in the coming years, it should
never be because it has forgotten that.

There is no doubting that the way forward for the Church
of Scotland between now and 2030 will contain unprecedented
challenges and will carry painful choices. While presbyterianism
may sometimes ask too much and give too little, God never does.
Believing that and being open to both what is asked of us and
what is given to us, is what will sustain and enable the work of
reforming the Kirk.

Appendix:
The Chalmers Lectures 2017

Lecture 1: Walls Without Church (Glory Without Power)
St Giles' Cathedral, 1 February 2017

I want to begin by thanking you warmly for coming or for clicking in if you are out there in cyberspace, by thanking the church for appointing me and waiting for me as Chalmers Lecturer and by thanking the Kirk Session and Minister of St Giles for making available this historic church as a venue for these three lectures.

That there are three lectures means that we will all have to pace ourselves. I want to try and lead an argument and make a case about reforming the church and to build it over these three weeks. We are going to move from the general to the particular, and the detailed suggestions I want to make for specific reforms are going to come mostly in the second and third lectures, so I ask for your patience in that respect, particularly in the questions, so that I have something left to say on 15 February.

Reasons for writing

Tell someone you are writing a book on the future of the Kirk and their instant response is likely to be some version of the quip 'So it has one?' Another favourite is: 'So it'll be a short book then.'

I have felt very inadequate in tackling this subject – I have a very clear sense of my own limitations – and if these lectures have any gifts to give to the church, among them will be the gift of being wrong. My hope is that they can serve the church by contributing to a positive and creative conversation about its future.

There have been some very important conversations about reform within the Church of Scotland since the year 2000 and some significant reports and proposals – some of which have led to change, some of which have been set aside. But given the scale of the challenges we are facing, I do not think we have yet done enough.

With some very honourable exceptions, too often, across the church, we treat our presbyterian identity and its institutional expression as a running joke; we are prepared to ironise it relentlessly and to complain about it endlessly, without putting enough serious effort into devising constructive options for reform. My growing suspicion has been that this reaction reflects a sense of disempowerment and even distress. People have been laughing instead of crying, because they did not know what else to do.

In the conversations I have had with a range of folk within the church, I sense that mood is beginning to change – the challenges are too serious and too imminent. As one person said to me, 'There's nowhere left to hide.' So I want to begin these lectures, as I begin the book, with this question: 'What just happened?'

What just happened?

There are two simple answers to that question, both of which are also very challenging and complicated when we begin to unpack them: *decline* happened and *secularisation* happened.

Decline happened

Table 4 sets out the turning point and the onset of decline in membership from the peak of the middle of the twentieth century:

Table 4. Church of Scotland Membership 1950–2016

Year	Membership
1950	1,271,247
1956	**1,319,574***
1960	1,301,280
1970	1,154,211
1980	953,933
1990	786,787
2000	607,712
2010	445,646
2011	432,343
2012	413,488
2013	398,389
2014	380,163
2015	363,597

*All-time peak membership

The Church of Scotland reached a peak of membership – in 1956, when it registered 1,319,574 members – in 2015 the membership stood at 352,912. At the current rate of decline, by 2020 we will have lost around a million members since 1956.

Between 2005 and 2015 there was a 30 per cent drop in membership, which meant that we declined faster than any other major denomination in the UK. The Church of Scotland has lost the equivalent of an average-sized congregation each week for the past ten years.[1]

In that same decade up to 2015, there was a 30 per cent drop in children, a 24 per cent drop in ministers and a 26 per cent drop in elders. As things stand more than 75 per cent of our ministers, of which I am one, are aged over 50–95 per cent are aged over 40. These are grim statistics.

Tracing the pattern of decline which set in from the early 1960s is not just a statistical and a sociological task, it is also a spiritual challenge for the Kirk. Not everywhere, but in most

---

1 The comparison was made to me by Rev. Dr Fiona Tweedie, Statistics for Mission adviser to the Church of Scotland.

congregations, it has been a story of relentless decline. It is psychologically significant that most people in the Kirk, along with most ministers, are unlikely to have ever had the experience of being part of a growing congregation. It is sociologically and missiologically significant that Church of Scotland membership is declining faster than that of any other major denomination in the UK.

A tale of two Censuses

Questions on religion were only finally included in the UK Census in 2001. After the Census, the Church of Scotland was braced for results which would highlight its decline, but the numbers in 2001 were not nearly as bad as some had feared. More than two million Scots identified their religion as 'Church of Scotland' in the Census returns, representing 42 per cent of the population, while just 27.5 per cent or 1.4 million said they had 'no religion'. While this represented a substantial decline from what the levels would have been in 1971 or 1981, it still bore witness to a prior Scotland, much of which had understood and felt itself to be culturally presbyterian. However, when the results of the 2011 Census came out, with the church again braced for bad news, as its own numbers continued to plummet, this time there was little comfort to be found. The number of those identifying as 'Church of Scotland' had fallen by 20 per cent to just over 1.7 million, while the number of those identifying as having 'no religion' had risen by 38 per cent to 1.94 million. It is known in the trade as the rise of the 'Nones'. Presbyterian Scotland – which was never all of Scotland – was not yet entirely gone, but it was fading fast. The Census, which perhaps functions best as a measure of a residual, cultural religiosity, was charting a rapid process of secularisation across Scotland, and the Kirk was topping the charts for religious decline.

The question 'What just happened?' is intended to reflect a sense of shock, dismay and, if you'll forgive the term, disbelief. I am not sure we have fully acknowledged the grief within the Kirk at how much has been lost – at how this has felt for those who have lived and ministered through these years. Nor have we properly begun to understand why the Church of Scotland has fared so badly in comparative terms.

As well as decline, the other answer to what just happened is that secularisation happened.

Secularisation happened

Classic theories of secularisation, as they emerged within the Western tradition of social science, held that a decline in the social significance of religion would be an inevitable accompaniment to the rise of modernity.

The predictions of most secularisation theorists until the 1990s were that institutional forms of Christianity, which had been powerful in Europe for over a thousand years, were now facing a relentless decline. In the 1990s, Scotland's own Callum Brown offered a postmodern challenge to the modernist determinism of classic secularisation theory – he argued for a more open account of religious change – but having redated it to the 1960s and linked its cause to issues of gender in Scottish society, he was clear that secularisation should from this point be understood as a powerful reality, that it was probably irreversible and that this was a very good thing too.

Scotland's former *makar* Liz Lochhead (b.1947) is an example of Callum Brown's generation of women who came of age in the mid-960s and quickly left behind the Church of Scotland (where her father had been Elder and Session Clerk). There were too many ways, Brown suggests, in which the Kirk did not seem to understand or resonate with their understanding of being a woman in a changing Scotland.[2]

Liz Lochhead's poem 'The Offering' begins: 'Never in a month of them would you go back./Sunday, the late smell of bacon/then the hard small feeling of the offering in the mitten.'

---

2 In conversation with her at Solas Festival in 2015, she told me her father had been Session Clerk.

It is one of a few post-1960 literary texts which are essential resources for understanding the decline of the Kirk in terms of what happened inside people's psyches, their hearts and minds.[3]

It would be rare if not impossible to find an academic working in this field who did not believe that secularisation was a very real phenomenon across western Europe. But there are different strands to how this is understood.

Some academics have questioned how secularisation relates to life beyond Europe. Christianity continues to grow as a global religion, as does Islam. Some areas of the world, including parts of eastern Europe, appear to have shown signs of desecularisation. North America and the USA in particular, despite also being advanced capitalist societies, continue to show much higher levels of religious participation than in Europe, although 'Nones' are on the rise there also.

Let me refer briefly to three other perspectives on secularisation.

The sociologist Grace Davie has drawn attention to the phenomenon of what she calls 'vicarious religion' across Europe, arguing that while religious participation is declining, religion is still valued by a silent majority who want it to be there, while not wanting to have much to do with it. This raises questions about what happens to religiosity when secularisation takes place – does it disappear, does it simply evaporate, or does it go quiet, go dormant?

Paul Heelas and Linda Woodhead's influential study *The Spiritual Revolution*[4] explored changing religious behaviours in the town of Kendal, drawing on philosopher Charles Taylor's theories of subjectification or a turn to the subject/to the self in Western culture. The classic example here is the person who says, 'I'm not religious but I see myself as a spiritual person.' The search for authentic ways of being a self, of being ourselves, is seen as driving what people do with religion and how they do it. What they call the holistic milieu – a constellation of spaces and practices for developing body, mind and spirit – is growing

---

3 Text is in Lochhead, 2011. For a brief critical commentary on 'The Offering' see Lochhead, 1993, pp. 71–2.

4 Woodhead and Heelas, 2005.

in response to this search, particularly among women over 40. Where churches were growing, they suggested it was most often where they offered vividly experiential and self-involving ways to practise Christianity and particularly where this also brought with it a sense of belonging to a distinctive community. Those least likely to attract people were congregations offering an inherited, external moral code, but lacking distinctive social identity and heightened personal experience.

Canadian philosopher Charles Taylor, in his 2007 book *A Secular Age,* offers a profound and subtle account of secularisation in which he describes how the ways we imagine and experience the world have changed over the past 500 years – from an instinctive and immediate awareness of spirituality to a more distant, buffered and sceptical experience of the world. As someone sympathetic to faith, Taylor describes a range of different ways in which human beings now imagine, pursue and experience what he calls 'fullness'.

'Our age', he claims, 'is very far from settling in to a comfortable unbelief.'[5] Taylor suggests that as secularisation advances within Western societies, we may reach a kind of fragile equilibrium which is capable of tipping in different directions. In some societies, he believes there may still be further movement towards a more secular outlook, with increasing numbers of people identifying religion as a problem and gravitating towards what he calls a self-contained, 'immanentist' view of life.[6] However, Taylor also offers a distinctive reading of 'secularisation and its discontents',[7] suggesting that in the twenty-first century the most secular societies may find that 'many young people will begin again to explore beyond the boundaries' of a 'waste land' of immanence. In these societies, blaming what has become a relatively weak religious domain for human ills will seem increasingly implausible. Not only that, the record and capacities of a now dominant humanism and secularism for meeting human aspirations to 'fullness' of life will be increasingly

---

5 Taylor, 2007, p. 727.

6 Taylor, 2007, p. 770.

7 The phrase, a punning paraphrase of Freud's 1929 book *Civilisation and its Discontents*, has been used by multiple authors, so no single attribution seems possible.

questioned.[8] Those of us living in the most secularised societies in the world may find that beyond the post-Christendom period we are currently living through, we may be about to experience, even if this happens patchily across Europe, a post-secular and post-atheist phase in our culture.[9] This, we should note, would not be the same as a revival of religion, although it might create conditions favourable to that. In the first instance, it would represent a feeling, a *zeitgeist* or cultural mood, in which secularism and atheism no longer felt like progressive forces, which had the cultural winds in their sails, but were themselves the object of increasing critique, scepticism and disillusionment.

What just happened? Well, decline happened and is still happening . . . secularisation happened and is still happening. But what comes next – and what should we do about it? I want to suggest that there are four great tasks in front of the Church of Scotland today:

1 Spiritual renewal – listening and responding to God.
2 Liturgical renewal – remaking the public worship of the church.
3 Missional refocusing – committing ourselves to a holistic theology of mission.
4 Institutional reform – reshaping and restructuring our institutional life.

In these three lectures, I am going to be focusing on the third and fourth of these – so I will say very little in particular about liturgical renewal – I have written on that before, and I hope to do so again.

Spiritual renewal

I am not going to say much on this – but I want to say something. I believe there are others in coming months and years who will

---

8 See Smith, 2014.
9 The ideas explored here are on the borderlands between sociology of religion, prophetic spirituality and missiology, and need to be held within an overarching understanding of divine providence. There is no claim of inevitability and no claim that technique or strategy can secure outcomes.

write more insightfully than I can on the call to spiritual renewal. I am expecting that a few people, not all of them well-adjusted, will write or email to scold me for paying attention to polity and structures when what the church really needs, is thoroughgoing repentance and renewed devotion to prayer and scripture. I am the last person to discourage either repentance or prayer or scripture reading and I am sure both I and many of you are in great and continuing need of them. My plea to such people would be that we do not need to see such prescriptions as alternatives to the kinds of refocusing and reform I am going to devote these lectures to.

So let me simply say this. I fully believe that unless the Lord builds the house, they labour in vain that build it. The Church of Scotland as part of the one, holy, catholic and apostolic Church, lives only by the grace and power of God, our maker and our redeemer. We live and die, we stand or fall by our faith in the Lord Jesus Christ, the incarnate Word of God, crucified, risen and ascended – the Saviour of the world – who was before us in the beginning with God and as God, who calls us to follow him in the present, who awaits us at the end when the kingdoms of this world become the kingdom of our God and of the Christ.

As the body of Christ, we live by and through the work of the life-giving Holy Spirit.

As a Christian, I believe that the fullness of life which Charles Taylor speaks of, which people in Scotland long for and strive for, is to be found in knowing this one, true, triune God and Jesus Christ, the one sent to us because God so loved the world.

I believe that a true spiritual renewal involves a holistic renewal of our Christian witness; which is why we need to test the spirits when people want to talk of revival or renewal. It is not true revival if people are anguished about micro ethics but shed no tears over macro ethics. If they care about temperance but not about Trident. It is not true revival if men lament their lust for women but not their sexism. It is not true revival if people speak in strange tongues, but do not speak out against injustice and speak up for the poor. It is not true revival if people throw their fiddles on the fire – if they create an unbridgable cultural gap between ceilidh and congregation. It is not a true spiritual renewal if it makes us less human, less alive, less loving, less merciful, less open to art and beauty and sensuality and life.

I can already sense some people out there reaching for the green ink . . .

Everything does depend upon the prayer – Come, Holy Spirit.

Liturgical renewal

I will say even less about liturgical renewal. Just this – that in a broad church, I believe it will take different forms. For some, it will come through classical music and finely crafted liturgy; for some, it will come through Messy Church and Matt Redman; for some, it will come through a renewal of intense and passionate expository preaching; for some, it will come through exploring gifts of the Spirit; for others, it will come through a recovery of ancient spiritual practices; for some, it will come through Rend Collective; for others, it will come through the Iona Community. We are a diverse church – God's tastes are wider than mine. As a reformed church, what all of these should share is a deep attentiveness to scripture, to hearing God's word – and what I dare to hope they also share is a more frequent celebration of the Lord's Supper.

When that renewal comes, it will move us on from the dull mediocrity of middle-of-the-road traditionalism, from joyless formalism, from trite pietism, from funereal Communions, from boring sermons, from musical snobbery, from liturgical correctness, from liturgical sloppiness, from evangelical privatisation of the gospel, from the liberal progressivist reduction of the gospel to social ethics . . . I could go on, but I won't. That's another lecture, another book, another rant.

Missional Refocusing

The third task confronting us in the Kirk, I want to call a missional refocusing. In becoming more vivid and life-affirming, our spirituality and our worship will bear witness to a new ecumenical consensus about mission. Lesslie Newbigin wrote of his hopes for such a theological consensus in the 1950s, which was then overtaken by a period of polarisation between liberals infatuated with religionless Christianity, who virtually equated mission with humanisation and social progress, and evangelicals who craved a tighter focus on evangelism and personal salvation. Here in Scotland, where that consensus had animated initiatives like 'Tell Scotland', the subsequent divergence pulled people apart. Newbigin's return to Britain in the 1980s was one catalyst in the emergence of a new consensus from the 1990s onwards, of which David Bosch's book *Transforming Mission* was a key marker. The theological lens through which this was focused was the idea of the *missio Dei* – the mission of God. There are often quoted definitions of this from Jürgen Moltmann and from James Torrance. The most succinct is perhaps Tim Dearborn's formulation: 'It is not the church of God which has a mission, it is the mission of God which has a church.' Mission begins in the heart of God, there is mission Bosch says, because God loves people. The *missio Dei* enables a post-colonial understanding of mission; no longer something done by the sending churches of the North to the global South, we are all the objects of mission before we are ever its subjects.

The *missio Dei* offers an overarching vision of the work of God in creation and redemption, of the life of the world in all its dimensions, called to be reconciled to God-in-Christ, through the renewing and life-giving work of the Spirit. And the mission of God has a Church. The words of the risen Christ in John 20.21 reveal the dynamic at work: 'as the Father has sent me, so I send you'. This is the word which incorporates disciples into the *missio Dei*, which confirms and ordains the Church as the church apostolic.[10]

In seeking the consensus which Newbigin and Bosch pointed us to, we can also see convergence today between the Lausanne Movement's 2011 Cape Town Commitment[11] and the World

10 See also Flett, 2016.

11 For the text of the Lausanne Movement's 2011 Cape Town Commitment (agreed by the 2010 Cape Town conference), see www.lausanne.org/content/ctc/ctcommitment.

Council of Churches' 2013 statement on Mission and Evangelism, *Together Towards Life*.[12] There are still some significant differences of emphasis between the two documents, but there is also an important degree of common ground – a common ground which I believe would be affirmed by the mainstream opinion of at least two-thirds of the Kirk today. I am open to being shown a better formulation if you have one, but I value the strength and clarity of the Anglican Communion's Five Marks of Mission:

- To proclaim the good news of the kingdom.
- To teach, baptise and nurture new believers.
- To respond to human need by loving service.
- To transform unjust structures of society, to challenge violence of every kind and pursue peace and reconciliation.
- To strive to safeguard the integrity of creation, and sustain and renew the life of the earth.

This is the kind of full-spectrum lens which I believe we need to refocus the life and work of the Church of Scotland. It calls evangelicals beyond individualism to social and ecological ethics. It reminds liberals of the importance of evangelism and discipleship. It is succinct and memorable enough to use in Christian education and catechising. It reflects what David Bosch called an 'emerging, ecumenical, missionary paradigm'.[13] It is a vision of mission which could unite and inspire the church. If we can find ways to improve the Five Marks without spoiling them, or alienating one another, we can do that as well.

This is the key insight which I think can be the star which guides us on the next stage of the Kirk's journey. It is not my insight – it is an emerging consensus across many churches today, especially those like ourselves which need to re-imagine our calling in the face of decline and secularisation. Missiology frames ecclesiology which frames ministry.

---

12 www.churchofscotland.org.uk/__data/assets/pdf_file/0008/20699 /Mission_statement.pdf.

13 Bosch, 1991, pp. 368ff.

Institutional reform

The final task confronting the Church of Scotland is the task of institutional reform – reform which is shaped by the missional refocusing of the church's life.

I want to begin here by thinking about two inheritances which have shaped the Church of Scotland: the traditions of Reformed theology and the traditions of presbyterian polity or governance.

In 2017, the year in which we mark the 500th anniversary of Luther's Wittenberg theses, we recall Luther's Reforming restatement of the *notae ecclesiae* – the marks of the Church, the true preaching of the word of God and the right administration of the sacraments, to which was added in the Scots Confession a third mark of ecclesiastical discipline, uprightly administered.

The reception of the Reformed tradition in Scotland led the church through a series of struggles, some of them bloody, to affirm that its government was presbyterian.

In this last section of the lecture, I want to reflect on the inheritance of presbyterianism – on its gifts and graces, its shadows and deficits, and its promise for the future.

Presbyterianism is, in essence, a system of church government – although, when we see that it has taken subtly and markedly different forms in different places and times, we might find that we need to talk about presbyterianisms. Ours is not the only game in town nor, I will argue, should it rest on the conceit that it is 'the original and best'. Although technically it is only a form of polity, in reality it has been more than that and it has birthed more than that within Scottish culture. It has acquired an ethos, a spirituality – a cultural persona; it has become a brand. If we are going to reform it, we need to reclaim it and re-evaluate it and rethink it.

Donald MacLeod, former Principal of the Free Church of Scotland College in Edinburgh, writes of the development of presbyterianism in Scotland:

John Knox, of course, set up no presbyteries, and this can easily lead to the conclusion that he was no Presbyterian.

But Presbyterianism is not government by Presbyteries, but government by *presbyters*, and the essential principles of such a polity were already set in place by Calvin in Geneva. Here already it was perceived that the words *presbyters* and *bishops* referred to one and the same office; and here, too, it was laid down that churches must be governed not by one individual, but by a plurality of such presbyter-bishops. There had to be a *presbyterion*: a college or council of presbyters, 'which was in the church what a council is in a city' (Calvin, *Institutes*, IV.XI. 6). Hence the Scottish presbytery, the Genevan consistory and the Dutch classis.[14]

MacLeod identifies Alexander Henderson's *Notes on the Government and Order of the Church of Scotland*, published in 1641, as 'the best succinct exposition of Scottish presbyterianism'. In particular, he is drawn to what he calls Henderson's brilliant summary of the genius of presbyterian polity; that it offers 'superiority without tyranny, parity without confusion, subjection without slavery'.[15]

Presbyterian governance is built around a tiered, hierarchical system of courts and councils, which is designed to offer this 'superiority without tyranny'. In addressing this, it addresses a perennial political problem, which is not so different in form, whether it is within the church or within wider civil and political society: how to unite, represent and involve people in governance.

Marianne Wolfe puts it succinctly: 'Each governing body makes its decisions by majority vote, the representatives of the larger part of the church having the power of review over governing bodies representing a smaller part of the church.'[16] The weighting and calibration of the system has changed in different places and at different times, but these family resemblances have persisted. The power of review is the presbyterian form of *episkope* or oversight,

---

14 Article on Donald MacLeod's website, published 6 April 2015: www.donald macleod.org/?p=483.

15 Quotation from Alexander Henderson's 1641 *Notes on the Government and Order of the Church of Scotland*, via www.freescotcoll.ac.uk/images/files/Classics /Hendersongovernmentandchurchorder.pdf.

16 In McKim, 1992, p. 283.

which is exercised communally by the courts and their representatives, not in a personal form by a bishop.

Because of the cultural critique of presbyterianism which has grown up in Scotland – think of Alan Jackson: 'O Knox he was a bad man, he split the Scottish mind, one half he made cruel, the other half unkind', or Tom Nairn, paraphrasing Diderot: 'Scotland will be reborn when the last Church of Scotland minister is strangled with the last copy of the Sunda y Post' – references like Henderson's to 'the genius of presbyterian polity' have become rare things. We are more likely to encounter or maybe even to demonstrate a grumpy Monty Pythonesque, 'What did the presbyterians ever do for us?'

So let me ask you – what did the presbyterians ever do for us? It's not a rhetorical question. If we ask the question seriously, we will find we get some very mixed answers. We will find ourselves with mixed feelings:

- We will recover the memory that presbyterianism was seen as subversive of monarchy and episcopacy and hierarchy – because it was.
- We will recover the memory that presbyterianism was a powerful political model which influenced the design of secular political systems and constitutions, not least, via John Witherspoon and others, the federal constitution of the USA.
- We will recover the memory of a federal system which aimed to represent diversity while maintaining unity, which created checks and balances to resist institutional bullying.
- We will recover the memory of a parliamentary system – the attempt to create a place for hope out of the violence of sixteenth- and seventeenth-century societies – to create forums where talking and deliberation would be an alternative to violence and schism.
- We will recover the memory of a law-governed system, where rules could empower the weak and restrain the powerful, where people had a right to vote and learned to use it.
- We will recover the memory of an assembly which, from 1707 to 1999, functioned in some ways as a surrogate Scottish Parliament.

If that seems like a rather romantic account of presbyterianism, perhaps that is no bad thing. I have been reflecting this week on some of the cultural lessons from Brexit and the first days of a Trump presidency – if we have no love for our institutions, if we simply ironise and denigrate them, we will not value and maintain them and we will not have the patience or the heart to do the work of reforming them.

On the less romantic side: if we ask what presbyterianism did for us and for Scotland:

- We will also recover the memory of an institution whose governance was monopolised by men for 400 years.
- We will recover the memory of an institution whose desire for godly discipline too often became prurient and Pharisaical.
- We will recover the memory of an institution which at its worst approved statements which were racist and sectarian.
- We will recover the memory of an institution which could be punitive towards rebels or dissenters.
- We will recover the memory of an institution which developed a cultural reputation for being formalist, miserabilist and Philistine. (The phrase 'joyless presbyterian' comes to mind more easily than presbyterian party planner.)

We will also recover the memory of an institution which contained elements of both representative democracy and participatory democracy, but in which the representative element has always been stronger. In his 1954 book, *Presbyterianism*, the Scottish scholar G. D. Henderson notes that 'Calvin would have called his system aristocratic and representation does develop rather an aristocratic principle of government.'[17]

And we will recover the memory of an institution which, while it could empower people by asking a lot of their participation, could also exhaust and overwhelm them and come to seem remote from them, particularly as its central bureaucracy began to grow from the middle of the nineteenth century onwards. To quote

---

17 Henderson, 1954, p. 61.

Henderson again 'It may be that Presbyterianism asked too much and gave too little . . .'[18]

With an eye to thinking about reform, I want to finish by reflecting on those last two points. If, as Henderson suggests, the elders and ministers, the presbyters, were presbyterianism's aristocrats, perhaps the role of the congregation is one of the key deficits within the evolution of Scottish presbyterianism. For too long, 'congregationalism' has been used as a kind of foil against which presbyterians have defined their own polity. In the Church of Scotland, the 'aristocratic' character of traditional representative presbyterianism has meant that a certain pride is taken in emphasising Cox's statement that, 'The Kirk Session is not answerable to the congregation but only to superior courts.'[19] Even today, on the floor of the General Assembly, a proposal may be effectively resisted on the grounds that it is taking us down the slippery slope to congregationalism. The downside to this way of defining presbyterianism is a failure to see the extent to which it has led to an overly negative construal of the role of the congregation and a reluctance to grant it any additional and significant powers. A failure perhaps to trust it with enough freedom or to give it enough responsibility.

My last point relates to the remark, which I confess to having been haunted by since I read it, 'It may be that presbyterianism asked too much and gave too little.' Henderson makes the comment when discussing how in the USA, presbyterianism was overtaken in the westward movement by the new frontier-friendly traditions of the Baptists and Methodists – which seemed to give more in terms of experience and ask less in terms of bureaucracy.

So I end by wondering aloud about two things. People in Scotland today have embarked in increasing numbers upon an unprecedented cultural experiment – the attempt to make sense of their lives without religion. Secularisation is built on the promise that we will find other ways to celebrate, to cope with suffering and death, to confront evil and to find meaning in the daily

---

18 Henderson, 1954, p. 154.
19 Cox, J. *Practice and Procedure in the Church of Scotland*, quoted in Wolfe and Pickford, 1980, p. 35.

rhythms of life – other ways apart from religion, which will bring us greater fullness of life. I am personally very doubtful about its ability to make good on that promise. So we should watch this space – this immanent frame.

But we also need to ask this – What kind of witness have we given to fullness of life in Christ? Why have we been declining faster than almost any other church in the UK? Have we asked too much and given too little? And if so, are there ways in which we are being called to reform our life and work, which might help to change that?

Next week I will focus on Money and Ministry, looking at both ministers and elders

On 15 February in the final lecture, I will focus on presbyteries and councils – looking at the federal balance of the church as a whole.

Thank you so much for your time and attention.

Lecture 2: Call and Response
St Giles' Cathedral, 8 February 2017

Tonight I want to take further a discussion of missional refocusing and institutional reform, and in particular I want to look at questions of ministry and money.

I have given this the title 'Call and Response' because I want to reflect on the importance of context for the development of theology, for the shaping of the church and for the ordering of ministry.

One of the definitions of culture offered by the anthropologist Clifford Geertz is that it is the ensemble, the set of stories, that we tell ourselves about ourselves. The dialogue with our history as a church is key to these lectures, because out of it come the stories we tell ourselves about ourselves.

Presbyterianism has been shaped by the different historical, geographical and cultural contexts in which it has existed, so that although it describes a family resemblance between churches, it is not only one thing. Within those different contexts, the church has had to try to hear God's call and to respond to it faithfully.

A prophetic church, a missional church, lives in the space and in the rhythm of call and response – a rhythm which is basic to the church's life. It is gathered in worship as the *ekklesia* and sent in mission as the church apostolic.

The critical thing for the church in changing contexts is to discern what it may not or should not change and what it may or must change in order to be faithful to its Lord.

If we begin with the call which was heard 500 years ago. The sixteenth-century reformers were prepared, for the sake of the mission of God, to reshape the church and to reorder its ministry, so they introduced reforms:

- They left behind the ideal of a celibate priesthood and they affirmed that ministers of the gospel could be married.
- They left behind the insistence on episcopal ordination and they affirmed that a church which was faithful to the gospel of Jesus Christ, to the apostolic witness, could create a new pattern of ordination for ministers.
- They left behind the idea of a hierarchical and episcopal structure of church government and they created a new form of government for the church, in which ordained ministers and what Calvin and Knox came to call 'elders' would share in governance together.
- They bound themselves into a national church, through a federal system of tiered courts, in which both ministers and elders would be represented at every level.

There is a big story, then, to tell about the sixteenth century. It includes a strong reaffirmation of the distinct office of the pastor, reserving to it the ministry of word and sacrament. It includes clear moves towards a rejection of bishops, although there was some flexibility about the use of regional superintendents – a sign that the early reformers could see value in some of the functions of that office, but they wanted to give it a different character and status.

It also includes the introduction of elders and deacons – initially, in the *First Book of Discipline*, these are to be appointed annually by 'common and free election'. On a night when we are going to be thinking about money, some of you may be inspired by the touching provision 'that the deacons, treasurers, be not compelled to receive the office again for the space of three years'. These elders and deacons shared in the governance of the church alongside the pastors, but for now they were not ordained.

By the time of the *Second Book of Discipline* in 1578, thinking about eldership had changed: as an office it included pastors and doctors, but it was also used to apply to those 'whom the apostles call presidents or governors'. Three new things were now being stressed: that this was a spiritual office, that those who entered it must be called to it through election and ordination (election here by the judgement of the eldership and the consent of the congregation) and strikingly, 'Elders once lawfully called to the office, and having gifts of God meet to exercise the same, may not leave it again.'

In the seventeenth century, the rhythms of call and response led us into protracted and bloody struggles over the role of the monarch, the role of bishops, the shape and content of liturgy, and the freedom of the church to call Assemblies.

In the 1640s, against the backdrop of civil war, the Westminster Assembly was summoned with the aim of reforming the Church of England. The ironies here are well known that while it had little influence in England, its documents or standards have played a crucial role in the Church of Scotland. If ever there was an example of contextual theology, the Westminster standards give it to us, with all kinds of theological disputes and tensions hovering behind tightly worded and fiercely negotiated paragraphs. Sometimes, where there was no agreement, an option is given – other times, a matter is simply passed over in silence. Interestingly, the ordination of elders is one of those areas, though it does not command enough support in the Westminster negotiations to make it into the final text of the *Form of Church Government*.

In the eighteenth and nineteenth centuries, some within the Church of Scotland felt the call of God to affirm the spiritual independence of the church and to uphold the rights of congregations to call a minister, over against the operation of patronage by landowners and others. Thomas Chalmers, for whom these lectures are named, responded by leaving to form a new presbyterian denomination. Others felt the call to stay and work out the issues within the old church.

For those who felt the call to leave, their response was to build a new rival and parallel presbyterian establishment from the ground up – as Henry Sefton once said, 'the seceders planted strategically, the Free Church planted competitively'.

Historical and economic context matters here also: at the height of the British Empire, this response, which took the form of a competitive fever of church building, was financed by the profits of Victorian industry – leading often to monumental church buildings glowering at each other across high streets in Scotland's towns and cities.

But after all the drama and all the sacrifice and all the reassertion, only four years after the Disruption, the Secession Churches felt the call to reunite and most responded by forming the United Presbyterian Church. Within a generation that same call to be one was heard again, and in 1900 most of the Free Church united with most of the United Presbyterians. The United Free and the Auld Kirk then eyed one another suspiciously. While theologians and ministers debated what the next move should be, waiting to see who would blink first and what they might concede, the enormous, devastating slaughter of the First World War came and went – churches which began the war in brash patriotism ended it in sorrowful humility.

The subsequent negotiations were still difficult and fractious, but in time they led to the 'glorious' union of 1929 when most of the United Free Church was reunited with the Old Kirk. Among the gifts the United Free Church came bearing were the newly merged sustentation and augmentation funds, the bureaucratic culture which had been created to build a centrally funded, national denomination from scratch, the offices at 121 George Street and, of course, the Chalmers Lectureship.

A powerful legacy of both world wars, was the impetus they gave to the ecumenical movement – in a bitterly divided world, there was a passionate sense that the churches needed to be a sign of unity. From the 1930s, the Church of Scotland began conversations with the Church of England, and also with the Presbyterian Church in England and the Scottish Episcopal Church.

In the 1950s, one fruit of these conversations, in which T. F. Torrance played a prominent role after the Second World War, would be the so-called Bishops' Report, which was rejected by the General Assembly in 1959.

Despite the church's ecumenical resolve in 1954 to seek closer relations with other churches, it was not possible to fully resolve theological differences over church government and the ordering of ministry either in 1959 or a generation later, when the Scottish Churches Initiative for Union or SCIFU was rejected by the General Assembly in 2003.

In 1964 and then in 1968 – while many within the Church of Scotland had heard this call from God for a long time – the church finally responded and took the decision to open first the eldership, then the ministry of word and sacrament to women on the same basis as men.

Context matters. As we look back on past controversies, we can see how it matters profoundly to the church's hermeneutics – its interpretation and understanding of scripture. And yet, all any generation can ever do, is to walk by the light they have and pray for more light. All we can do is to try and ask what God is calling us to in our time and how we should respond.

For both of tonight's issues, ministry and money, the stories we tell ourselves about our own history are profoundly important, but so is our own context.

Ministry

The conversation about introducing reform to the ordered ministries of the church has, for the past 70 years, been dominated by ecumenical concerns. While I have a strong commitment to ecumenism, I believe this conversation now needs to change direction.

Our debates about reforming ministry have been shaped by the inhibitions of the ecumenism of late Christendom; they now need to be decisively shaped by the missiology of post-Christendom.

I do not believe that Christian witness to the gospel in Scotland has suffered greatly in the twentieth and twenty-first-centuries, from the existence alongside one another of the Scottish Episcopal Church and the Church of Scotland; nor do I believe that there are too many parishes today where organic union would lead to a greater missional synergy or effectiveness.

What has been damaging to our witness are the older sectarian divisions within Scottish society between Protestants and Roman Catholics; and in some communities, the divisions between the Kirk and the smaller conservative presbyterian denominations, all of which oppose the ordination of women.

I do not believe that either of those more damaging examples is fixable in relation to full recognition of ministry in the fore-seeable future. We are decades away from the Roman Catholic Church ordaining women, if it ever does. We are also, I suspect, decades away from the Free Church doing it, if it ever does. What we can hope for, in both of these very different cases, is as much friendly, peaceable co-operation and as many positive alliances on key issues as we can healthily achieve.

Relationships between the Kirk, the URC and Methodists in Scotland are good – there are few real barriers to joint working, to setting up LEPs or even to union, although there seem to be few felt incentives either. If there are people around in the Kirk who believe that SCIFU would have released and resourced new and dynamic energies for mission within Scotland, they have been very quiet over the past decade or so.

My sense is rather that there were too many unfinished conversations going on within our own denominations – we have needed to allow these to develop organically and see where they would lead.

If we had voted for SCIFU, we would be on a different course. But we did not, and in the end neither did the Scottish Episcopal Church. Sheilagh Kesting has commented that this was seen as yesterday's 'top down' model of ecumenism adding, 'It is unlikely that there will be further talks of this nature in Scotland for the foreseeable future.'

I want to suggest, therefore, that the call to us today is to move away from the inhibitions of late-Christendom ecumenism and embrace the imperatives of post-Christendom missiology. My thinking here has been influenced by the work of Jürgen Moltmann in his 1977 book *The Church in the Power of the Holy Spirit* – a book which has not always been very popular, perhaps because it was ahead of its time. Moltmann draws what I think is a useful distinction between the *charges* given to the church, which do not change – to preach the gospel, to make disciples and to celebrate the sacraments – and the *assignments* made within the church, which he believes are historically variable, and which can vary in different missional contexts.

This is an area where we still have theological work to do. We have, I think, inherited an understanding of ordination which is too rigid, too singular and too compressed – there are some very real tensions between the New Testament witness to a diversity of ministries within the body and the way we compress so many of these into a single office. I think our understanding of *ordination* is too restrictive and our understanding of *commissioning* is too weak and too underdeveloped.

We are already painfully short of ministers and we will soon be dangerously short of ministers. As I said last week, I am both aware of and excited by the opportunities which can come from a less minister-centred church, but I am also very aware of the threats.

It is irresponsible, even when well intentioned, to exaggerate the speed and ease with which an institution like the Kirk can make the transition to radically different models of ministry. Both unity and continuity are hugely important to making such a transition.

So, the call I am hearing in our context is not to go full steam ahead for a radical dismantling of current structures of ministry – it is not even to go as far as my own convictions might allow me to go – but it is to go further than we have gone until now, seeking to find a way forward that will not divide or destabilise the church and will not leave our existing ministers and elders feeling alienated or devalued.

The future of eldership

To turn to the eldership first, the ecumenical issues I raised earlier are less significant here. Ecumenical documents are usually polite about the eldership, but nobody else really understands what we are on about and certainly not why we ordain elders. That is not entirely surprising – my colleague Sandy Forsyth has written a superb paper on the history and theology of eldership which you can download from the church's website. We have already noted how 1560 said one thing, 1578 said another, while 1645 rowed back a bit – from the sixteenth century onwards, one strand of reformed theology and even of presbyterian theology, has clearly not believed we should ordain elders. T. F. Torrance of course stood in that tradition, while another strand has defended this practice.

What is also clear is that, in recent years when proposals to reform the eldership have been brought before the church, they have not won support. My sense of why that has been is that our elders – who do so much of the gracious working, the faithful caring, the heavy lifting and who take with great seriousness that they are ordained to a spiritual office – have felt such proposals to represent a devaluing of their ministry, which would also move the balance between minister and elders in the wrong direction.

I hear that. At the same time, I believe that we urgently need more flexibility within our system. We very much need a new generation of younger people to become elders between now and 2030, and I know that for significant numbers of people the prospect of being permanently ordained into a lifelong office which 'they may not leave again' is something they find offputting.

The third chapter of *The Second Book of Discipline* begins like this: 'Vocation or calling is common to all that should bear office within the kirk.' I believe that a way forward may be for us not to overturn our existing traditions, but to add to them. What if we continued to think of the eldership as a single office within the church, but we affirmed that there were different ways to be called into it?

Some might enter the office as elders do now and have done for hundreds of years, through ordination to a ministry which they understand as a permanent and lifelong vocation. Others might enter the office in a new way, elected as Commissioned Elders, who would serve for a period of three years, after which they could step down; or if there was mutual agreement, they could serve again for a further term.

Those who were experiencing a call to serve as elders could discern, with their minister and other elders, which of these they believed they were called to. There would be no other difference in status or function. This would allow a gracious flow of change to take place, without conflict or compulsion, without injuring the calling or status of existing elders and without preventing others from being ordained in the future. At the same time it would open our Sessions to full participation by those for whom commissioning for three years feels like a more natural and appropriate way to fulfil their spiritual calling.

Ministers

I want to move on to ministers. We urgently need to address the growing shortage of ministers. There are really only four ways of doing that:

1 Recruit more ministers.
2 Reduce the number of charges.
3 Add new forms of ministry.
4 Introduce greater flexibility around ministerial assignments.

I now want to explore each of these in turn.

Recruit more ministers

The area of vocations or recruitment is one on which some important research has been done by Catherine Skinner. Her conclusion was that between the 1990s and the early 2010s not enough work was done on nurturing and supporting vocations, at a time when other trends were reducing the pool of likely candidates. The excellent 'Tomorrow's Calling' initiative has been informed by that – I believe we need to support it and we need to work on a number of other initiatives to increase numbers:

1 First of all, through 'Tomorrow's Calling' we need better communication and support for vocations.

2 We also need a clearer and more generous package of financial support for candidates, many of whom have to make real sacrifices to go and study.

3 In addition I want to suggest that we consider three targeted initiatives to help address supply in the next few years:

a *Give us ten*

Recognising the age weighting within our church membership, we should consider making a specific appeal to some of our members to consider taking early retirement and to give us the last ten years of their working lives. In support of this, we would set aside money from reserves which could be used by agreement to compensate for pension losses they might occur.

b *Give us five*

We should consider making a formal approach to the PCUSA, which is well supplied with ministers and ordinands just now, to develop an initiative for ministers from the USA to come and serve in Scotland for five years, with a programme of induction and support.

c *A woman's place*

We should make a fresh appeal within 'Tomorrow's Calling' to women, who are still under-represented in our ministry, emphasising how much their gifts and experience are needed and welcomed in the ministry – as they say these days, a woman's place is in the White House, is in the resistance and is in the ministry.

4 Finally, still on recruiting more ministers – I have argued for some years that, like the Church of England and the Methodist Church, we need a new pathway to candidate directly for Pioneer ministry, linked to a national strategy for church planting between now and 2030.

Reduce the number of charges

Taking initiatives to reduce the number of parishes has been one major way in which the Kirk has addressed the shortage of ministers as well as responding to the oversupply of churches

which was a legacy of the Secessions and the Disruption. A programme of union and readjustment over many years has been
replaced in recent years by the Presbytery Planning process. This
has undoubtedly been part of the pain of decline – people form
strong attachments to the churches in which they were baptised,
or married, where family funerals have taken place. These attachments die hard. Some unions are a model of grace and mutual
care – others are resisted, resented and finally boycotted by those
who feel that their church has been taken away from them. The
last round of presbytery planning was driven not by a shortage of
money but by a concern to spread ministers across all of Scotland's
parishes in a relatively just and even-handed way. This meant a
distribution of ministerial posts per presbytery being agreed by
General Assembly and implemented by presbyteries. It was difficult to do and it was painful for those who felt they lost out. In
fact, it was so painful and so difficult that few seem to feel the
church has the stomach to do it again in the same form, despite
the situation which called for it continuing to worsen.

Last year in their report Ministries Council floated the idea of
ministry 'Hubs', making clear the idea was still at a formative
stage. The key difference from the previous presbytery planning
model seems to be the promise of linking more, while uniting and
closing less. This addresses the original problem not by solving it,
but by making it change shape and also, potentially, by making
the role of the minister change shape. The only way Hubs can be
effective in addressing the question of shortage is to make more
stipendiary ministers into 'team vicars' with charge of a group of
parishes. Although Hubs give with one hand, they take away with
the other – but this time round, we may want what they can give
and be prepared to adjust to what they take away.

Add new forms of ministry

A third way to address a declining supply of ordained ministers
is to create more of them by other means. This is a major route
which the Church of England has embraced, reflecting the fact
that the pattern of a weekly parish Communion is now normative,

unlike the Kirk, in which quarterly Communions remain common. In order for the normal pattern of Anglican worship to continue as numbers of stipendiary clergy fell, it has been necessary to provide a new supply of Eucharistic presidents, and this has been achieved through very significant increases in the numbers of 'Self-Supporting Ministers' and 'Ordained Local Ministers'. Of the 28,000 licensed ministers in the Church of England, 65 per cent do not receive any stipend and 30 per cent of parish clergy are non-stipendiary.

This stands in stark contrast to the Church of Scotland. Neither Auxiliary Ministry, nor the newer Ordained Local Ministry programmes have been anything like as successful as these Church of England schemes in drawing in new ministers. Within the Kirk, these seem to be suffering the same fate as the stipendiary ministry, in failing to attract enough new candidates, although we can hope that 'Tomorrow's Calling' may be of help here as well.

Introduce greater flexibility around ministerial assignments

The final way to address a crisis in the supply of ministers is to think more flexibly about the nature of ordination itself. This is an option which in the past has struggled to gain support for two main reasons. The first is the ecumenical caution I discussed earlier, about making it harder to achieve some future mutual recognition of ministries. The second is a concern, particularly on the part of ministers, that this might somehow undervalue their role and their formation for that role.

I believe the time is right for the Church of Scotland to change tack on this question and to introduce provisions to allow elders to assume new responsibilities. If we compare ourselves to other sections of the Reformed family of churches, this is not such a drastic step to imagine ourselves taking. We would be joining the United Reformed Church and the PCUSA if we enabled presbyteries to authorise suitably trained and experienced elders (who could be commissioned or ordained elders in terms of the suggestion made above) to preach, baptise and preside at

Communion. The question of what to call them I will leave as an open one. The PCUSA calls them Commissioned Ruling Elders, having previously called them Commissioned Lay Pastors.[20] I find that terminology on the clunky side, although I agree with moving away from the language of 'lay' which does not belong in the Reformed tradition. The word 'pastor' is a friendlier term but if, as I have already proposed, we were embracing and developing a more expansive theology of commissioning, we might prefer to opt for Commissioned Local Minister (CLM) to sit alongside OLM. In the PCUSA, they are commissioned for up to three years at a time and can conduct worship, including sacraments, weddings and funerals – working, as OLMs do, under the oversight of an ordained minister. They could work either in a vacant charge or alongside an existing minister within their congregation. If we followed the US model, then CLMs could also be paid.

If we were convinced that we could justify this theologically, there would still be the concerns of existing ministers to address, and there are various ways in which this could be done. Commissioning would be local and time-limited; commissioned ministries would be subject to oversight from ordained ministries (which is how they might work in a Hub anyway); CLMs, if paid, could be paid less than ordained ministers (although I have some reservations about that) and they could have stricter requirements for ongoing CME and training.

In that way we could maintain the distinction between this ministry and ordained stipendiary ministry, the potential erosion of which has worried many ministers. However, as with OLM, I think we would also want to create pathways from CLM to OLM or to nationally recognised ordained ministry – in some cases, this would prove to be a way of people discerning such a calling.

I recognise that some will have theological and ecumenical concerns about this change. But I want to stress I am not asking the Church of Scotland to row dangerously far away from its ecumenical moorings – if we row out into this part of the river, we will be moving alongside the PCUSA, the URC, the Methodist Church,

---

20 http://oga.pcusa.org/section/mid-council-ministries/clp/.

the Scottish Baptist Union – all of whom allow this already in some form.

I am referring to very few people by name in these lectures – however, at this point I do want to mention Iain Torrance (and I feel I can say this because he knows how much esteem and respect I have for him) he really is a renowned theologian,[21] unlike myself, who is more of a jobbing theologian – I think he spoke too soon when he responded to this issue at Assembly.[22] If I can throw out a wee challenge, I hope he and the Theological Forum will consider how this question relates, not just to a late-Christendom ecumenism, but to a post-Christendom missiology.

I said there were four ways in which we could act as a church to address a potentially destabilising decline in the number of ministers, and I have now discussed each of them. So which should we pursue? For me the answer is very clear – that we will need to pursue all of them. None of them on their own is likely to be enough. Not only that, but all of them are only ways to work on a broader and even more important ministry objective – which is the one set out in Ephesians 4.12: to equip the saints for the work of ministry, for building up the body of Christ.

Money

In the final section of tonight's lecture, I want to offer some thoughts about money and reform.

There is a long and complicated historical story to tell ourselves about the Kirk and money, one which includes teinds and glebes, heritors and patronage, the establishment principle and the rise of voluntarism – I will address this in more detail in the book. The nineteenth century saw crucial changes. When he came to believe Disruption was inevitable, Chalmers set about preparing financially for the task of building a new denomination from the

---

21 This was a reference to the Church of Scotland pre-publicity for the lectures, where press releases had (over) described me as a 'renowned theologian'.

22 Professor Torrance had been discouraging about such a proposal on the floor of GA 2016 in response to a question from a commissioner.

ground up. Soon there were three contrasting presbyterian financial cultures – alongside the older establishment expectations of state, heritor and teind support in the Old Kirk, two new voluntarist models were in operation: the UP Church operated an *augmentation* fund while the Free Church established a *sustentation* fund. The first topped up local funds from a central pot, the second gathered funds locally, sent them to a central pot and redistributed them to local congregations.[23]

As these various presbyterian establishments grew and then merged, the sustentation model prevailed alongside the traces of establishment support. The whole post-1929 church then worked with a system which was introduced as a response to a particular historical call and context – that of building a new national denomination from scratch. So my former teacher, the late Douglas Murray once commented:

It was in the later 19th century that there was an increase in the centralised bureaucracy of the Kirk. The Free Church in particular had to raise its own funds and this led to a more centralised structure and power tending towards the Assembly Committees and their Conveners. The '121' syndrome is very much a Free Church phenomenon.

By contrast, the churches which would come together to form the PCUSA have stayed with a less centralised system and one which overall was more Darwinian. For them there was and still is strong emphasis on local responsibility to raise money to pay the stipend. With that comes flexibility about how much ministers are paid and about how many people the congregation can employ locally. Once again, I make the point that there are different ways to be presbyterian.

Today in the Church of Scotland we have a financial system which is strong on solidarity and central control. That has its strengths. For one thing, you could argue that it has worked reasonably well. We are not broke. In fact, congregational giving

---

23 Gibson, 1961, p. 43.

has held up remarkably well in recent years, despite the decline in membership.

The 64 thousand dollar question – or closer to $64 million in the case of our annual Ministries and Mission figure – is whether this highly centralised system, with its rather rigid mechanisms for administering solidarity, is the one best suited to the new context we find ourselves in.

I will admit to being disappointed at General Assembly 2016, that the high-level working group reviewing the Kirk's financial systems for the Council of Assembly, recommended virtually no change to present arrangements. The Council of Assembly report is clear why this was done: because for now, income is still holding up well and to embark on change seemed to be to introduce too much risk.[24] The danger is that this is a missed opportunity. We need a persuasive vision for the future of the system as well as a sober assessment of its present. I am not sure that this recent review took enough account of the risks posed by how congregations are feeling in the wake of presbytery planning and how they will react to a future which includes more and longer vacancies.

While there is real commitment to the principles of financial solidarity which must be present in a presbyterian system, there is also disquiet and discontent across the church. I want to reflect on where I think the current system stands in need of change:

1 While properly reflecting solidarity with the poorest congregations in the poorest areas, the current formula for weighting resources to priority congregations does not seem sustainable – it needs to be revised – and we need to develop new ways of expressing that solidarity which are less damaging to other parts of the church.

2 The attempt to remove stigma from congregations being 'aid-receiving' has weakened a proper and healthy sense of aspiration to become self-sustaining.

3 Although the current system is simple to operate, it is uninspiring and unimaginative – it contains too few incentives and offers too little flexibility.

---

24 RGA, 2016.

4 There is suppressed liberality within the system; many people wish to give for local ministry and mission, but feel that too much of their money will be skimmed by the wider church; while this does raise some concerns, I think we are too mistrustful of this.

5 Vacancy allowances need to be increased, particularly where those vacancies are prolonged or where they have become guardianships; there are limits to how far fewer people will go on paying more to have less.

6 Some churches are so alienated from current arrangements that they are sheltering money from assessment – this is not a healthy way to protest the system.

7 As well as showing solidarity with the poorest, we also urgently need to support larger churches and help them to grow. We need our strongest churches to get stronger – they have crucial gifts to bring to the denomination as a whole.

8 We need to consider whether some expressions of solidarity should be invited in the form of a pledge, rather than imposed in the form of a tax.

9 We need to stop micro-managing so much of congregational spend on fabric at presbytery level. You really don't need me to vote on the budget for your new kitchen units – it's disempowering to congregations and a waste of everyone's time.

Devising new formulas for congregational assessment is a process fraught with difficulty. It is essential but not interesting, vital but not enlivening, strategic but not sexy. As is the case with any kind of tax policy, it requires an alchemy of technical skills, psychological understanding, theological/ethical integrity and creative instinct. In thinking about this, my mind has often returned to the parable of the dishonest steward in Luke 16. This process calls for 'design' skills, to build new formulas around memorable images and ideas, to strike a balance between simplicity and adaptability, to strike a balance between positing ideals and anticipating behaviours. It has to minimise the resentments of the poorest and the richest. And it has to work. The formulas have to raise enough money to meet existing commitments, to pay salaries and provide for pensions. They have to maintain responsibility and incentivise liberality. Small wonder, when the system seems to be coping under pressure, that we have been cautious about changing it. We are mindful of the medical maxim – to first Do No Harm.

Devising new ways forward must be a collective task. I would like to see a phase in which we do some more creative and exploratory work on a new funding formula – when we generate ideas and discuss options. Here I can only offer a few tentative thoughts as a contribution to that work.

The funding formula should have a nominal *floor* and *ceiling* to it.

- The floor should relate to the basic cost of parish ministry, currently around £50,000 for a full-time post and should represent a healthy aspiration and challenge for as many congregations as possible to become self-supporting.
- The ceiling should act as a maximum figure for assessed contributions from wealthier congregations and might be set at £100,000. The decision to leave more money with these congregations would reflect a judgement that the whole Kirk would benefit from encouraging such congregations to grow further. It would be part of a deliberate institutional strategy to support the development of a greater number of larger churches.
- A ceiling would have the effect of reducing the funds available for subsidy, so it would be necessary to draw more congregations towards being self-sustaining, as well as possibly creating new pledged funds, as a means to maintain sharing and solidarity.

Congregations must be supported where necessary, but should also be incentivised where possible. A missional refocusing might encourage us to think more creatively about where our own congregations fit within the financial ecology of our church.

Some congregations are Solidarity Congregations. We must continue to make a core commitment to fund ministry within our poorest congregations, but in ways which do not take so many ministry posts from a limited pool. Above and beyond the core commitment, we need routes to additional funding via dedicated solidarity funds held at national and presbytery levels.

Some might best be seen as Development Congregations. Some congregations may respond best to working with a match-funding formula, which could be geared differently for different circumstances. For some congregations which are able to cover their core costs and make a contribution to supporting ministry and mission elsewhere, a key incentive may be the knowledge that, having reached an agreed figure, they retain any additional money for local use.

We could imagine a range of Self-Sustaining Congregations/ Contributor Congregations/Invester Congregations. In these three cases, for example, reaching the floor figure of £50,000, the ceiling figure of £100,000 or a midpoint between the two could mean the congregations kept 80, 90 or 95 per cent of any additional income.

These are rough-and-ready designations and rough-and-ready figures[25] – they are offered only as thought experiments, throwing my hae'pence worth into a conversation about money which I believe needs to be opened up more candidly and creatively.

Conclusion

Next week, in the final lecture, I will be reflecting on presbyteries and councils and on rebalancing the federal identity of the church. Once again, I very much appreciate your time and attention.

Lecture 3: Grand Designs
St Giles' Cathedral, 15 February 2017

In tonight's lecture, I turn to broader questions of institutional reform, though still looking at those questions through the lens of holistic mission. I will take a wide-angle looking at the federal structure of the church as a whole and the ways in which we try to keep our institutional balance across different levels of governance and organisation.

---

25 They are offered here as rough illustrations.

As with other issues that I have addressed in the lectures, the questions here are not new and nor are many of the proposals. So, much of what I will be doing is reflecting on why I think the questions still matter and why this might now be the right time for the proposed reforms.

I want to recognise from the outset that it may seem like hubris for anyone to presume to redraw the shape of the church as a whole. I am very aware of that – so the title for tonight's lecture, 'Grand Designs,' is both a joke at my own expense and a signal to you that I know how this may look.

That said, I also want to go on to make a serious point about the kind of questions we are dealing with here, a point which I think also helps to explain why previous attempts at introducing major reforms have not – in that time-honoured phrase – commended themselves to the mind of the church.

In the first lecture we looked at presbyterianism as a polity, a form of government, order, organisation for the church, which has a federal character. Federalism is sometimes seen within British political culture as a fancy European idea, which those rebel Americans took up with but which we lucky Britons blessed with an unwritten constitution have no need for. At the root of federalism is the idea of a covenant – which is of course a rich theo-logical and theo-political idea. We often stress that theologically it means something more than a contract, but when we use it in political terms or in polity terms, its meaning is not so different – it describes a relationship between different elements of a pol-ity. A federal system is a social and political contract about how to divide power and where to locate functions within a system. In particular, it lays out the relationship between the local, the regional and the national.

To spell it out then, in the Church of Scotland our Kirk Sessions are local courts overseen by presbytery, which is a regional court overseen by General Assembly, which is the highest court of the national church. We have rules which govern their relationships, which include checks and balances – a session or an individual may appeal to the General Assembly against the decision of a presbytery; a General Assembly ruling may need a majority of presbyteries to vote in favour of it under the Barrier Act. We also have rules which govern the composition of the courts: both presbytery and General Assembly have to be representative of the church geographically and they have to balance representation of ministers and elders.

For many centuries there was another tier within the system – the synod – but the 12 synods were abolished in Scotland 25 years ago this year. So we have these three tiers or levels of governance within the Kirk. We also have our central councils, as they have been known since 2004. (There are six of these – the Council of Assembly which has a co-ordinating function, then Ministries Council, Mission and Discipleship Council, Church and Society Council, the World Mission Council and the Social Care Council, known as CrossReach. Alongside these we have 27 additional committees, departments and agencies.

The first thing I want to say tonight is that, if we imagined all those who serve on those six councils and who work on their staffs, all those who oversee and service those 27 other bodies – if they were gathered in one place, I think we would want to say, we in the church are in your debt. You are muscles and sinews within the body, you are the salt of the earth and the light of the world – your work and commitment and care are precious to the church, and, we believe, precious to God.

If I worry about proposals for reform seeming presumptuous, I also worry about them seeming ungrateful. I have many friends who work at 121, whose work and witness, whose dedication, gifts and vision I admire greatly.

When we talk about reforming a system, we are not disrespecting those who work within it as it stands, and nor are we forgetting about them. What I will present tonight are only my thoughts, although they owe many debts to the work of others, in this context they have no other weight or backing – but even so, none of us should even argue for reform without realising that our thought experiment is someone else's life, job, salary, home-base, ministry and vocation.

Having said that, I am going to open up some radical options tonight. I wanted to make it clear that I do realise this is about real people and real lives, but it is also the case that in any major institutional reform of a university or a government department, of the NHS or a major charity or a private company, some things will have to be done which will prove to be very difficult for some of the individuals affected, but which are done in the hope that they will be for the good of the institution as a whole.

- *Effective institutional reform* refocuses an institution on its core mission and its core values. It reorders work and spend and time according to the priorities which flow from that mission. It does not know the price of everything and the value of nothing, it seeks to know the value of everything and to relate the price of things to their value. It is brave without being callous, bold without being reckless.
- *Ethical institutional reform* consults and cares for those affected by its actions.
- *Ecclesial institutional reform* understands that reform is a spiritual task, is prayerful; seeks to be guided and animated by the Holy Spirit, has a theology of mission and ministry at its heart. It is neither institutionally 'pelagian' – believing that it can do God's work in its own strength, through its own effort, by depending on its own strategies – nor is it institutionally 'docetic', forgetting that God works through ordinary human processes, methods, structures and strategies. It cares about the peace and unity of the church – it values the church as a community of discernment and decision. Its great motto comes from Acts 15: 'It seemed good to the Holy Spirit and to us', and it should always be haunted by 1 Corinthians 13 – the concern that if we do this without love, then we are nothing and we gain nothing.

So why do we need reform? Why does our federal identity need to be rebalanced?

- For the sake of mission.
- To support and empower congregations.
- To develop and enhance presbyteries.
- To refocus and renew central bodies.

For the sake of mission

Remembering all that was said in Lecture 1 about the *missio Dei*, about the church being the object of mission before it is a subject – about the church receiving mission before it is recruited to be part of it, we may go on to say this:

- In mission, the church stands before the world on behalf of God – not to build up its own status or position, but believing that God wants the world to know fullness of life.
- In mission, the church stands before the world in the way of Jesus Christ, believing that in Jesus, the Word made flesh, we see and know God more clearly and truly than anywhere else, that in his life and death and resurrection the world was reconciled to God and that God is making an appeal to us and then to the world through us, to be reconciled to God.
- In mission, the church stands before the world in the power of the Holy Spirit – believing that the Spirit's life is renewing our life and is the power of God's life and love at work in the world.

As women and men are called to be reconciled to God, to find fullness of life in God, we believe they are called into that same rhythm which is the heartbeat of the church's life – being called together in worship and sent in mission – in worship where Jesus is named as Lord and in mission where Jesus is proclaimed as Saviour, as Liberator, as Friend, in both word and in deed.

We want our churches to grow, not out of vanity or insecurity, but because we want to see as many people as possible find meaning and hope through their faith in God and find a community and family of faith which can be home to them.

We recognise the mystery of God's sovereignty, but we also recognise our calling to be witnesses – witnesses to what we know of God's truth, to what we can show of God's love. Witnesses to the mercy, to the grace, to the justice, to the beauty of God.

So we want our churches, in those poignant words of John Bell's hymn, to be places where 'Christ makes with his friends a touching place'. Where people can be in touch with the love and mercy of God.

Bill Hybels has said powerfully that the local church is the hope of the world. This is a vision for Aberfeldy and Uist, Kirkwall and Castle Douglas, Bearsden and Whitfield, Renfrew and the Raploch – that congregations of the Kirk, for all of their limitations and faults, can be touching places, can be places of hope.

And, yes, why would we not say this – a vision that they can be that for as many people as possible. And be that in spiritual and ecumenical partnership with everyone else in those places who shows the true face of the Kirk.

I know there are Christians in Scotland who believe that God is finished with the Church of Scotland, or at least is finished blessing it and blessing Scotland through it. But I don't believe that. At least not yet . . . What comes first is the integrity of our witness, because we understand throughout history there have been successful churches that were not faithful and faithful churches that were not successful.

But as we try by the grace of God to bear witness faithfully, a second faithful and heartfelt concern may be that we long to see our congregations grow and as they grow, be salt and light, be communities which bless and enrich the parishes they are called to serve.

Reform is for the sake of mission – and it is a demanding task. There are no books out there on how to undertake the successful reform of a presbyterian church. What examples there are come from other contexts, where the choices made may have been right for them, but might not be right for us.

What makes this a demanding task is that it has to help us to do five things. In the years between now and 2030, we will have to:

- close unsustainable churches;
- manage declining churches;
- enable declining churches to grow again;
- support growing churches in their development;
- plant new churches and replant some we have had to close.

The work of doing those five things simultaneously presents a huge challenge for us over the next 13 years. With this challenge comes the question of whether our institutional structures are ordered as well as they can be to support this work. There are no definite answers to that question. It is a judgement call, a strategic judgement for us to make together as a church – we don't get to test it in advance in the lab and we won't get to see the counterfactual scenario afterwards. But that's true of most things in life.

Why do I think we should consider radical change? There is one overriding reason: *we need to offer more effective support to the witness of local congregations.* For me, that is the decisive concern of reform. It was, of course, the key concern behind the 2001 *Church Without Walls* report. So we need to ask if a programme of reform could help us to do this.

When that is put into a wider institutional context, I think it points to one other conclusion: *the key level at which this support has to be delivered is the presbytery.* So the question about supporting local congregations is also a question about making presbyteries work.

It is intrinsic to a federal structure that it works as a system, which is why, although it might seem like hubris to talk of reforming the system as a whole, in fact it is the only way to do it. If you don't adjust both central councils and regional presbyteries simultaneously, you almost by definition end up making it impossible to properly reform them separately. I think it is hard to draw any other conclusion from the 2001 *Church Without Walls* report, the 2001 *Tomorrow's Presbyteries* report, the 2006 Structure and Change Commission, the 2011 *Review and Reform* report – if you sit down and read them together, this point is made in every one of them.

Since 1975, we have had 46-2[26] Scottish presbyteries, which vary in size from well over 100 to fewer than ten charges. It's not uniform, it's not at the same level in all cases, but there is a high level of dissatisfaction across the church with how presbyteries work. Because many of them don't work particularly well at the

---

26 Three prebsyteries merged into one, so the list still goes to 46 with two numbers vacant.

moment, it's hard to imagine giving them more power or more functions, and many of them are too small to cope with that.

One significant change since 2011 is that the presbytery planning process has further exposed the pressures on congregations and has strained the bonds between some local congregations and their presbyteries.

If we approach the question from the other end, we need to consider how effectively our current system of councils works. I am completely sincere in saying that within them as they stand there are many outstanding individuals who do creative, effective and invaluable work, but I have spent the past ten years deeply unconvinced by the current division between Ministries and Mission and Discipleship in particular – I don't think it makes theological or missional sense in terms of where the church should be heading. Nor am I convinced about the articulation of the relationship between church and society and mission and discipleship, in terms of developing and enabling holistic models of witness.

I can therefore see convincing, perhaps even compelling, reasons to introduce reform, for both the regional and the central church and to rebalance the federal identity and organisation of the church.

- We need stronger missional leadership at regional level.
- We need more effective training and support at local level.
- Too much power, resource and initiative is held centrally, and not enough regionally and locally.
- The church is too bureaucratic, *it asks too much of too many to too little effect* – it has been observed by a number of commentators, including former Principal Clerk Finlay MacDonald in his 2004 book on 'a changing church',[27] that the Church of Scotland consumes too much of its members and ministers time and energy in keeping the system going. Our processes and procedures are too expansive, too exhausting and too expensive. We have too many meetings, which consume too many people hours. We pay too many sets of travel expenses and employ too many administrators to clerk and service committees.

---

27 MacDonald, 2004.

In 2016, the church's Nominations Committee reported that they had been busy preparing to fill 127 vacancies on central committees and councils to replace those who had moved on in that year, out of a total of some 493 members who comprised those bodies. That is before we add in the hours spent locally in Kirk Sessions and their sub-committees and the hours spent attending presbytery committees and working groups – and it's before our elders and ministers have ventured out to take part in ecumenical forums or community councils or be active within political parties and voluntary organisations.

- The current division of councils, along with their relative autonomy in finance and governance, perpetuates a silo mentality, which includes both competition for resources and defence of council prerogatives, with no adequate management mechanism other than the General Assembly itself, for integrating the work of different councils. The Council of Assembly has improved co-ordination, but it has never been given a true management role, and probably cannot be given it within the system as it stands.

So what should we do? I believe that there are five key structural reforms which, if enacted, could help the church to respond more effectively in fulfilling its missional calling to the people of Scotland and, crucially, to support the witness of local congregations.

1 *Presbytery reform*
  The currently existing 43 Scottish presbyteries should be reduced to 12 regional presbyteries, each of which should have a stipendiary elected Moderator holding office for a five-year term and a salaried appointed Clerk. The new presbyteries would be given substantial devolved financial responsibility for deploying and resourcing ministry within their bounds. They would be governed by a council and would meet in full presbytery (on a Saturday) two to four times a year.

2 *Council reform*
  The four main central councils should be merged into one single Church of Scotland Mission Agency, which would work with internal ministry divisions, but under a single

management structure. There would be a distinctive arrangement for CrossReach.[28] The numbers working for central councils and bodies would be reduced by around a third and new congregational support posts would be created within the new presbyteries.

3 *Central Governance Reform*

The work of the new central agency should be governed by a properly federal Council of Assembly, comprised of elder and minister representatives from each presbytery, which could include the Presbytery Moderators. A Mission Agency Secretary would lead a team of senior managers.

I want to pause here and reflect on how this rebalances our federal identity. We have traditionally been allergic to the idea of a strong central management. This suggestion would create one, but it would offset it by devolving substantial power from the centre to the presbyteries. It envisages a leaner, tighter central spine to the institution, and balances this with fewer, stronger presbyteries. For the first time, it imagines a properly federal central council, made up of presbytery representatives from across Scotland.

4 *General Assembly*

The model I am describing imagines many fewer members sitting on central councils and committees. The danger with that is of a loss of connection and participation. What offsets that, I suggest, is a continuing annual General Assembly which, of course, remains the highest court of the church. This is how we bring in a wider perspective, while easing the burden of populating councils and committees. We embrace the General Assembly as an asset, both in governance terms and as a symbolic witness which projects the identity of the church; we build on the success of Heart & Soul – which is the Kirk in festival mode.

---

28 I have nothing invested in this particular name; for convenience I am following the example of the PCUSA here, who have a single central Presbyterian Mission Agency. CrossReach has a distinctive status and should be treated separately, still under the Assembly and Agency overall, but with its own distinctive pattern of governance suited to its operational needs.

5 *Congregations*
   In line with the case made during the first lecture, the legal
   rights and functions of congregations and congregational
   meetings in relation to Kirk Sessions should be clarified and
   strengthened.

You may be wondering if I have worked out in detail all of the
anomalies, difficulties and tensions which would be created by
such a system – and the answer is of course, I haven't. For example, I have nothing invested in there being 12 presbyteries rather
than 9, 11 or 14.
   I want to add a few more notes to this grand design and then
consider one final question.

1 One thing to stress is that the full-time Presbytery Moderators
   would emphatically *not* be bishops – read my lips . . . *not bish-*
   ops. What draws me to the idea, though, is seeing how effectively some dioceses within the Church of England have begun
   to mobilise and reform themselves for mission. The Mods
   would work alongside the Rockers/new generation presbytery
   clerks, most of whom would not be ordained, who would focus
   on the managerial, financial, legal and administrative spheres.
   The key charge to the Mods would be to support mission and
   support ministers. The big question for Scots presbyterians is,
   could we bear to, and dare we try, to incorporate stronger personal ministries of initiative and support within presbyterian
   governance, while maintaining a clear emphasis on corporate
   episkope?
2 Another point to recognise is that larger presbyteries could of
   course still feel remote. Like the Panel on Review and Reform
   in 2011, my sense is that churches would still want to meet
   in more local settings, but that these would try to recover the
   original functions of presbyteries in promoting mutual encouragement and support. Business and governance would be done
   at the regional level by local representatives. Three or four local
   meetings each year could focus on training, consultation, worship and fellowship, without the burden of a business agenda.

And we would still have met on fewer occasions per year than many presbyteries do.

3   My hope for the new Mod posts and for the stronger presbyteries is that they would help us to be more strategic and creative about mission, and they would help us to get much better at resourcing and supporting ministers, deacons, readers, elders and members – to equip them for the work of ministry.

4   If there were to be a single new Mission Agency, one priority for me would be to not simply turn the existing four council domains into new ministry divisions, but to think creatively about new ways to assign work.

5   It feels to me that we are overdue a moment of refocusing, of streamlining, of simplifying – there is a kind of Victorian gothic quality to our institutional architecture. It's time to knock some solid walls down, take out some pews, put up some new glass partitions, and create some cleaner, clearer, fit-for-purpose spaces.

6   Talking of spaces – the key symbolic focus of some of what we need to move on from is the building at 121 George Street itself. If we can ever make it work in terms of stewardship, we should treat ourselves to a new beginning somewhere else. The ideal would be a building which could be built or converted to somehow be an architectural statement of the kind of holistic witness we want to offer to twenty-first-century Scotland.

I am nearly done. I may have done enough already to send you running back to George Street, to embrace the old pillars and say all is forgiven – we took a look at an alternative future and it was horrible.

In my defence, I have tried to do what I hope the church might want its academics to do – to think aloud in public, to think theologically about church practice and to speak the truth in love.

I have tried to be provocative without being annoying, to be bold without being naive, to be cautious without being timid. As I said in the first lecture – and I meant it – if these lectures have any gifts to give to the church, among them will be the gift of being wrong; hopefully in ways that can help others to be less wrong in future.

The final question – and I have tried tonight to be briefer and to leave more time for your questions and comments – but my final question is: Would it be worth it?

On the best-case scenario, it's a lot of work, a lot of hassle, a lot of upheaval – could it ever be worth the time, the energy and the angst it would take to deliver?

Some people I have interviewed for these lectures and the coming book, including some who dreamed of reform in the past, are now worried that it would not be, that it could instead be a dangerous distraction. The only way I can think to answer that is: it depends. I can think of three tests:

- Could it better enable the mission of the church?
- Does it commend itself to the mind of the church?
- Could it be done in a way which maintains the peace and unity of the church?

The Kirk, as we know, is pretty good at 'departing from matters' which it is not convinced by. It is far more important that we love one another than we improve our institutional architecture. Love covers a multitude of presbyterian sins.

We have enough that is divisive to contend with, so if we still could not find a convincing measure of agreement, that would I think be clear enough guidance to leave it alone and work well with what we have.

I said at the outset there were four great tasks in front of the Kirk – spiritual renewal, liturgical renewal, missional refocusing and institutional reform. If there is no way to progress the fourth, the other three can still be transformative.

The management guru Peter Drucker famously said that culture eats strategy. No amount of structural change, even when well conceived, will overcome a culture that does not embrace or endorse it, that does not itself commit to grow and change. But culture also *floats* strategy. Culture is, as Geertz said, the set of stories we tell ourselves, about ourselves – and it's the life those stories reflect and sustain.

I want to thank you for being so generous and patient with my storytelling over these three weeks.

Now to God who by the power at work within us is able to accomplish abundantly far more than all we can ask or imagine, to God be glory in the church and in Christ Jesus to all generations, for ever and ever. Amen.

Bibliography

Aisthorpe, S., *The Invisible Church*, Edinburgh: Saint Andrew Press, 2016.

Berger, P., *The Desecularization of the World: Resurgent Religion and World Politics*, 1999.

Beveridge, C. and Turnbull, R., *The Eclipse of Scottish Culture*, Edinburgh: Polygon, 1989.

——*Scotland After Enlightenment*, Edinburgh: Polygon, 1997.

Bliss, K., *We the People: A Theology of the Laity*, London: SCM Press, 1963.

Bosch, D. J., 'Theological Education in Missionary Perspective', in *Missiology: An International Review*, 10(1), 1982, 13–34.

——*Transforming Mission: Paradigm Shifts in Theology of Mission*, Maryknoll, NY: Orbis, 1991.

Brown, C. G., *The Death of Christian Britain* (2nd edn), London: Routledge, 2009.

——*Postmodernism for Historians*, London: Pearson Education, 2005.

——*Religion and Society in Scotland Since 1707*, Edinburgh: Edinburgh University Press, 1997.

Brown, S. J., *Becoming Atheist: Humanism and the Secular West*, London: Bloomsbury, 2017.

——*Religion and Society in 20th Century Britain*, Harlow: Pearson Education, 2006.

——'The Social Vision of Scottish Presbyterianism and the Union of 1929', *Records of the Scottish Church History Society*, 24(1), 1990, 77–96.

——*Thomas Chalmers and the Godly Commonwealth in Scotland*, Oxford: OUP, 2003.

Bruce, S., *Scottish Gods: Religion in Modern Scotland 1900–2012*, Edinburgh: Edinburgh University Press, 2014.

Brueggemann, W., *Worship in Ancient Israel: An Essential Guide*, Nashville, TN: Abingdon, 2005.

Buchan, J., *The Kirk in Scotland*, Dunbar: Labarum Publications Ltd, 1985 (Hodder and Stoughton 1930).

Burleigh, J. H. S., *A Church History of Scotland*, Edinburgh: Hope Trust, 1983.

Cencrastus 10, Edinburgh: Cencrastus/Ross, 1982.

Chapman, W. E., *History and Theology in the Book of Order*, Louisville, KY: Witherspoon Press, 1999.

Chartres, C. (ed.), *Why I Am Still an Anglican*, London: Continuum, 2011.

Craig, C., *The Scots' Crisis of Self-Confidence*, Glasgow: Big Thinking, 2003.

Davie, G, *Europe: The Exceptional Case*, London: Darton, Longman & Todd, 2002.

Dearborn, T., *Beyond Duty: A Passion for Christ, A Heart for Mission*, Marc, 1998.

Faith and Order Advisory Group of the Church of England (FOAG), *The Mission and Ministry of the Whole Church: Biblical, Theological and Contemporary Perspectives*, 2007.

Feldman, S. (ed.), *Religion and Law: A Critical Anthology*, New York: NYU Press, 2000.

Flett, J., *Apostolicity*, Downers Grove, IL: IVP, 2016.

Forrester, D. B. and Gay, D. (eds), *Worship and Liturgy in Context: Studies of Theology and Practice*, London: SCM Press, 2008.

Forsyth, A., 'The Apostolate of the Laity', unpublished PhD thesis, University of Edinburgh, 2017, at: www.era.lib.ed.ac.uk/bitstream/handle/1842/10587/Forsyth2014.pdf?sequence=2&is Allowed=y.

——'History and Theology of the Eldership', at www.churchofscotland.org.uk/__data/assets/pdf_file/0016/36124/History_and_Theology_of_the_Eldership_Paper_Dec2015.pdf.

——*The Hoe and the Sceptre*, Eugene, OR: Pickwick Publications, 2017.

Fraser, Ian, *Bible, Congregation and Community*, London: SCM, 1959.

BIBLIOGRAPHY

Ganiel, G., *Transforming Post-Catholic Ireland*, Oxford: OUP, 2016.

Gay, Douglas, 'Faith In, With and Under Gordon Brown', *International Journal of Public Theology*, November 2007.

——'Gordon Brown and his Presbyterian Moral Compass', in Scott, P. and Graham, E. (eds), *Remoralising Britain*, London: Continuum, 2009.

——*Honey From the Lion: Christianity and the Ethics of Nationalism*, London: SCM, 2014.

——*Remixing the Church: Towards an Emerging Ecclesiology*, London: SCM, 2011.

——'Scotland, Church and World', unpublished PhD thesis, University of Edinburgh, 2006.

Geertz, C., *The Interpretation of Culture*, London: Hutchinson, 1975.

Gibson, A. J. H., *Stipend in the Church of Scotland*, Edinburgh: William Blackwood and Sons, 1961.

Graham, E., *Transforming Practice*, London: Wipf & Stock, 1996.

Guder, D. L. and Barrett, Lois, *Missional Church: A Vision for the Sending of the Church in North America* (The Gospel and Our Culture Series), Grand Rapids, MI: Eerdmans, 1998.

Hauerwas, S., *In Good Company*, Notre Dame, IN: University of Notre Dame Press, 1995.

Hazlett, I. W., 'A New Version of the Scots Confession, 1560', in *Theology in Scotland*, 2010, 33–41.

Healy, N., *Church, World and the Christian Life*, Cambridge: CUP, 2000.

Heelas, P. (ed.), *The Spiritual Revolution*, Oxford: Wiley, 2005.

Henderson, G. D., *The Scottish Ruling Elder*, London: James Clarke & Co. Ltd, 1935.

——*Why We Are Presbyterians*, Aberdeen: Church of Scotland Publications, 1954.

——*Presbyterianism* (The Chalmers Lectures), Aberdeen: The University Press, 1954.

Highet, J., *The Scottish Churches: A Review of Their State 400 Years After the Reformation*, London: Skeffington, 1960.

Holmes, A. T., *All Truth is God's Truth*, Grand Rapids, MI: Eerrdmans, 1977.

Jinkins, M., *The Church Faces Death: Ecclesiology in a Post-Modern Context*, NY/Oxford: OUP, 1999.

Kärkkäinen, V-M., *An Introduction to Ecclesiology: Ecumenical, Historical and Global Perspectives*, Downers Grove, IL: InterVarsity Press, 2009.

Kernohan, R. D., *Scotland's Life and Work*, Edinburgh: Saint Andrew Press, 1979.

Kesting, S. M., 'Ecumenism in Scotland', *International Journal for the Study of the Christian Church*, 4(2), 2014.

Kraemer, H., *A Theology of the Laity*, Lutterworth: London, 1958.

Küng, Hans, *On Being a Christian*, trans. Edward Quinn, London: Collins, 1977.

Kuyper, A., 'Sphere Sovereignty', in *Abraham Kuyper: A Centennial Reader*, ed. J. D. Bratt, Grand Rapids, MI: Eerdmans, 1998.

Leeman, J., *Political Church: The Local Assembly as Embassy of Christ's Rule*, Downers Grove, IL: IVP Academic, 2016.

Lochhead, E., *Dreaming Frankenstein and Collected Poems 1967–84*, Edinburgh: Birlinn Books, 2011.

——*Liz Lochhead's Voices*, ed. R. Crawford and A. Varty, Edinburgh: Edinburgh University Press, 1993.

Louden, R. S., *The True Face of the Kirk: An Examination of the Ethos and Traditions of the Church of Scotland*, London: Oxford University Press, 1963.

MacDonald, C. F., *Confidence in a Changing Church*, Edinburgh: Saint Andrew Press, 2004.

Maley, W. and Swann, A., '"Is this the Region . . . That We Must Change for Heav'n?": Milton on the Margin', pp. 139–52, in Coleman, D. (ed.) *Region, Religion and English Renaissance Literature*, Farnham: Ashgate, 2013.

Matthew, Stewart, *Session Matters: A Book on Eldership*, Edinburgh: Saint Andrew Press, 1990.

McKim, D. (ed.), *Encyclopaedia of the Reformed Faith*, Louisville KY: WJKP/Edinburgh: Saint Andrew Press, 1992.

McKim, D., *Presbyterian Questions, Presbyterian Answers*, Geneva Press: Louisville, KY, 2003.

McLaren, B., *A Generous Orthodoxy*, Grand Rapids, MI: Zondervan, 2014.

McNeill, J., 'The Doctrine of the Ministry in Reformed Theology', *Church History*, 12(2), (1943), 77–97, Cambridge University Press/American Society of Church History.

Miller, K. (ed.), *Memoirs of a Modern Scotland*, London: Faber & Faber, 1970.

Moltmann, J., *The Church in the Power of the Holy Spirit*, London: SCM, 1977.

Murray, D., *Rebuilding the Kirk*, Edinburgh: Scottish Academic Press, 2000.

Newbigin, L., *The Reunion of the Church: A Defence of the South India Scheme*, revd edn, London: SCM Press, 1960.

——*Unfinished Agenda: An Updated Autobiography*, Eugene, OR, Wipf & Stock, 2009.

Newlands, G. and Baillie, J. & D., *Transatlantic Theology*, New York, Peter Lang, 2002.

O'Donovan, O., *The Desire of the Nations*, Grand Rapids, MI: Eerdmans, 1996.

Paas, S., *Church Planting in the Secular West*, Grand Rapids, MI: Eerdmans, 2016.

Petersen, D. L. and O'Day, G. (eds), *Theological Bible Commentary*, Louisville, KY: WJKP, 2009.

Simpson, P. Carnegie, *The Life of Principal Rainy*, London: Hodder & Stoughton, 1909.

Skinner, C., 'Facing the Future: How Can the Church of Scotland Increase its Numbers of Ministers in Order to Remain Viable as an Institution in the Twenty-First Century?', Edinburgh Napier University Business School MBA Project (unpublished), 2013.

Smith, I., 'The Economics of Church Decline in Scotland', *International Journal of Social Economics*, 20(12), 1993, 27–36.

Smith, J. K. A., *Desiring the Kingdom*, Grand Rapids, MI: Baker Academic, 2009.

——*How (Not) To Be Secular: Reading Charles Taylor*, Grand Rapids, MI: Eerdmans, 2014.

Storrar, W., *Scottish Identity: A Christian Vision*, Edinburgh: Handsel Press, 1990.

Taylor, C., *Modern Social Imaginaries*, Durham, NC: Duke University Press, 2004.

——*A Secular Age*, Cambridge MA: Belknap/Harvard University Press, 2007.

Todd, M., *The Culture of Protestantism in Early Modern Scotland*, New Haven, CT: Yale University Press, 2002.

Torrance, T. F., 'The Eldership in the Reformed Church', *Scottish Journal of Theology*, 37(4), November 1984, 503–18; also published under the same title as a booklet (Edinburgh: Handsel Press, 1984), and as a chapter within *Gospel, Church and Ministry* (Eugene, OR: Pickwick Publications, 2012).

Volf, M., *After Our Likeness: The Church as the image of the Trinity*, Grand Rapids: Eerdmans, 1998.

Wells, S., *Transforming Fate Into Destiny*, Carlisle: Paternoster Press, 1998.

Wesley, J., *The Works of John Wesley*, New York, NY: J & J Harper, 1826.

Wightman, A., *The Poor Had No Lawyers*, Edinburgh: Birlinn Books, 2013.

Wilkie, G., *The Eldership Today*, Glasgow: Iona Community, 1958.

Wolfe, J. N. and Pickford, M., *The Church of Scotland: An Economic Survey*, London: Geoffrey Chapman, 1980.

Woodhead, L. et al. (eds), *Peter Berger and the Study of Religion*, London, Routledge, 2001 (includes a Postscript by Berger).

Yoder, J. H., *Body Politics*, Nashville, TN: Discipleship Resources, 1992.